Lasting the Course

BY THE SAME AUTHOR

Alliss Through the Looking-Glass (*with Bob Ferrier*)
Easier Golf (*with Paul Trevillion*)
Play Golf
An Autobiography (*with Bob Ferrier*)
The Shell Book of Golf (*with Michael Hobbs*)
Bedside Golf
More Bedside Golf
Bedside Golf 3
The Duke (*a novel*)
The Who's Who of Golf (*with Michael Hobbs*)
The Open: The British Championship
since the War (*with Michael Hobbs*)

Lasting the Course

Why, Where and How You Should Play Golf

Peter Alliss

with Michael Hobbs
Illustrated by Chris Perfect

Stanley Paul

London Melbourne Sydney Auckland Johannesburg

To my father and to the original Old Boys at Ferndown Golf Club, who played such a large part in my early golfing development

Stanley Paul & Co. Ltd

An imprint of the Hutchinson Publishing Group

17–21 Conway Street, London, W1P 6JD

Hutchinson Publishing Group (Australia) Pty Ltd
PO Box 496, 16–22 Church Street, Hawthorne, Melbourne, Victoria 3122
PO Box 151, Broadway, New South Wales 2007

Hutchinson Group (NZ) Ltd
32–34 View Road, PO Box 40-086, Glenfield, Auckland 10

Hutchinson Group (SA) Pty Ltd
PO Box 337, Bergvlei 2012, South Africa

First published 1984

Set in Monophoto Ehrhardt

Printed and bound in Great Britain by
Butler & Tanner Ltd, Frome, Somerset

British Library Cataloguing in Publication Data

Alliss, Peter
Lasting the course.
1. Golf
I. Title
796.352'3 GV965

ISBN 0 09 158390 x

Contents

ACKNOWLEDGEMENTS

My sincere thanks to Michael Hobbs for all his hard work in putting this book together. For me, and I hope for him too, it has been a lot of fun. Many thanks also to Chris Perfect for his excellent illustrations

PHOTOGRAPHIC ACKNOWLEDGEMENT

For permission to reproduce copyright photographs, the publishers would like to thank Peter Dazeley Photography, Sport & General Press Agency, the BBC, Action Photos, Syndication International, the *Evening Standard*, Phil Sheldon, Bob Drummond, Golf Photography International, the *Dundee Courier*, Ian Joy and the BBC Hulton Picture Library

Golf is the most skilful of all games; it has baffled mankind for centuries, and, because of its inherent qualities and subtleties, will continue to do so for all time.

GEORGE GREENWOOD

I Why Golf?

Why golf, you may be asking yourselves. Well, one very good reason that immediately comes to mind is the experience of literally hundreds upon hundreds of men and women who have come to the game relatively late in life – over the age of thirty-five, shall we say. Whether they achieve a little or a great deal of success, at club or county level, with one voice they come to me and say, 'Oh, how I wish I'd started earlier!' Usually they have been active in other sports and have only come to golf when their abilities at more strenuous sports began to wane.

Then there are others who have played no sport at all since leaving school. The waist has expanded a little and the spouse or doctor has said, 'You really must take some exercise.' I make no bones about it. Golf is very good exercise indeed. The average golf course is some 6000 yards long, plus walks between green and tee, and more to be added when, alas, the ball flies none too straight. You will also be carrying a bag of clubs or pulling a trolley over usually undulating ground. Finally, there is the game itself, which involves swinging a club in a way that brings into use about every muscle in the body.

If you are starting in early middle age, I am not about to argue that you have any chance at all of matching the achievements of a Bobby Jones or a Jack Nicklaus. Although there are a few exceptions, most of the very best golfers began young. I, for instance, first swung a golf club at the age of twenty months and, into my fifties, I am still learning. So, although I don't want to try to persuade you that you can begin late and still be great, I would argue that a late beginner can become highly competent and have year after year of enjoyment. After all, there are examples of people still playing at a ripe old age. There are few sports indeed of which that can be said!

Most of my readers will have some notion of golf. The game is frequently shown on television, and who has not had a go on a putting green, perhaps during a day out at the seaside? A chip and putt or pitch and putt course is another introduction to the game. You might also have had your fifty or so whacks at the driving range, venting your feelings on that little sphere and experiencing the thrill when it all comes together, with the ball boring away at a velocity you would never have believed possible and hanging there against the sky before eventually plunging downwards.

However, none of these is real golf, enjoyable though they may be as ways of starting. I am often asked by people I meet on my travels around the world just what the appeal of the game is and I sometimes warn them that it can often be annoying, frustrating or even infuriating. Any game has drawbacks and can be thought of as a stupid way to pass the time, but there is no denying that, as my late colleague and friend Henry Longhurst used to say, 'Golf takes you to such beautiful places.'

The Surroundings

Many courses are laid out on land by no means designed by nature for the game. At worst, I have sometimes found nothing more than a flat, cold, clay field with views of factory chimneys, cramped Victorian housing or even a prison wall. Yet there will still be a few birds aloft, trees growing and the feeling of being in the open air. However, the majority of courses in the British

The beautiful woodland setting of Woburn

Why golf? Because it takes you to so many beautiful and varied places: Gleneagles, Troon, Woburn and La Moye

Isles and elsewhere are set in far more attractive landscapes. Many are a delight to all the senses.

You may have come across Dylan Thomas's poem 'Fern Hill', in which he recalls time spent in his youth on a Welsh farm. I grew up from the age of seven at a golf club with a similar name, Ferndown, some six miles north of Bournemouth on the Dorset–Hampshire border. My father, Percy Alliss, a travelling Yorkshireman who had jobs in Wales, Buckinghamshire, Yorkshire, Essex and even Berlin, where I was born, came there in 1938 and remained as a professional until the late 1960s. It was there and on other courses in the Bournemouth area that my golf game developed. My liking for birch and pine woodland has never left me. I was not a keen ornithologist nor did I know the proper botanical name for the many wild flowers, but the feeling of the still glades – even after taking 3 putts – always remained with me.

As my game progressed, I began to play on courses farther afield. Today, if faced with the choice, I would play out my days in the golfing landscape of my roots, a few miles from our Ferndown home those many years ago.

Many golfers would disagree with me. For them, the great delight of golf is those rather barren stretches of land hard by the sea, with rearing sand dunes, rushes, gulls shrieking and whirling and the crash of waves on the shore. For many, links golf is the only real golf, and they scorn courses that meander amongst ancient oaks or carve their way through pine forest. The British Isles is fortunate in its wealth of links terrain. It is found along the Kent and Lancashire coasts, in eastern and western Scotland and elsewhere. If kept in good condition, the turf seems designed by nature for a golf ball to lie neat and clean, asking to be struck. The bunkering may be entirely natural or only need the surface to be scraped away. The greens ought to be fast and true – even in winter – but subtly undulating. Nowhere else will the golfer be so closely in touch with the weather. Inland, the day may be still and humid, but on linksland there is always the freshness of the sea and a light breeze. For some lovers of links golf, working the ball low into a stiff northeasterly is the thing. Others relish a soft summer evening with the skylarks swooping overhead.

But, of course, golf has long since spread inland. I am not prepared to enter into the argument over whether our game owes its birth to the medieval *kolven* of Holland or originated in Scotland. However, there's no doubt that it was the Scots who spread the game throughout Britain and around the world. Golf has come to be played in every type of landscape. There are courses on Japanese mountainsides, in Burmese jungles, in the desert, manufactured by huge earth-moving machines in America, in rolling parkland, on downs where the wind blows free, and on the heaths of Surrey, Yorkshire and Germany. Only the Communist states seem to have resisted the appeal of golf; perhaps it's too individual a game for them. But even so there have been rumours of Russian plans, and Arnold Palmer has designed a course in China.

So I suggest that you first take the time to look around you and see what appeals; golf in surroundings that give you a lift, however badly you may be playing on a particular day, is to be preferred. Having made your choice about which club to join, you will then have to see if you can get in.

Joining a Golf Club

Most golfers concentrate their interest on either the course or the clubhouse. For some, clubhouse facilities, atmosphere and even elegance are of supreme importance. Others are interested only in the course and little more than a wooden shed with a corrugated-iron roof (yes, they still survive here and there) is sufficient as a place to change their shoes and have a drink when the game is over. You'll know your own preferences, but, once you have come to a decision, this is what you do.

In golf you *ask if you can join*; you do not inform a club that you have decided to become a member. The normal procedure is to fill in an application form with the signatures of two members prepared to say that they have known you for a reasonable length of time and consider that you would be suitable as a member.

However, you may not know anyone who is a member, particularly if you have just recently moved into the area. If you are a Walker Cup man or rather a good player, you will have little in the way of a problem. Your low handicap will do your talking for you. Most clubs – but not all – are keen to recruit very good performers.

If you don't have these credentials and know no one, probably your best course is to write to the secretary and/or captain asking if you can make an appointment to see him. An alternative is simply to call in at the club and knock on the secretary's door. In either case, you will have the opportunity to explain your problem and, provided he thinks that you will fit in with the rest of the club membership, he will be able to smooth your way to joining.

However, all this presupposes that the club's membership list is not already full. You must be prepared for disappointment and may well have to look elsewhere. Some clubs have a waiting list as long as five or even ten years if they have a particularly good course or clubhouse facilities or are simply enjoyable places to be. They may offer five-day membership (excluding weekends) until full membership becomes available. Difficulties in gaining admission are mainly found in highly populated areas, and around London in particular. The chances are that elsewhere you will be able to gain almost immediate admission or only have to wait until the beginning of a new golfing year.

Undoubtedly it is by far the best to have your golf club on the doorstep so that you can nip along on a summer's evening early enough to join in the 'Friday night school' for those who come straight from office or factory, or simply potter about on the practice ground by yourself. If your club is really near at hand, you will have more opportunity to practise. Half an hour on the practice ground as often as possible will do your game an immense amount of good and should bring your handicap tumbling down.

But do not rule out courses farther afield. Our present road system means that clubs even fifty miles away are within your reach, especially if you are only able to play once a week anyway.

If you are looking for the sumptuous in clubhouse amenities, you are likely to be disappointed in Britain. Many of our clubs were founded fifty, sixty, even a hundred or more years ago, when golf was far more basic in every sense. A member then required somewhere to change his shoes, and a place to have sandwiches, beer and whisky after the game. Many are the tales of those early clubs where members were on their honour to put threepence a nip into the box provided. Alas, such clubs would go bankrupt nowadays! All in all, there isn't a single golf club in Britain that can fully compare with hundreds in the USA for multiple bars, deeply carpeted locker rooms and all the amenities Americans expect of their golf and country clubs. I recall playing in one Open Championship at St Andrews and hearing an American star loudly demanding to know where the showers were to be found. He complained in amazement when informed that there were none. However, a stalwart servant of the club had the best of the exchange when he said, 'I'm very sorry, sir. But you see, their lordships are accustomed to retire to their castles when they wish to bathe.' Closer to home, we cannot quite compare with the elegance of more than a few clubs on the Continent, France in particular.

But sumptuousness and elegance cost money and it has always been the pattern in Britain that golf should be as cheap as possible. Rises in the annual subscription are often bitterly opposed, with calls for the resignation of a committee responsible for the latest extortionate rise of £5 a year.

When you have been admitted to a club as a beginner you may find one condition: that you take a course of, say, six lessons from the club professional. This can only do you good. Most would-be golfers begin with a poor grip, a bad set-up to the ball and a hazy idea of the golf swing. Without good guidance, bad habits can quickly become ingrained and may remain with you for ever. So, whether your new club insists on it or not, take a course of lessons, preferably packing them into a short space of time. If you have one every couple of weeks you may well find that what you learned last time has gone. It's just like learning to drive a car. You do it, if possible, in a concentrated dose.

By this time, you may well be wondering how much all this is going to cost you. Well, friends, it's not cheap. Few things that are worthwhile are.

The first year is the worst. You will have to pay not only the annual subscription but the entrance fee as well, which is normally the same as the subscription. It can sometimes be a lot; but, on the good side, in these days of high unemployment and recession, it might not be too expensive – £30 to £50 with a bit of luck.

Annual subscriptions vary enormously, depending on the standard of the golf course, the quality of its maintenance, and the clubhouse facilities and services. A wooden shed ought to mean low fees – perhaps £50 a year – whereas a clubhouse with luxurious changing rooms, a choice of bars, haute cuisine restaurant, sauna, indoor swimming pool and lavish furnishings does not come cheap. In my experience, the highest British rate for family membership is more than £1000. Yet even this is not quite so much as it sounds if you consider that it provides substantial entertainment for husband, wife and three or more children. Excluding the London area, the national average, giving you an acceptable standard of both course and clubhouse, is between £100 and £150 annually.

Certainly that may seem a lot of money when paid out in one go. Yet consider what you will be getting for your outlay. If you intend to play both summer and winter – as most keen golfers do these days – on average a couple of games a week, £100 works out at little more than £1 a game. The more you play, the more of a bargain you have, especially if you compare your outlay with what a visitor pays at a club. The national average for a visitor is now reckoned to be about £6. At the very top end of the market, the Gleneagles green fee for the King's and Queen's courses is likely to be raised to £20 for 1984, while Turnberry was not much less in 1982 and 1983.

Choosing Your Equipment

The first thing I want to stress is that you do not need to dash off and buy yourself a glittering set of new irons and woods at a cost of £200 to £500, or even more if you are buying the latest in space-age technology. Neither do you need alligator-skin shoes, a vast bag, armfuls of slacks, mink head-covers and fourteen cashmere sweaters. Like a new car, the clubs will lose almost half their value after a few games.

Also, even the most expensive golf clubs may be wrong for you. There are several things that make a golf club suit you. Take length for a start. Some of you will be tall with short arms; others short with long arms. The distance between hands and the ground can't be the same in both cases. You will also have no idea, when starting off, whether you will eventually prefer heavy or light clubs. There is also a great range of difference in the flex of the shaft. Will extra stiff, stiff, regular or whippy suit you best? Only time will tell, but I can give you a little guidance. If you are a hard hitter you will need fairly stiff shafts, whereas those who swing the golf club almost always fare better using something with more give in the shaft.

I myself had a great deal of success with a very heavy driver weighing 17½ ounces. Like Sam Snead, I found that a heavy club seemed to help my control of a full-out swing. Yet I remember my surprise when picking up the clubs of Jack Nicklaus, Arnold Palmer and Tom Weiskopf, amongst others. In each case the shafts were stiff and the heads light. Swinging them was rather like using a stick.

Most top professionals do not use a matched set of clubs. A typical bag may well contain a 'safe' driver (one that gets the ball on the fairway more often than not), a fairway wood of a different make, with a variety of manufacturers' names on the 1 iron and the 3, 4 and 5 irons, and an even more bewildering selection of the pitching clubs. These men and women have found, by trial and error, what suits them best and gives them confidence. I remember the story of the great Bobby Jones. Over his career, before the days of machine-made clubs, he built up his collection of hand-crafted ones. Such was his feel for shaft and clubhead that when eventually they came to be tested it was announced that Jones had assembled a perfectly matched set of clubs – except for one. 'Ah, yes,' said Jones, 'I was never really happy with that niblick' (the equivalent of an 8 iron today).

But, of course, as a beginner, you will not want to spend half a lifetime selecting the ideal clubs for you. What I suggest you do is go to a professional and tell him that you are looking for

A rueful Fred Trueman, waiting for yet another new ball

FRED TRUEMAN
Slazenger

a secondhand set, at least until your swing and natural way of playing the game have become established. He will probably ask to see you swing and fit you out with a set that will do you very well indeed for a while. Remember that a golf professional is also a shopkeeper. If the pro you first see hasn't anything suitable in stock there are others in your area. You don't have to be a club member to go to a club's shop, and some professionals now have a very fine range of both new and used equipment. Obviously the range of choice varies, so shop around.

I am uneasy, however, at the thought of your going to a golf shop or the sports department of a multiple store. Although the staff may be knowledgeable about sports equipment in general, they may have little knowledge of golf. They are mainly interested in selling new equipment anyway.

Having made your choice, you may find it a lucky one. The 'temporary' set which cost you perhaps £50 to £70 may prove to suit you and serve you many years. Old clubs are by no means necessarily 'worn out' ones. In my golf career, for instance, although I put great strain on my shafts because I was a long hitter, I have broken only one in fifty years of playing the game. Occasionally I changed a shaft because I came to feel it was too stiff or too whippy – but that is a very different matter.

Although my father was one of the great British professionals of his day, I, too, began with a secondhand set of clubs which he acquired in part exchange from Sir Edward Durrant. Probably they were none too suitable for me as the shafts were rather too whippy for my youthful strength, but I used them in the 1946 Boys Championship and they got me through to the final. Next I came by a set of John Letters White Heather which I had longed for when they stood in my father's shop at Ferndown. Eventually he relented and let me have them below cost price. Thereafter, as I became a tournament golfer, I was contracted to the Slazenger sporting goods organization and seldom had to put my hand in my pocket for golf equipment. Yet this did not mean I appeared on the first tee with a new set every month. In fact, including those cast-offs from Sir Edward, I have had no more than six sets of golf clubs.

Of course, I tried other clubs in plenty. All professionals have a favourite driver, fairway wood, perhaps an individual 1 iron, and those vital short pitching clubs. Putters are another story. Many of the great players have remained faithful throughout their careers to a single club – once they have been lucky enough to find the one that gives them confidence. Yet players such as Arnold Palmer, Sam Snead, Max Faulkner and Henry Cotton have had hundreds between them – they never felt they had found quite the right one. Tony Jacklin had a boxful in his garage in Jersey and I suppose I've bought some forty or more in my time – just about one a year, not that extravagant for someone making his living at golf.

The great Peter Thomson, five times British Open Champion, used the same set of irons until the grooves on the clubfaces were almost worn away. Of course, from time to time he would try out others, but when things began to go wrong for him he would return to the old faithfuls. It was his special set. I dare say he has them still, just as I have a few old favourites and give them an airing now and then. One of the best drivers of a golf ball ever, Sam Snead, for most of his career used a club given to him early in his competitive life by a fellow pro. The particular driver was heavier than the ones Sam had been using. The extra weight helped him control the full-out swing and, once he was confident with the club, Sam could hardly bear to be parted from it. As it became more and more battered, he would abandon it temporarily – but if a quick hook appeared he would return to his early love. There is a story that Snead was once playing with it in a tournament when the head flew off. He let out a howl of anguish and ran off down the course in a desperate search which ended happily in deep rough.

So if you find one of these special clubs that suits you, stay with it when you change your basic set – the driver in particular; you may never find one you like as well again.

When buying your first secondhand set, however, pay particular attention to the grips; after all, they are your only point of contact with the club. If you can see areas of wear, perhaps a depression where the thumb of a former owner has rubbed deep into the grip over the years, have the grips changed. It will only cost you a couple of pounds a club. Many – perhaps most – club golfers do not look after their grips properly. Give them a good scrub with a nail brush and washing-up liquid and the improvement will be dramatic. If they are still too smooth, rub them gently with a fine grade of sandpaper and then rinse them off.

Leather grips are a little more difficult to look after, but they are becoming increasingly rare. Again, give them a thorough clean, followed by a little castor oil. If you are still not satisfied, consult your pro. He has the experience to know what should be done. Good leather grips have still not been bettered by modern compositions – but they need a great deal more care to keep them fit for play. Jack Nicklaus is one player who insists on leather.

There is a useful alternative to the secondhand full set of clubs – the short set. All you actually need to begin with are five irons – the 3, 5, 7, 9 and the sand wedge (which can also be used for those little pitches over bunkers) – a putter and a 3 wood. There is one very positive advantage in having few clubs: you will be more likely to learn the difficult art of playing a greater variety of shots with the same club. Take the 9 iron, for instance. The distance the ball travels from an iron shot of any kind depends a great deal on the angle that the clubface makes with the ball at the moment of impact. If you have your hands well ahead of the clubhead and the ball is also set back in your stance, you have changed the loft to something like a 6 iron. Because of the shorter shaft, the ball will not fly quite so far, but it will travel much lower and farther than when you play from the standard position with the ball just inside the left heel. Move it forward and you increase the loft of the club and get a higher and, of course, a shorter shot, a wedge distance, more or less. Think of Seve Ballesteros. His golf began when he was given a 3 iron. He had to use it for maximum length, for pitching, for getting out of bunkers and even for putting. It tremendously benefited his golfing imagination and taught him to use his hands. He had to learn how to get results with a tool not designed for the particular task. As a result, he can now shape shots with all his clubs, when something more complicated than a full shot is needed.

But, of course, I am talking of a man with a genius for the game. For most of us, golf is a lot easier if we use the same basic swing for every shot and let the loft of the club and length of shaft adjust the distance for us.

How Difficult Is Golf?

There is no hard and fast answer. Undoubtedly it is one of the most difficult games to play to a very high standard. Every course is different, and even when playing the same course all the time – as many golfers do – you will find that it is wholly or subtly different from one day to another, or even from hour to hour. You may find yourself in winter or summer trying to keep your hands and club grips dry, while pulling a trolley, holding an umbrella, and writing down the score to boot. In golf, play is abandoned only if the course becomes unplayable through flooding or snow cover or presents a danger to life from lightning. No concession is made to the players' comfort!

People coming to golf from sports which involve reflex actions and a moving ball find it difficult. It looks so much easier. There is that little white ball quietly waiting to be hit. It's all up to you. Nothing your opponent can do should affect your own ability to swing the club back and through. I remember Prince Philip saying to me that he hadn't taken up golf because it was 'Too easy. Try polo. That's hitting a ball with a club, but it's moving and you've got to ride a horse as well.' True enough, but in the little polo I have watched, I noticed that they missed the ball a lot and the pony seemed to do all the work.

In many sports you have no time to think of the *consequences* of what you are about to do. A ball hurtles towards you and you react instinctively. But what happens, however, when the player *has* got time to think? There's the penalty at soccer, for instance. Whoever takes a penalty has quite a long time to think how easy it *ought* to be to place the ball in the net, but how many penalty kicks go rather feebly straight to the goalkeeper? The kicker has not kept his nerve. The horrid thoughts of failure have got to him. In rugby, similarly, most things happen at a fairly high speed – but you need nerve at fullback as a high up-and-under is hoisted into the air.

How frightful to drop it in front of a packed house at Cardiff Arms Park with a historic win against the All Blacks in the balance! Or think of tennis. The players dart about the court and the ball flashes to and fro across the net, sometimes in a marvellous volleying sequence too fast for the eye to follow the flight of the ball. But what happens when a player is serving? Now he is almost in a golf situation: he or she has to toss the ball gently in the air and strike it when almost stationary. How often someone serves a double fault in a crisis of the match. And finally cricket on a village green. The fast bowlers have had their say and the score is clicking along nicely. The fielding team is glum. Are they going to bat through the day? Oh well, let's give old Charlie a go. Old Charlie ambles up to the wicket and sends down his standard delivery: a lob up in the air that takes some time to arrive with the batsman. 'Easy,' thinks he. That is just the trouble. He does have time to think – and time to doubt and change his mind. Another wicket for old Charlie.

So, then, golf is a very difficult game to play to a high standard, but it's one of the easiest games to play well enough to enjoy. After all, the ball is stationary. You don't need much natural reflex ability or great strength to see you through. Strength can be a disadvantage. My father once taught an Olympic weightlifter who never succeeded in hitting a golf ball more than 180 yards. Never was a man more frustrated and eventually he gave up the game.

The ability you most need to hit a golf ball long and far is to be able to make a clubhead move fast, to accelerate it. Other considerations come into striking a golf ball a long way, but you must get the clubhead moving fast. But don't despair, it doesn't take great strength or clubhead speed to move the ball over 200 yards and that will be enough for you to be able to compete enjoyably at golf. Hand and arm speed undoubtedly are very important and later I shall be explaining a few ways in which these can be improved, although they depend to some extent on how naturally gifted you are. But you must be prepared to give the necessary time to developing your game.

If you have been successful at other ball games you will begin with certain advantages. Above

A selection of backswings from the world's greatest – take your pick

all, you will have learned how to *compete*, how to keep your nerve in a crisis in a match, how to steel yourself to play a shot when you lack confidence in your ability to play it. You will also have to unlearn some of the skills you bring to golf from other sports. All manner of marvellous shots, for instance, can be played at racquet games when the player is off-balance, but in golf an off-balance shot is seldom a good one. The basic mechanics of the swing must always be right. Nevertheless, such people have already learned one of the essentials of golf: how to swing an implement *through* the ball not merely *at* it.

I would always, for instance, back a good-class batsman at cricket to attain a relatively low golf handicap. Certainly driving a ball straight for 6, with a full backswing and follow-through, closely resembles what we are after in the golf swing.

Even so, the cricket backswing is much shorter than that necessary for golf – indeed, some players have no backswing at all. Many golfers, such as Bernard Hunt and Doug Sanders, have prospered with short backswings – barely to the vertical – but such short swings often cause problems, particularly as regards rhythm, an essential ingredient in golf.

My father, Percy, had an encouraging message for beginners. Unlike me, he reckoned it was an easy game. It was 'us' who made it difficult, particularly through not accepting limitations and allowing little or no time at all for practice. Remember, no other game has so effective a handicapping system; the poor player can compete with the good, provided that each plays to his or her handicap.

The Handicapping System

The new golfer is not immediately awarded a handicap by his club. He must first work at his game to develop a sound swing and at least modest skill at the great variety of shots that go to make up our game, particularly on and near the green. He or she may find, if lucky, that the ability to hit the ball a fair distance comes quickly but that touch on the short game takes very much longer. I found that I could always hit the ball vast distances easily, without forcing every ounce into the shot. I was also a fairly good putter. Yet it took me many years to develop what skill I had at those little high-floating shots or low runners from 70 yards and closer to the flag.

First, then, work away on a driving range or practice ground before venturing on the course. There may also be open ground near your home where the grass is cut close – disused aerodromes or playing fields perhaps.

The next stage is to play a few rounds either on your own or with another beginner of similar standard. Don't jump in at the deep end by asking some of the better players at your new club if you can play with them. Your incompetence may embarrass you and they will look the other way the next time they see you coming!

Once you have earned your handicap, however, all changes. You should be able to compete with anyone and should seek out the better players. Your concentration will be improved and you will find yourself tested to emulate the shots that your club's stars are capable of. You will also not be lulled into thinking you are better than you are, which can happen if you settle into the pattern of a regular fourball and you are the best player amongst your friends.

The next stage, once you can manoeuvre the ball around your home course without too many disasters, is to begin submitting scorecards so that the handicap committee can assess your standard. Let us suppose they allot you a handicap of 23. By this time you will understand what this means in strokeplay: if the standard scratch of your course is 71 and you go round in 94, you have played exactly to your handicap when your 23 strokes' allowance is deducted. Such a score has won not a few monthly medals.

There are minor differences for matchplay. Suppose you find yourself playing a singles match against a player with a handicap of 9. The 9 is subtracted from your 23, giving a difference of 14. You now receive only three-quarters of the difference, or 10½. Half or three-quarter strokes are rounded up to the next number, so you will receive 11 shots. Now look at the card for your course. One column is headed 'Stroke Index'. You will receive a stroke start on each hole with an index number between 1 and 11. If both of you play close to your handicaps, a closely fought game is bound to result.

Armed with your handicap, if you can play to it, there is no reason at all why you should not be able to give Tom Watson, Jack Nicklaus and Seve Ballesteros something to think about on the golf course. In what other game would this be possible? There are a few like tennis or squash – but with the important difference that you would be given a huge start and the greater skills of your opponent would still dwarf your efforts. In golf, if you play your own game – against the course, not your opponent – you will survive and even prosper.

The Appeal of Golf

Earlier I said that one of the wonders of the game of golf is that it is almost always played in beautiful or at least attractive surroundings. Yet

Ace driver James Hunt plays a delicate pitch – one of the most competitive players I know

many players are concerned only with the game itself. Although it is the methodical touch players who usually come out best, I would by no means decry the sheer animalistic thrill of smashing full out into the ball with a driver. I remember the days of my youth at Ferndown when I used to pick up every cut ball I could lay eyes on and save them until the end of the round. Then I would go to the edge of the putting green and try to drive across what were then the eighth and ninth fairways and on up into the woods that bordered Lone Pine Caravan Camp. Ah, the bliss of it all when everything in the swing was exactly right at full power!

Perhaps few of you, especially if you come late to the game, will experience the joy of sending a ball a journey of 300 yards. Yet the appeal is little different when, within your capabilities, you launch into the ball and everything goes far better than normal. Perhaps this will be a drive of 220 yards – but the feeling is much the same if 190 yards is the distance you're used to.

What does the average keen golfer so delight in about the game that he will go out every day of the week, come rain, shine, high winds or chilled hands?

Golf is as highly competitive as any other game and there is little to equal the thrill of a

THE PICCADILLY MEDAL

first win in a club competition, perhaps with a trophy to stand on the mantelpiece for the rest of your life or at least until the next club annual dinner. Yet many golfers ignore club competitions almost entirely. Perhaps they play in a sufficient number to retain their handicap – or never bother to have an official handicap at all. But there will still be competition. It may be the chap you play with every Sunday morning or a regular fourball. In either case there is the pleasure of winning – and, of course, the frustration of losing a match which was nearly in your grasp. Above all, the game is there to be enjoyed. Don't ever allow yourself to wander the course in a cloud of gloom.

Although I've begun by emphasizing long driving as a basic delight, that is just a small part of golf. One of the strongest features of my own game, for instance, has always been long-iron play. Many would say that the feel of a perfectly struck 1, 2 or 3 iron loses nothing in comparison with the perfect drive. It's a test of accuracy as well; how near that distant flag has the ball come to rest? Long-iron play is the part of golf where the greatest weaknesses show themselves. Several years ago, performance analysis at a Dunlop Masters tournament, which hosted the year's most successful players, showed that even the tournament players were relatively unsuccessful in hitting the target from around the 180- to 200-yard mark with the long irons.

As you move to the short irons you are into the precision game. It is no longer a matter of how far you can hit the ball, but whether you have chosen the right club and hit the ball the right distance along the target line. There is perhaps a different kind of delight in deciding just what sort of shot you want to play and then judging and executing that shot to perfection.

Ah yes, putting, the game within a game, at times the great equalizer of both small fry and the great names alike. As the old-time Open champion Willie Park used to declare, 'The man who can putt is a match for anyone.' Obviously any idiot ought to be able to get the ball into the hole from, say, 8 feet. Yet all too often we have to shrug our shoulders as the ball pulls up short or tantalizingly curls around the rim. From 2 to 4 feet it is even more infuriating when the ball obstinately remains above ground.

1969 saw my last tournament victory. Here I am with the Piccadilly Medal trophy on the balcony of Prince's Golf Club

This distance was my greatest weakness as a tournament golfer. As a youngster I had no difficulty in rattling them in without pause for thought, but then a world-famous professional told me that I would never be much of a putter with the grip I was using. I heeded the great man's words – and never felt comfortable again. However, I was never quite as bad as my reputation and my car number plate – 'PUT 3' – imply. I must have holed plenty to win some twenty tournaments and five national championships, but there were not a few others that slipped away as the short putts slid past the hole.

If you can play the long shots steadily, pitch reliably and putt consistently, you will, off your handicap, indeed be a match for anyone.

The Nineteenth Hole

Yes, perhaps the most famous hole in golf, yet it has little if anything to do with the game. It's the favoured place in the clubhouse for a drink and companionship. After the game is over, the conversation flowers over an orange juice or whatever you fancy. For many, this part of the golfing day – especially if the golf has not prospered – may prove to be the most enjoyable. Here every man and woman becomes an expert – in their own eyes at least! We can complain that the new sand being tried out in the bunkers is really quite unsuitable – 'Why don't they use the same kind as at so and so golf club?' 'Why, for heaven's sake, haven't they started to scarify the greens yet, and why is that greenkeeper planting all those trees just where my drive normally finishes at the fourteenth?' 'This new handicapping system is dreadful. The wrong people seem to be winning all the competitions.' 'What do you think of this new steward they've got hold of? Do you know, he refused to get me bacon and eggs at 4 a.m. when the card school broke up.' 'The new secretary's a tartar. Ordered me out of the bar last week because I still had my golf shoes on. Fellow seemed to think I was

dropping grass and mud all over the place. It's just like being at home.' 'Who's that lady member? Haven't seen her before. Is she new? Mmm, might ask her to play in the mixed foursomes next week.'

The talk ranges freely. Few topics are actually banned, though perhaps politics should be treated with caution. There's one subject above all to be avoided. No one, absolutely no one, is interested in how you played your last round. You have to be a Nicklaus or a Ballesteros in a crowded press tent to find an interested audience, and even they have long ago learned that their fellow players care not in the least. As the great Bobby Locke used to say in kindly tones, 'How did you play today, Master – but please start at the eighteenth!'

I learned this lesson myself many years ago. I was in the company of my father, the Whitcombe brothers and Abe Mitchell, the greatest player to fail to win the Open Championship. Into the clubhouse came a dejected young man, Bill Laidlaw, an assistant to Henry Cotton at Ashridge. He was a most promising player whose career never came to fruition because he was killed in the war. Seeing his dejection, Abe Mitchell said, 'What's the matter, son?' This was a mistake. Bill proceeded to go through his round stroke by horrid stroke. There was the opening drive out of bounds, an iron shot ruled on the flag that kicked sharp right into a pot bunker, a four-putt where the hole had been set just at the top of a rise and the ball returned to Bill's feet rather too often. So the account went on, the minutes ticking away. But we heard him out. When the tale of disaster came to an end, the generally kindly Abe Mitchell leaned forward and said, 'Yes, it's a sad story, lad. But remember this, no one but you gives a bugger.'

So, dear friends, take heed. It's a self-centred world. Don't launch into a wordy account of the state of your game, and if anyone asks you how went the day, limit your reply to a dozen words. Perhaps 'Not bad, but I couldn't get a putt' or 'Had four birdies' or 'Couldn't have hit my hat' or 'Thirty-three on the outward half and 52 home.' That will be quite enough for your audience, unless you are a raconteur accustomed to having your fellow men rolling in the aisles.

Otherwise, let the conversation flow where it will, but now it is time for me to tell you how to play the game.

An amazing picture of Bobby Locke. Who says the club must point to the target at the top of the backswing?

2 Beginning at Golf

I am a great believer in getting as many things right as possible before you start. Most important of all, what is your eventual aim in golf? Are you prepared to work at the game? Do you have the time available? Are you looking for a little healthy exercise on balmy summer evenings? Have you been an excellent player of another sport and expect to be competitive at golf?

However modest or ambitious your aims, I suggest you begin by taking a series of lessons. At this stage you do not need to be a member of a club. You may find a course of lessons, especially during the winter months, at a technical college or sports centre. Here the instruction will be in groups, but it will usually enable you to pick up the rudiments of the basic golf swing and there will be time also for brief individual pointers from the professional taking the course. You can also ring around the golf clubs in your area and find out if their professionals are putting on group classes in which you would be welcome. In this case, the courses will usually be held on spring and summer evenings. Few golf clubs have indoor facilities.

But most of us prefer individual instruction. This is available at well nigh every golf club. It is naturally more expensive, but, say, £50 is well spent if it gives you a good grounding in the basics.

It's worth asking around amongst your acquaintances for their recommendations as regards good teachers, especially of beginners. As with all teachers, some are better at correcting the faults of advanced players and others have more flair at instilling the basics of the game.

Some of my pupils warming up

The ideal golf lesson lasts half an hour. Most of us can only concentrate at a peak for a fairly short time; an intense half-hour will be better spent than a more leisurely hour, with thoughts going in one ear and just as rapidly out the other.

However, though I recommend short lessons, I must emphasize again that these should be close together. Try to have two a week – or even more – for a total at this stage of something between eight and twelve lessons. As your game develops later, you can return to your favourite professional for check-ups and more advanced instruction.

The Grip

The clubhead is the only thing that hits that little white golf ball. The golfer's only connection with it is his grip on the top of the shaft. You'll seldom see a golfer of quality with a bad grip. Instead, his hands seem to fall naturally and exactly into place as if born to hold a golf club.

But we must beware of the word 'natural'. For many, the natural way to hold a golf club may be highly unsuitable. Think for a moment of a batsman at cricket. Although there are grips for the bat considered ideal in cricket, not a few top players have not only got by but prospered with the unorthodox. In other words, the mechanics are not always vital; but, I must warn you, they are in golf.

Let me give you an example drawn from my own experience. My father, who was among the leading tournament players of the 1920s and 1930s, was a very good teacher indeed and had a perfect grip of the club. Not so, young Peter Alliss. I began to play on my own and in due time devised a grip to give me distance. My game

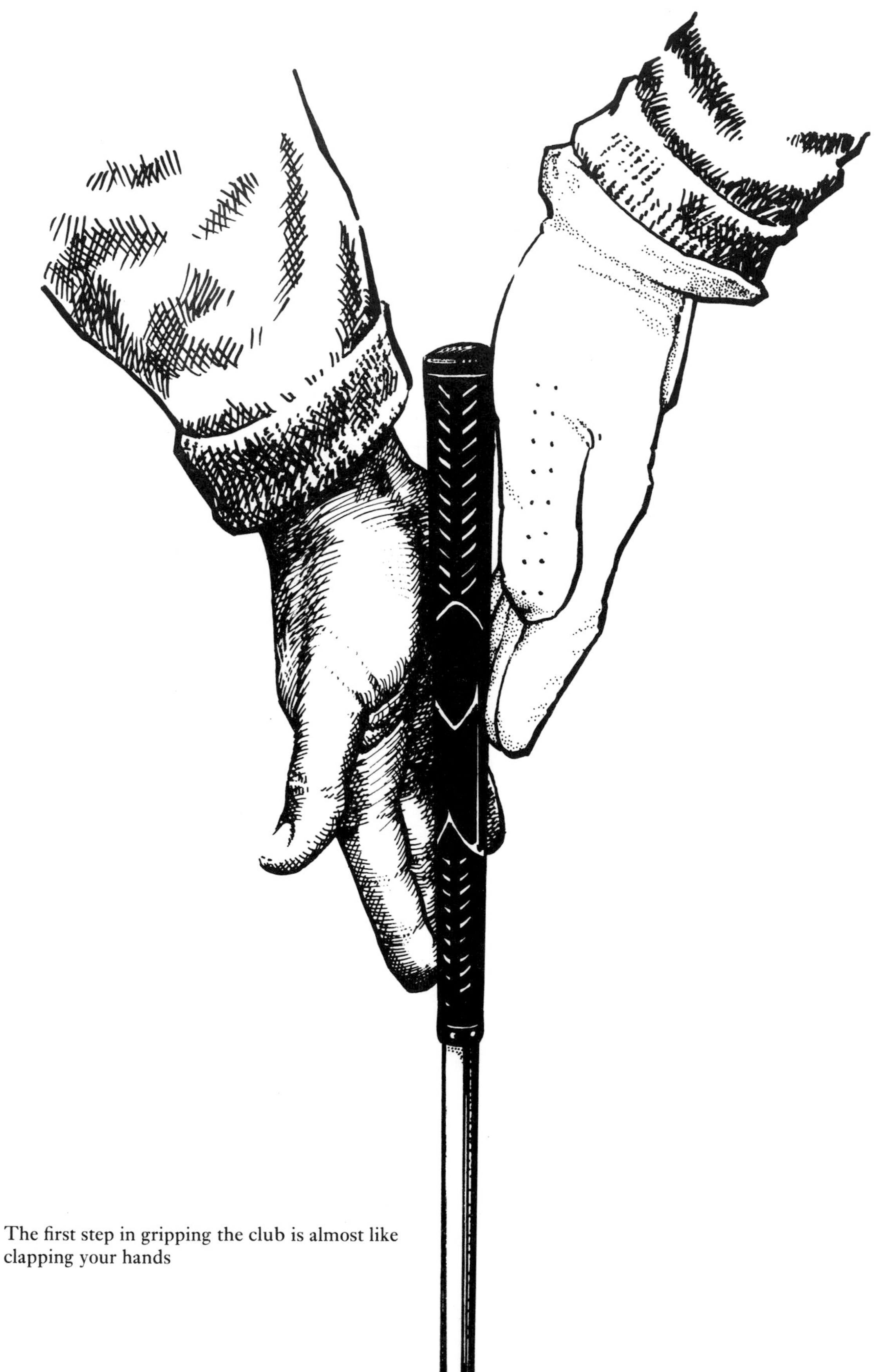

The first step in gripping the club is almost like clapping your hands

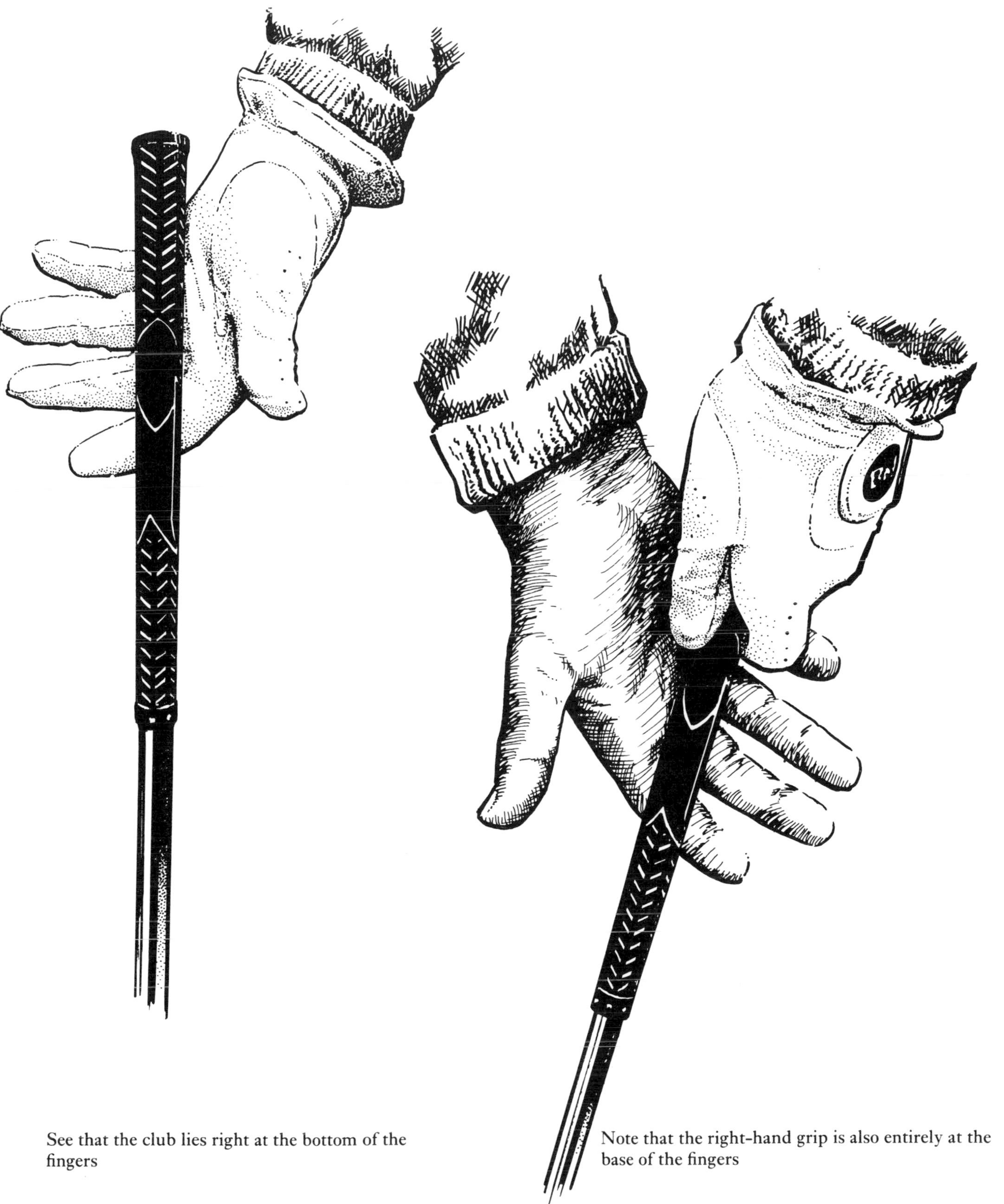

See that the club lies right at the bottom of the fingers

Note that the right-hand grip is also entirely at the base of the fingers

progressed to quite a good standard, though I used to spend rather a lot of time searching far, far away from the fairways for my ball. Eventually my father decided to check on my grip and was horrified at what he saw. He told me that there was no chance that I would progress unless I changed to the Vardon, one of the three standard grips. Because my faulty grip had become second nature, I had a nightmare time. All I could do was give the ball a little chop away to the right. But I knew my father was the expert so I persisted.

All this heartache could have been avoided if I had started out the right way. Fortunately there was a happy ending. The ball began to go in the right direction and the power came back, step by step. This is the grip he taught me.

The Vardon grip

Take out a golf club (if you haven't got one handy, plenty of other things will do – a hammer or a reasonably thick stick, for instance). Now stand sideways on to a target of some kind. If you are on a golf course, a flag perhaps; if not, a lamppost across the street or an object in the room. Now place the palms of your hands together with the back of your left hand and the palm of your right facing the target. Keeping the hands in that position, place them on the grip of the club. You are now about halfway there, for in some ways golf is a simple enough game.

Let us now concentrate on the left hand for a while. Have the shaft of your club, stick or hammer running across your hand in this way: the top should be in the butt of the hand about halfway between the heel and the roots of the little finger. It then runs diagonally across the hand, resting at the roots of your middle finger and ending in the crook of the forefinger. Although all your fingers close around the shaft, the top two fingers press the shaft into the palm while the next two grip it without assistance from the palm. The left-hand grip, therefore, is part in the palm, part in the fingers.

Now the thumb. Place that straight down the shaft, offset just a fraction to the right. Now check. Is the back of your left hand still facing the target? It is? Good, we can now deal with the right hand.

Here I want to start by stressing that the right-hand grip is entirely in the fingers. If you let the club rest in the palm, you will end up with a grip with little feel and will also lose the ability to accelerate the clubhead through the ball. Again, the shaft will nestle in the finger roots and end in the crook of your forefinger. Now check that the palm of your right hand is facing the target. It is? Good. We can go on to deal with the little finger.

Some cricketers grip a bat with the hands apart. This will not do in golf. In golf, the hands must work together as a unit. Neither hand can be allowed to dominate in the golf swing. They must work together as one.

Golfers began to appreciate this late in the last century and some began to weld the hands together using the little finger. Because Harry Vardon was the greatest player of that time, the grip took its name from him. What Vardon and others did was to slide the little finger of the right hand close up to the left and then allow it to slide up over the forefinger of the left hand and let it rest on the knuckle. Place your thumb down the top of the shaft but this time offset slightly to the left.

And that, friends, is it: the Vardon grip, which, with subtle differences mainly caused by different sizes of hands, thickness of fingers and length, is how most of the world holds a golf club – or those who hold it correctly, perhaps I should say.

Now look down at your hands on the shaft. If you have followed the palm drill correctly and what I have told you about finger placement, this is what you should see.

Take your left hand off the club. The nail of your right-hand little finger should be in sight but no other fingernails, otherwise you will have placed the hand too far 'under' the shaft. Of knuckles, the forefinger's will be plain and a glimpse of the middle finger's is permissible. More than this and you have your right hand too much on top of the shaft, a very weak position.

If all is not well, go back to the palm drill. Check that the palm is facing the target.

Next place your left hand on the shaft again and carry out this simple check. You should see the thumb and the knuckles of the first two fingers of your left hand.

The Vardon grip is virtually identical to the baseball grip except the little finger of the right hand rests on top of the first finger of the left

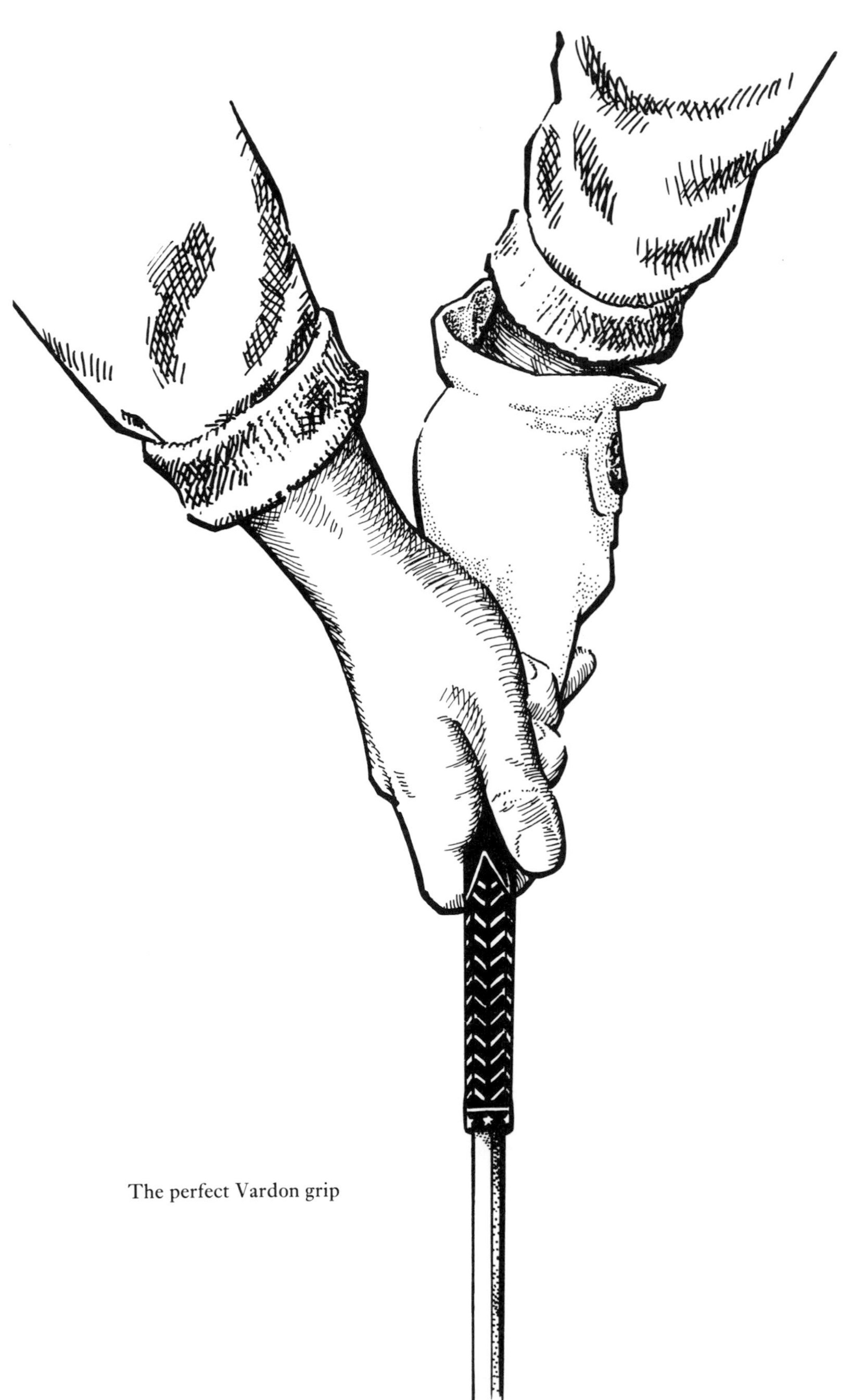

The perfect Vardon grip

The baseball grip

This is identical to the conventional Vardon grip, with one exception: the little finger of the right hand doesn't ride over the left forefinger. Instead, it's fully on the shaft of the club doing its share of gripping. The alignment of the hands towards the target is exactly the same.

Many feel that there is one definite disadvantage to this grip. Because the two hands are less closely linked together, the right hand may tend to dominate the grip and even overpower the left. I do not agree. Provided both hands are pushed close together, there should be no problem. One of the greatest British professionals ever, Dai Rees, agreed with me. He felt that golf is a difficult enough game without losing the use of one finger!

This is a more comfortable grip than the Vardon because it is undoubtedly more natural. I have tried it myself at times but decided that the Vardon happened to suit me best. In part, it will depend on your physical characteristics and I suggest you experiment with both on the practice ground. You may notice that when you use the Vardon grip it is more difficult to have a firm hold of the club with the third finger of the right hand, so the forefinger and middle finger do even more of the work. Although the Vardon is almost universal, this is because it is what everybody teaches. See what suits you best.

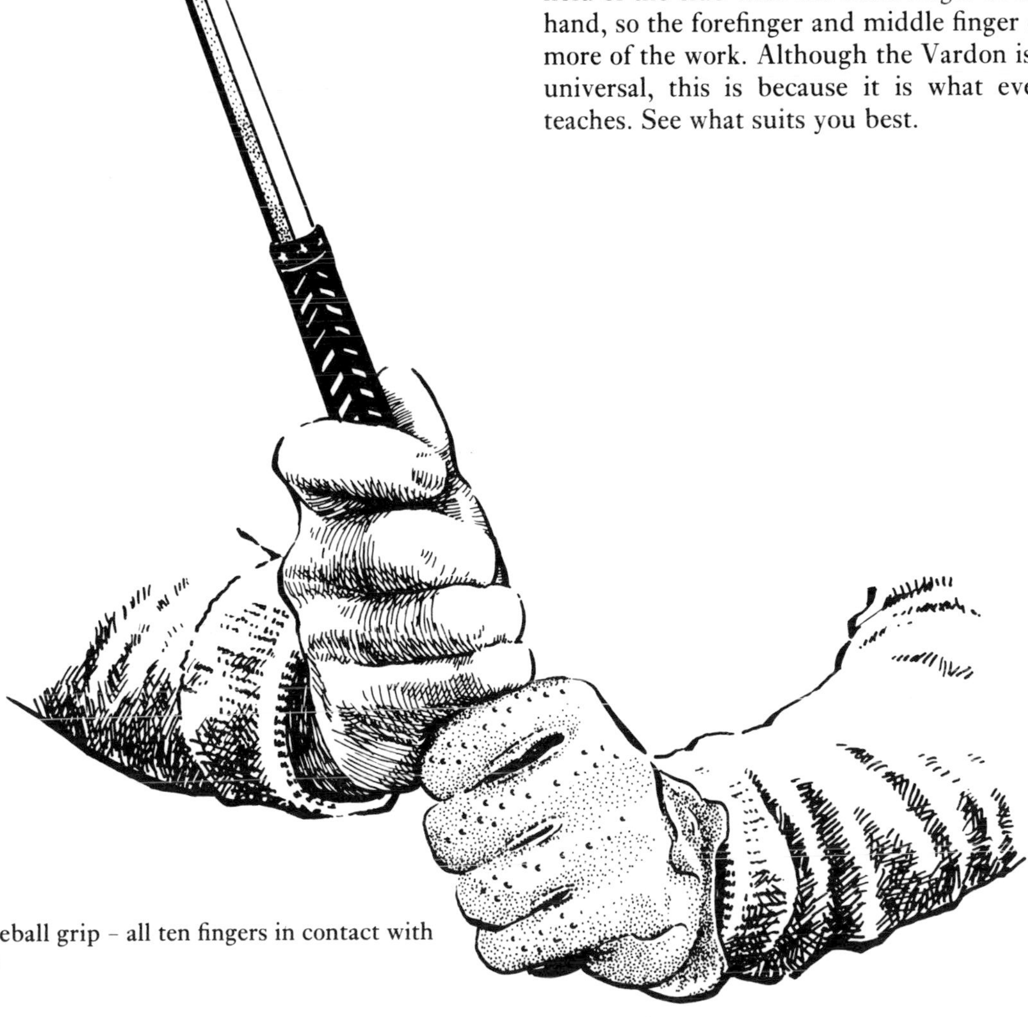

The baseball grip – all ten fingers in contact with the club

The interlocking grip

This is the third of the standard golf grips and is at the extreme from the baseball grip - with the Vardon about in the middle. Again do the drill of palm and back of the hand facing the hole and grip the club very loosely in both hands. Now slide your right hand up the shaft until the little finger reaches the gap between the left fore- and middle fingers. Tuck it in there, lift your left forefinger and place it in the gap between your right little finger and third finger. Now you will have just six of your eight fingers fully on the shaft. Far fewer people are comfortable with this grip than the other two - but it has been used rather successfully by Jack Nicklaus throughout his career. Its best feature is that it encourages use of the last two fingers of the left hand in gripping the club more than the other two grips do.

These three, then, are the only grips I would recommend. They are the same in essence and differ only in how closely the hands are brought together and, I must emphasize, this must be very close indeed. As a check, whichever of the grips you are using, look at the fingers of each hand. There should be no gap between them, except for the right forefinger. This accelerates the clubhead as you come into the ball.

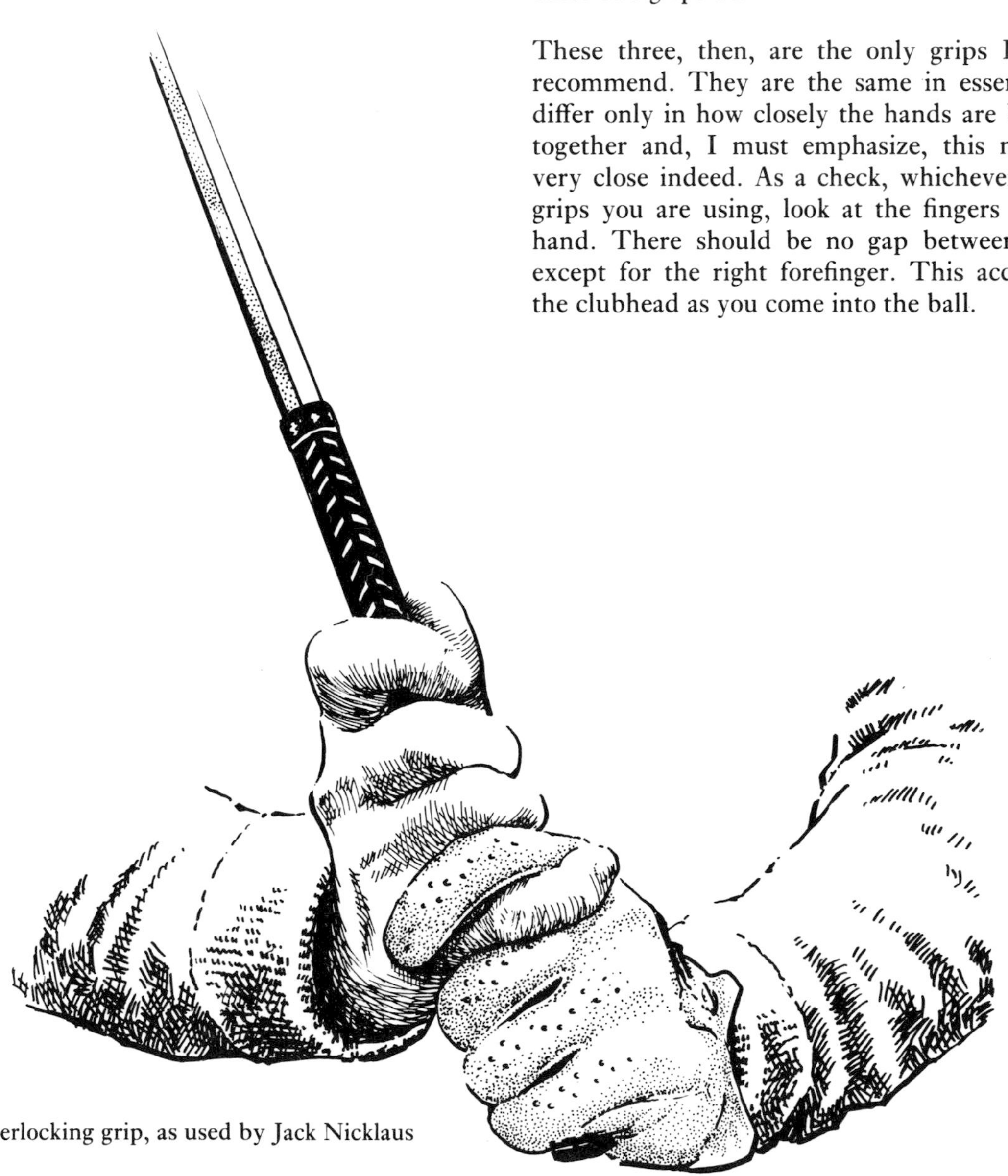

The interlocking grip, as used by Jack Nicklaus

Grip pressure

I am often asked how tightly a golf club should be held. The answer is not tightly at all – but firmly. Your grip must be firm enough so that the club does not move in your hands at any point in the swing. The danger times are at the top of the backswing, when there may come a temptation to 'let go' with the last fingers of the left hand, and in the hitting area.

A good test of whether your grip is firm enough has been suggested by Henry Cotton. He says you should be able to hit two or three golf balls without needing to regrip in between shots. If you can, this proves that you are not allowing the club to twist in your hands as you strike the ball.

Of course, this needs reasonably strong fingers and below I outline some exercises that will help you.

Gripping too tightly is a very common fault. Players do this not just because their fingers are not strong enough but because they are nervous. The results make a good golf swing almost impossible. The muscles of arms and shoulders become tight as well and you can't swish the arms through freely. Often a heave with the body, not a swing at all, can be the result.

And now those exercises. The best is to play a lot of golf. No one who does this comes out of it with weak fingers, but, alas, this is not possible for all of us. However, you should be able to find somewhere inside or outside your house with enough room to swing a club. Go there and swing the club fiercely. Even though there is no ball in the way you will still have to hold on very firmly indeed and will develop just the finger muscles needed in the golf grip.

Alternatively, carry a small hard ball around in your pocket and squeeze it with all the fingers and with each one separately. Another simple exercise is to place the tips of all your fingers and thumbs together and force them against each other as hard as you can. This is good for other muscles as well: forearms, upper arms and shoulders.

Pick up a golf club in one hand and hold it out horizontally. Then try gripping with thumb and forefinger only, then between fore- and middle fingers (oops, you dropped it?), then between middle and third, and finally between the last two fingers. Concentrate particularly on the last two fingers of the left hand because a firm grip with these is so important.

If you haven't room for the full swing in the house, an alternative is to hold a club out away from you and wave it backwards and forwards, stopping the swing with your hands so that the clubhead travels only a total of about 3 feet. It's the stopping that strengthens your hands.

Of course, there is a host of other exercises not particularly connected with golf, such as press-ups. You will have to judge for yourself or consult your doctor as to what it's safe for you to attempt.

With a good grip you have given yourself at least a chance of becoming a good golfer. With a bad one you have no chance.

The Stance

I will begin with your feet. Most people walk with their feet in a position somewhere about ten or five minutes to one o'clock. This is about the ideal for your foot position when standing to a golf ball.

Years ago, when Henry Cotton was the greatest name in British golf, people noticed that he stood pigeon-toed to the golf ball. 'Ah, ha,' they said. 'So that's his secret, is it? Must give it a try.'

Alas, it was not Henry's secret at all, merely the way he naturally walked and stood to the ball. Such a stance locks you up, both on the backswing and the downswing. Similarly, of course, just one foot pigeon-toed or even square will lock part of the swing. On the backswing, it will force you to take the club outside the line and you will then only be able to chop down at the ball; on the downswing, you will be unable to swing through and on with any real freedom.

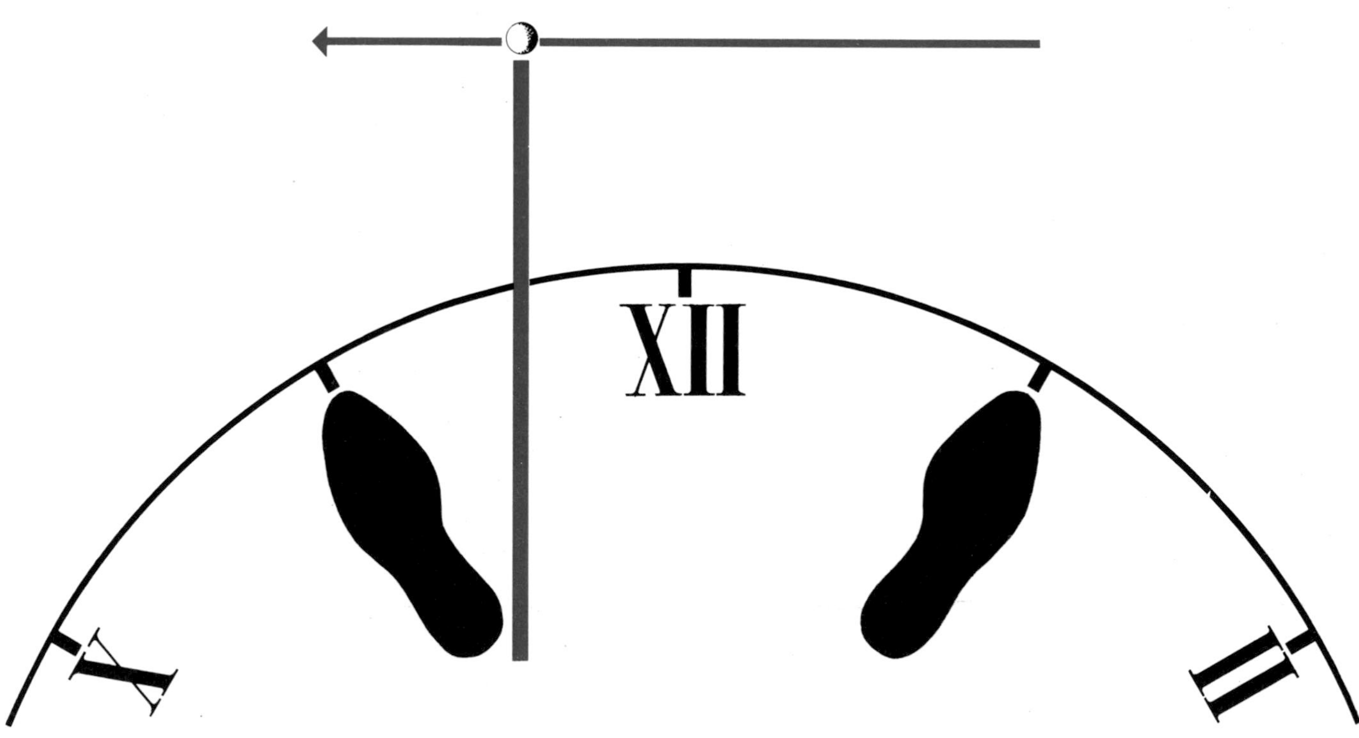

The 'five to one' foot position

Width of stance

The old cliché is that the feet should be the same width as the shoulders and there is little wrong with this except that people have the oddest notions about how wide their shoulders are. Ian Marchbank, professional at the Gleneagles Hotel courses, once gave me a good tip which is easy for the beginner to grasp. 'Take your normal walking stride,' he advised, 'then stop and just swivel around square to an imaginary ball. It's your natural stride length and that's how you will be best balanced because it's what your body is used to.'

Let's see what happens, however, when you stand with your feet too wide apart. Do it and now try swinging a club. Your legs will seem rather stiff and it's difficult to feel at all balanced. Now try the reverse, the feet close together or even touching. Then take a full swing. Did you fall over? If you didn't, you have good natural balance, but you are making the game more difficult for yourself. Even though one of the all-times golfing greats, Bobby Jones, stood with his feet just a very few inches apart, he was very much an exception. However, swinging a golf club with your feet close together may well improve your balance and rhythm and help to get the feet rolling.

So we should by now have the right grip, the feet set correctly and the right distance apart. We are now going to relate all this to a ball.

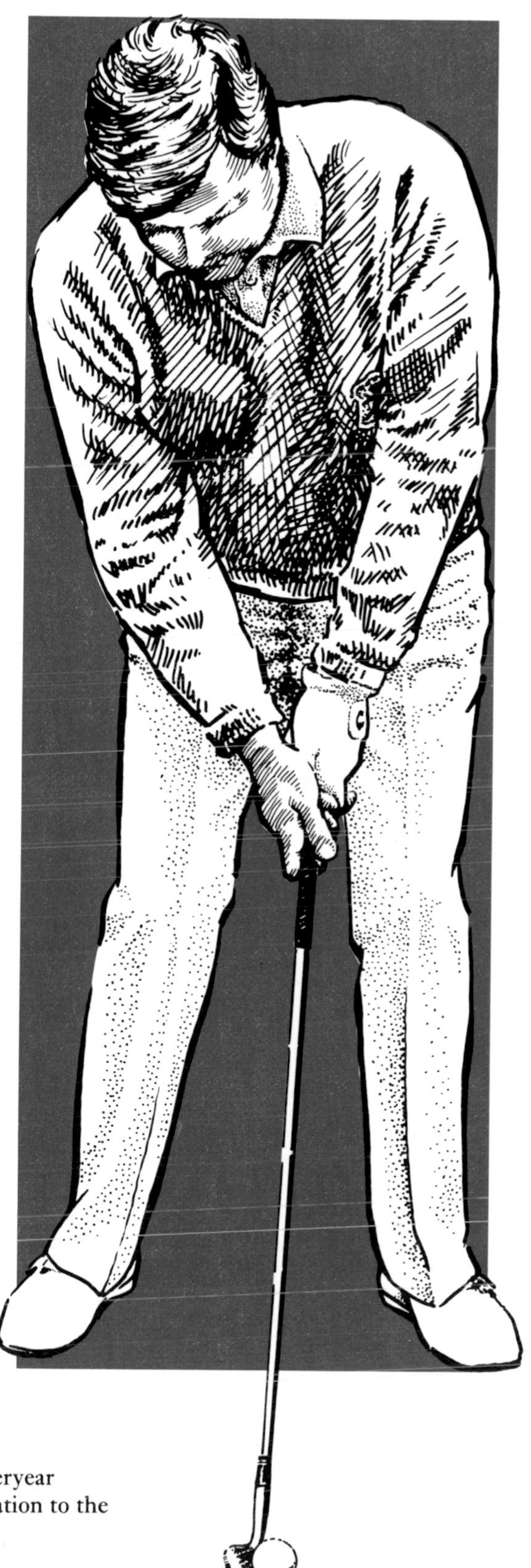

The easy-looking Alliss stance of yesteryear showing the width of the stance in relation to the shoulders

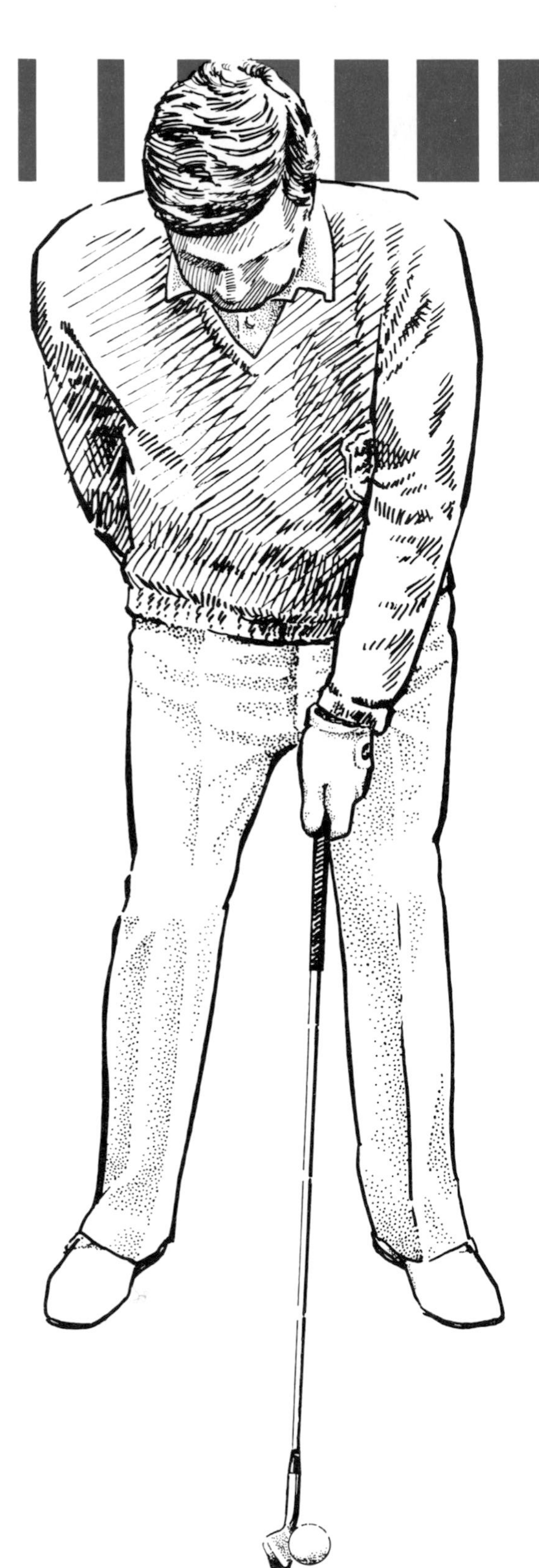

Addressing the Ball

Distance from the ball

Many beginners stand too far away from the ball. They find themselves having to crouch or reach out off-balance in order to get to it. Others have the ball too close and then have little room to swing the club. How, then, do we find the right distance between these two extremes?

Stand erect but not stiff, flex both knees a couple of inches or so and also 'sit down' slightly as if on a high stool or a wall only just below the height of your bottom. Now hold your club and left arm out towards the ground in a straight line (but without the arm being stiff) until the blade lies flat on the ground and just inside the line of your left heel. That is the distance away from the ball that suits your height and length of arm.

'Ah,' you may say, 'but I've seen lots of tournament professionals ground the club behind the ball with their *right* hand first and only then put the left on the club.' This is true. But remember, they are thinking of aiming only. After years of play and practice, they can feel how far away the ball is without needing to carry out a drill.

The easy left arm and club position. No rigid straight lines

Putting the Right Hand to the Club

Well, this sounds simple enough, but there is one 'don't' and one 'do'. It's farther to the right-hand position on the grip of the club than to the left. To get there, you must not bring your right shoulder round but instead reach *under*, your shoulders tilting from left to right. When you've finished, your shoulders and your hips must be side on to the target. You should have the feeling of having to look towards the target over your left shoulder. If in doubt, place a club across shoulders and hips in turn. Each time the club should point directly towards the target.

If all is well, now look along the line of your left arm towards the ball. The ideal is as near a straight line as possible. If there is a distinct kink at the wrists your hands are set too low, so raise your left wrist until you get that straight line and let your right hand follow. If you even have an arch in the left wrist, that's acceptable. It's seen in some top players.

The right shoulder lowers slightly as the right hand is placed on the club

The back

If your back is fully erect you will not be able to reach the ball. However, you should get down to the ball using that sitting-down movement I told you about and by flexing the knees a little. You should have the feeling of 'standing tall', without drawing your neck in like a tortoise.

Looking at the ball

As in any ball game, the ball must be watched at least until impact. Look at it with both eyes, but *don't* look at the top. You are going to be trying to get the clubhead into the *back* of the ball. Looking at the top is no help at all. You want to have the feeling of your swing coming in at the back and through the ball on the same line.

Note the angle of club and wrist – the wrist is not too low or arched too high

Aim

To allow for the difference between where your clubhead and the ball are and where your eyes are, aim just a little to the left of your target, say about 10 yards.

Weight distribution

Quite a lot of nonsense has been written about this over the years, with people declaring that when playing this and that kind of shot they have 35 per cent on one foot and 65 per cent on the other. I don't know how they arrive at these figures – unless they take two sets of scales out with them. In my own swing, however, I like to have the feeling that I am evenly balanced, though I will lean just a little to the left when I want to hit the ball low – and vice versa.

The Swing

The takeaway

This is, roughly, the first couple of feet of the backswing. It should begin with shoulders, hips, arms and hands moving in unison, nothing leading and nothing lagging behind. Keep the clubhead almost brushing the ground and travelling straight back. We must avoid either lifting the club or bringing it sharply inwards.

Easy position at the top of the backswing. Club pointing to the target. Left knee looking down on right foot

Nearing the top

Simply continue swinging the club back with hands and arms while your shoulders and back turn away from the ball until your back is square to the target. You must at no point *lift* the club into any position. The golf swing is a turning, swinging movement. As long as you don't let your wrists break very early on, it doesn't matter when this happens, but the later the better because this helps the rest of the body to turn and swing to the full.

The top of the swing

This differs with each person. Golf can be played with very different lengths of backswing. Doug Sanders, as I have pointed out, did not get the club up much above his shoulders, while others get beyond the horizontal. The two vital elements, if we are to make a swing of any real power, are a full turn of the shoulders and getting the hands well away from the ball, as far as you can comfortably manage and certainly above shoulder height.

Beginning the downswing

So far, the golf swing I have been teaching you has been a matter of first getting the stationary bits right and then swinging the clubhead back fairly slowly and in a relaxed way. Things are now about to speed up and troubles often start when the backswing is completed and the golfer begins to swing back to the ball. It is here that players show their anxiety. Psychologically, they may be afraid of making a bad shot or of missing the ball. There comes a sudden jerk as they try to get the whole thing over with. But we should be in no hurry.

We want no sudden jerk or heave of the shoulders; the arms should swing down and through the back of the ball with the feeling of hitting it *forward*. As you begin that movement, you should feel the muscles of your left side doing most of the work, pulling that clubhead into the hitting area. Your hips will take care of themselves, turning naturally until square to the target by the time you hit the ball. Your shoulders will also turn naturally, but you will do better if you feel they are still side on as you reach the point of contact between ball and clubhead. If you let them turn away too soon, the path of your swing will be from right to left and you will cut across the ball, losing both distance and direction. If your clubface is closed as you strike the ball, it will fly straight left; if square or open, it will curl weakly away to the right.

In the hitting area

What happens in the hitting area is mostly the result of what has gone before: swinging back and beginning the downswing in the way I have described. But what, you may ask, about the hands? They come in late on in the swing, as you approach the ball, providing the final acceleration. Remember, I am saying 'final'. Use them too early and you will push the clubhead way in front of your hands and that powerful pulling movement will be gone.

But that's by no means the worst effect. Think back to how you began the backswing. You set the club to aim precisely at your target. That is the position that the whole swing aims to reach once again at the moment of impact between clubhead and ball. But it is impossible if the hands take over too early and *throw* the clubhead at the ball. Allowing the head of the club to meet the ball with the hands behind rather than leading is the single most common fault amongst relatively poor golfers.

However, it's rather difficult for the golfer to know when he's developed this fault because this is the high-speed area of the swing. We can't see what's happening. But most, perhaps all, of you should be able to feel that pulling movement all the time until after the ball has been struck.

If not, it's easy to observe the results you will achieve when you let the clubhead get in advance of the hands. Topped shots, for instance, will be frequent, but above all there will be very little consistency. The ball will fly to right or left equally unpredictably because in the split-second timing of the hitting area, with very narrow margins for error, the clubhead will not reach the ball in the same position twice running.

Swing speed

For the downswing, all players, when hitting more or less full out, want as much acceleration as they can generate and control. You'll soon learn just what you can control and what you can't.

The speed of the backswing, however, is very much an individual matter. Top professionals, for example, vary a very great deal. People used to say that Dai Rees swung the club back as fast as down – an exaggeration, of course, but it was a quicker movement than the eye could follow. Another contemporary of his, former US Open champion Dr Cary Middlecoff, swung the club back extremely slowly and then came to a dead halt at the top. He felt the pause enabled him to make a smooth and balanced transition from the backwards to the downwards movement. Though Middlecoff was a prodigious tournament winner, I don't recommend it for lesser mortals. With that kind of pause, you will probably lose all rhythm – and even get stuck up there! Stranger things have been known.

For two modern examples, we need look no farther than Jack Nicklaus and Tom Watson. Nicklaus is slow, Watson fast. As models, both are probably a little too extreme; something in between is required.

What you must aim at is a balanced rhythmic change of direction as you begin to move down to the ball again. There should be a fleeting moment when you feel nicely poised and in the right position to pour everything down towards the ball and beyond. You also need to feel your right wrist underneath the shaft and your left ready to lead the right.

Undoubtedly this is more easily achieved if your backswing is slow rather than fast. All of us have to resist the tendency to swing back more quickly when tension is at a height; it's often then that a golfer with a fast action comes to grief.

The follow-through

This is the part of the golf swing that matters not one jot. Once the clubhead has met the ball, you can fall flat on your face if you like. At the other extreme, the most elegant of statuesque finishes to the swing will gain you nothing at all. The ball is long gone, for better or worse. The follow-through is simply the result of what has gone before. How you finish is useful in highlighting faults – as I pointed out in discussing the right-sided heave at the ball – particularly after a cut shot. However, the perfect follow-through does not mean that a perfect shot has been played, only that you made a good swing which may well have not been on exactly the right path. I remember a photo caption which said: 'The poise of the follow-through is excellent. Unfortunately the ball only just missed my left kneecap.'

Leg action

In the backswing, the legs move in sympathy with the rest of the body. As you progress into your one-piece takeaway, your left knee should bend, more or less directly, towards the right foot, though this is quite a small movement, say about 6 inches and no more. The right leg moves far less, just a twisting movement as it follows your torso action, eventually resisting towards the end of the backswing. The leg will be fairly taut, but by no means stiff, when the hips have completed their movement. This is through about 45 degrees rather than the 90 degrees or more of the shoulders. The feet should tend to roll and the left heel can be allowed to leave the ground, though preferably not.

Broadly speaking, on the downswing the legs will take care of themselves. Certainly, for a beginner, I do not recommend your getting yourself involved in the theory you may come across about leg drive and how it increases distance. Severiano Ballesteros has played a round of golf in about level par on his knees. There is negligible extra distance to be gained from leg action. What is important is that the legs should follow the rest of the body and move away from and back into the ball smoothly and on the right path.

Keeping Your Eye on the Ball

There are two particular points I want to make which apply to every stroke from drive to putt. Do not merely look at the ball. This means that you will probably just be aware of the top, whereas it is the back you are always trying to find. Throughout your backswing, the ball must remain in view. Notice particularly what happens at the top of the swing, for it is at this point your head may be pulled by the tug of shoulders on neck. If this happens to you, a trick worth trying is to set your head a little to the right before you start swinging, as Jack Nicklaus and many other players do. The head must be kept still, though unavoidably it slides a little right and then left during the two parts of the swing.

The other moment of danger comes when the player wants to see the result of his shot. As the brain works more quickly than the body, it is instinctive to think the ball has been struck before it has. If you aren't looking at the ball in that final instant, it matters little in theory, but other faults follow. After all, we do not lift just our eyes to follow the flight of a ball, but our head and shoulders as well. If this happens, there is no possibility at all of making good contact with the ball. All too often a topped shot is the result.

The old Ryder Cup player, Irishman Harry Bradshaw, drilled himself not to follow the run of the ball at all. Instead, he kept his head down and listened for the sound of the ball rattling into the hole. Try it. Of course, this does not do for long shots. Lost balls will result!

Through the green, then, I suggest that either you drill yourself to try to see the clubhead strike the ball (impossible, of course) or watch the back of the ball until your brain accepts that it has gone.

Listen for the Swish

I have been telling you how the golf swing is a pulling, not a pushing or throwing, movement. If I haven't convinced you, I want you to try a simple little experiment.

Make a smooth unhurried backswing and then give your all in a right-handed bash at the ball. Try that again, this time listening for the swish your club makes through the air. And again. Keep the fastest sound you made in your mind and now go back to the swing where you have the feeling of pulling into the ball. It's a great deal faster. That feeling of strength in your right side is a bit of a cheat. You are using only about half your natural ability to accelerate the clubhead through the ball. If you pull with the left side, you bring all your ability into the swing. The right side has its say too – but late in the downswing, not near the beginning. When it actually comes into play is mostly a matter of letting nature take its course. It cannot be really deliberate because at that stage everything happens at such a high speed.

So far, I have been talking about the basic golf swing for all full shots, irons as well as woods. There is very little difference in the swing whatever club you are using, but I want to discuss those differences, such as they are.

The Drive

Although a ball position just inside the left heel is recommended, you may benefit from moving the ball forward in your stance just an inch or so. Most golf shots are struck both forward and down. For the drive, however, a descending blow costs distance because a little more backspin is put on the ball. The shot may be impeccably straight (although it is apt to be a slice), but the result is a ball that flies higher than ideal and has very little run. Instead, the clubhead should come into the ball on a horizontal line (parallel to the ground), or just after it has reached the bottom of its arc and begins to rise on the upswing. There will be a little less backspin, resulting in less height and more roll. This is really the meaning of the old saying, 'Tee it high and let it fly.' When a player sets his ball high, he has the feeling that his club will go up at the

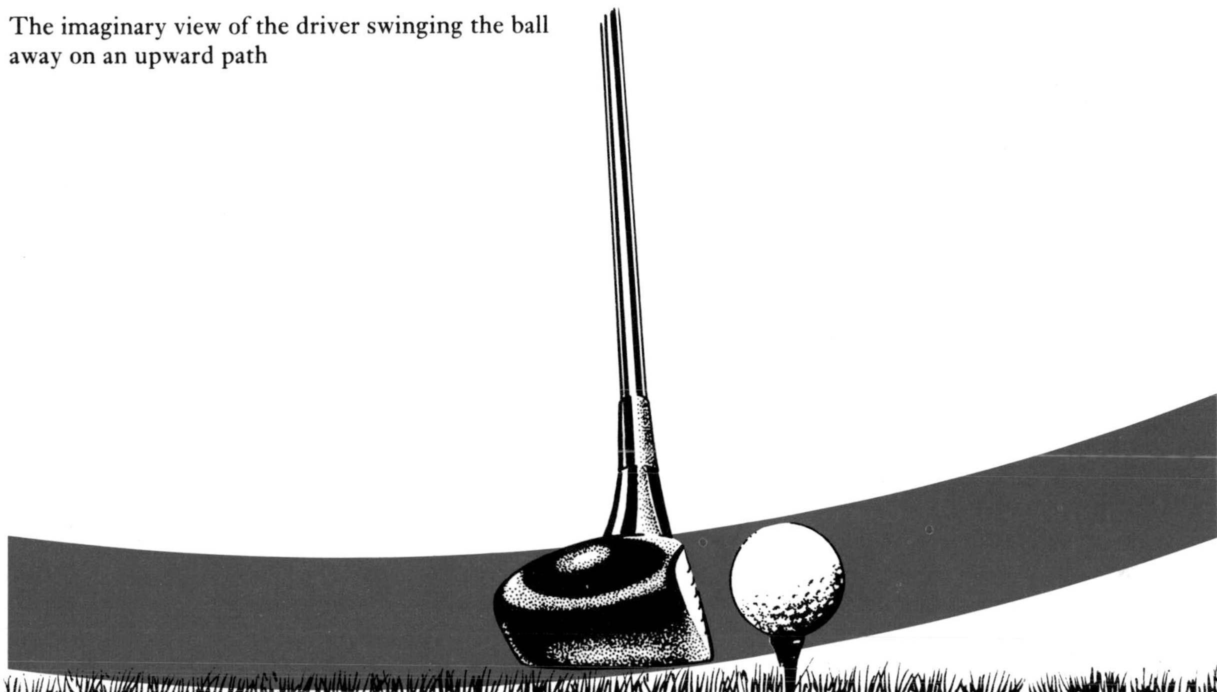
The imaginary view of the driver swinging the ball away on an upward path

ball. So place the ball a little farther forward and tee it up at whatever height gives you the feeling that you are striking through and very slightly up at the moment of impact. The actual height is a matter of personal choice and will result from trial and error.

And remember, your swing path must ensure that the clubhead is travelling along the target line when it reaches the hitting zone and the club-face is square to the target line. A ball with a lot of sidespin on it – a quick hook or slice – loses direction as well as length.

Fairway Woods

Assuming that you have a good fairway lie, there are two ways of striking a fairway wood. One is to sweep the ball away clean either without touching the turf or just brushing it. This gives the maximum distance. The other is to deliver a slightly descending blow with, naturally, a divot being taken. The latter is suitable when the ball is sitting low and a sweeping shot would be likely to result in your taking turf before hitting the ball or topping your shot. You will lose a little length, but this is usually less important for a fairway shot than for the drive. When playing with woods it's also possible to develop a punched wooden-club shot. This can be useful when playing from a divot mark or when the ball is well down in the grass.

When in the rough, don't be afraid of taking a wood, but do be sensible about it. It's sometimes possible to have a lie good enough for a driver, when kindly providence has perched the ball, say, an inch above the ground. If the lie is not quite perfect, a fairway wood is better than a long iron, which has to cut, rather than push, through the grass. If the ball is set well down, only a player with fast, strong hand action should consider using a long iron. Think of Arnold Palmer. He lost the 1966 US Open when in a dominating position because he took long irons from doubtful lies – and there's never been a more powerful man with a long iron than Palmer.

When using a wood from a moderate lie in the rough, always choose the club with the smallest head for it will travel through the grass more easily. The 4 wood will often be suitable and some players have a number 5 or an even more lofted club.

Do not strive for maximum length. Good contact with the ball from a controlled swing is what you are after.

If you decide the lie is not good enough to be worth risking a wood, you should then switch your choice to a fairly lofted iron, certainly no straighter in the face than a 5 iron.

Fairway woods can also be used from fairway bunkers, but do be sensible. Ask yourself if you're an accurate enough striker for it to be worth the risk. If you take sand before the ball, you will get very little distance indeed and a topped shot will almost always remain in the bunker.

Long Irons

As with a driver, many golfers feel that they have to hit the long irons full out. This is a great mistake. (I am referring here to 3 irons since 1 and 2 irons are only advisable for the very low handicap player.) Remember, all irons are supposed to be precision clubs. I advise you to hit, say, your 3 iron no harder than you would a normal full shot with a 7 or 8 iron. If you feel the need to thrash away at the ball, you would be far better off playing a controlled wooden-club shot. I've seen handicap golfers in their thousands using an iron at long par 3 holes when they have no real chance of reaching the green, except with a once-in-a-lifetime shot. The silly fellows don't like to take a wood because the hole is 'only' 190 yards – quite possibly the distance they get with their average drives.

Remember that the long iron is the most difficult club in the bag to hit well. If you are a golfer who finds them difficult, a 7 wood might well be worth the purchase price. I have seen some club golfers' games transformed when they have acknowledged to themselves, sometimes as a result of growing older, they they cannot play long irons effectively.

As well as for play to the greens, the long irons are invaluable for tee shots to the fairway on those days when your driving is off. Remember also that on many fairly short par 4s a good architect will have put a premium on placement of the tee shot. To be in the right or left half of the fairway may well be far more important than being 50 yards farther on but on the 'wrong' side, with the approach menaced by rough and bunkers or the flag set in a difficult position.

You must, however, devote a lot of time to practice. Undeniably, a long iron requires more skill and experience than, say, a fairway wood, but the rewards are greater.

Mid-Irons

Basically these are the clubs 4 or 5 through 7, the easiest to use in your bag. You may meet problems with the other irons, either because of lack of loft or because of too much loft for your particular swing faults. This problem should not occur with the mid-irons; whatever your faults, you should be able to get the ball up in the air and not sky your shots too much.

Just use your normal golf swing and, once again, don't hit full out. There are no special prizes for getting on to the green with a 7 iron when others are using a 5. It's simply where the ball finishes that counts.

I would also suggest that you become particularly friendly with your 5 iron. It will move the ball a fair distance and can come in very useful for keeping the ball in play when you are horribly off form, as happens to all of us.

The Approach Clubs

Here I am mainly talking about the 8, the 9, the pitching wedge and the sand iron, when you are using a full swing. The main difficulties with these clubs comes from variable length. On the one hand, there are golfers who hit all of them rather too high and, on the other, those who hit them too low. In the first case this is usually caused by the hands being behind the clubhead, thus increasing the clubhead loft; in the second, the hands are too far ahead, which, of course, has the reverse result. And check your ball position, which can affect either case a great deal. If this is satisfactory, the fault must be in your hands in relation to clubhead position. This is far less easy to check. On the practice ground try to get the feel of your position at the point of impact. Better still, try to get someone to film you with a video camera or take still photos.

You may now be asking why very high or very low shots should be avoided. The main reason is that either the pattern of play produces too great a variety of distance, especially with the pitching wedge and the sand iron, where control of dis-

Variations in ball position for iron play, but beware of exaggeration

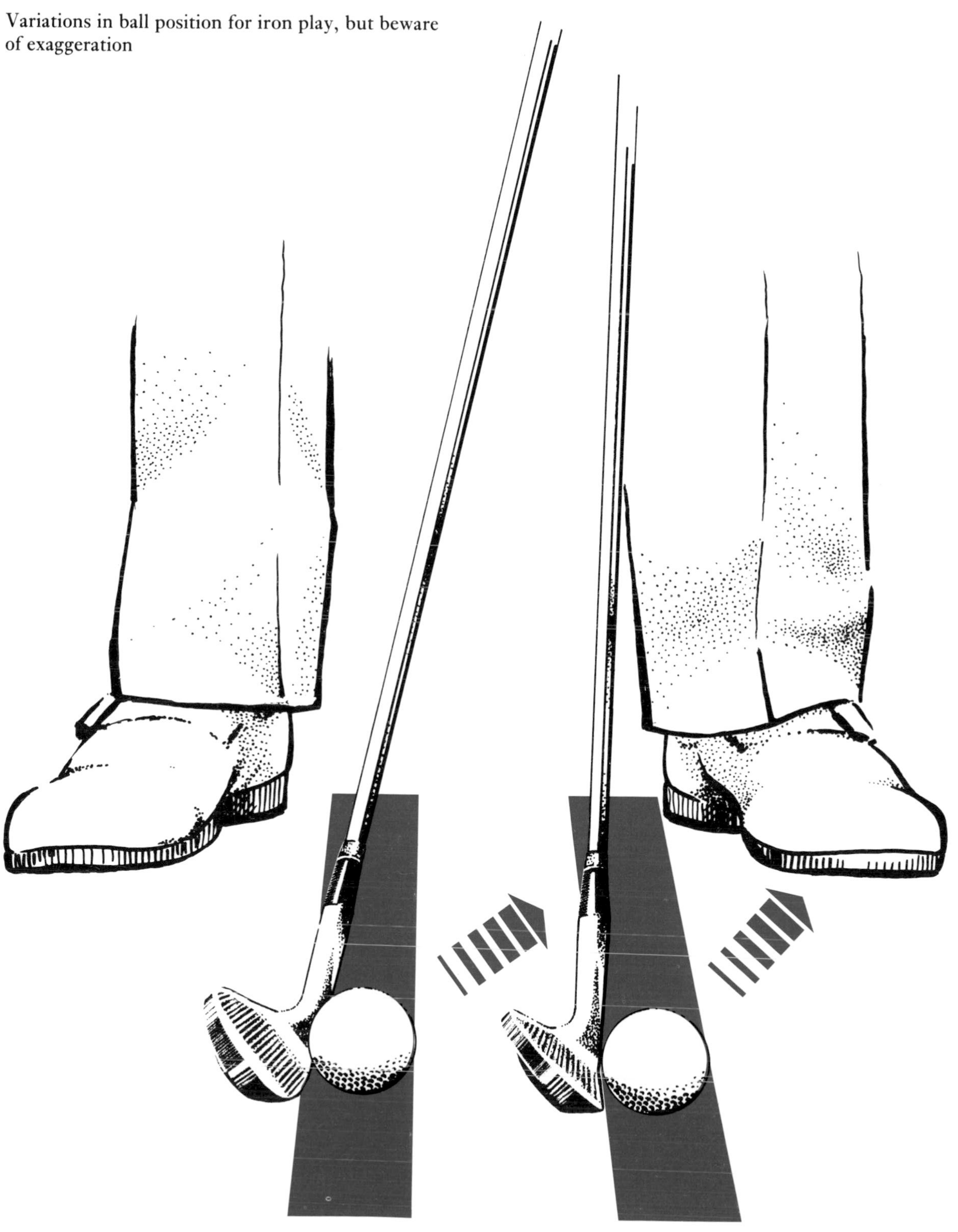

tance means the difference between being up to the flag, short of the green or well through the green.

Let me give you an example. I have heard club golfers – and professionals as well for that matter – boast that they can hit a sand wedge 120 yards. If true, all this means is that they are losing a great proportion of the stopping power of the club. They are hitting the ball an exceptional distance, but the flight is low, perhaps with some hook on the ball. The obvious result is that the ball will run on farther than required. The reverse is also unhelpful. With very high shots, you will begin to hit harder in order to get extra distance, whereas it's precision and control that are desperately wanted – and that's the name of this part of the golf game.

Move the ball back in the stance if you are hitting too high, forward if too low. You can also vary the position of your hands on the grip. Holding the club right at the top of the shaft tends to produce high shots. The lower down you grip the club, the lower the ball will fly.

Above all, remember that these are precision clubs. It doesn't matter in the least which club you use or how far you hit it. What matters is how close to the flag your ball finishes.

Putting

It's not just a game within a game, but two, perhaps even three, games in one. From, let's say, 20 yards you are trying to get the ball near the hole; from a few strides the aim is to leave your ball on the lip or at the bottom of the hole; our third category is holing out in the range where it is really a bit shameful to miss – those 2- to 4-footers, or even less.

Of course, the putting stroke is exactly the same for all these distances, though the mental attitude is not. From a long distance, you ought to be trying to get the feel of the yards to be covered into your finger and arm muscles; at medium range you must leave the ball nestling by the hole, but you are really hoping to hole out; while from pointblank range you simply must not miss.

Whatever the range, most golfers do not realize that many of their failures can be put down to poor striking. One who did was Bobby Locke, who, despite the incredible averages that both U S and European Tour players achieve per round nowadays, was the best putter I have ever seen. Locke believed that most golfers cut across the ball and so he devised a method that made this well-nigh impossible: he putted with his left foot well in advance of the right and swung the club back quickly inside and almost, it looked, around his right ankle. The Americans, on whose Tour he was so successful, claimed that he hooked the ball into the hole and perhaps they had a point, for Bobby Locke certainly always aimed for the right half of the hole. He felt that his method gave him consistency in striking – and that's what you should aim at. Every putt is a straight one, once you have decided the line to hit it along, but you must strike the middle of the back of the ball with the sweet spot of your putter. If you do not, you may have judged the strength to perfection, but you will always finish short of the hole.

Bobby Locke did not in fact have the perfect putting stroke any more than Lee Trevino or Jack Nicklaus has a perfect golf swing. What all great champions have is a method that they can repeat, so that their worst efforts are not too far away from their best.

So what are the ingredients of an effective putting method?

First, you have to have the right tool for the job. I know of one man who persisted for years in using a putter he had bought in a junk shop for a few pence when he started playing the game. He never thought to blame his putter for his fairly woeful efforts. Eventually he began to experiment and then found he was really quite effective with just about any club – except the one he had failed with for so long. As a beginner, experiment. I do not suggest that you buy a whole trunkful of putters, but try out any that you can borrow for a little light exercise on your club's putting green. You may well discover which of the many types suits you best. Remember that the great putters have come up with very different answers to the problem of getting the little white ball into the hole. Johnny Miller and Isao Aoki, for example, almost always use centre shafts. Jack Nicklaus and Gary Player favour the blade type. Tom Watson and Severiano Ballesteros always use putters with the weight evenly balanced between both the heel and toe. Of course, there are plenty of others for you to choose from. Some that look like branding irons or mallets; others with hickory shafts and/or marble heads; yet others may be a combination of all the ingenuities yet devised by man. Find something that suits you.

Whatever putter you eventually choose, some basic rules must be followed. The most important is that, as you strike the ball, your putter must be moving towards the target and parallel with the ground. You cannot putt consistently well if you jab downwards at the ball, lift up as you strike or do not have the clubhead moving towards the target in a straight line.

I believe the Locke method is best for most of us: hit from inside to out and, above all, avoid cutting across the ball in a right-to-left movement. You needn't carry this to his extreme. Straight back and straight through will also do very well, as long as the clubhead is carrying through towards the hole as you come into contact with the ball. Keep the club low to the ground throughout, for it is far more difficult to get it there as you hit the ball if you have lifted it up as you swing back.

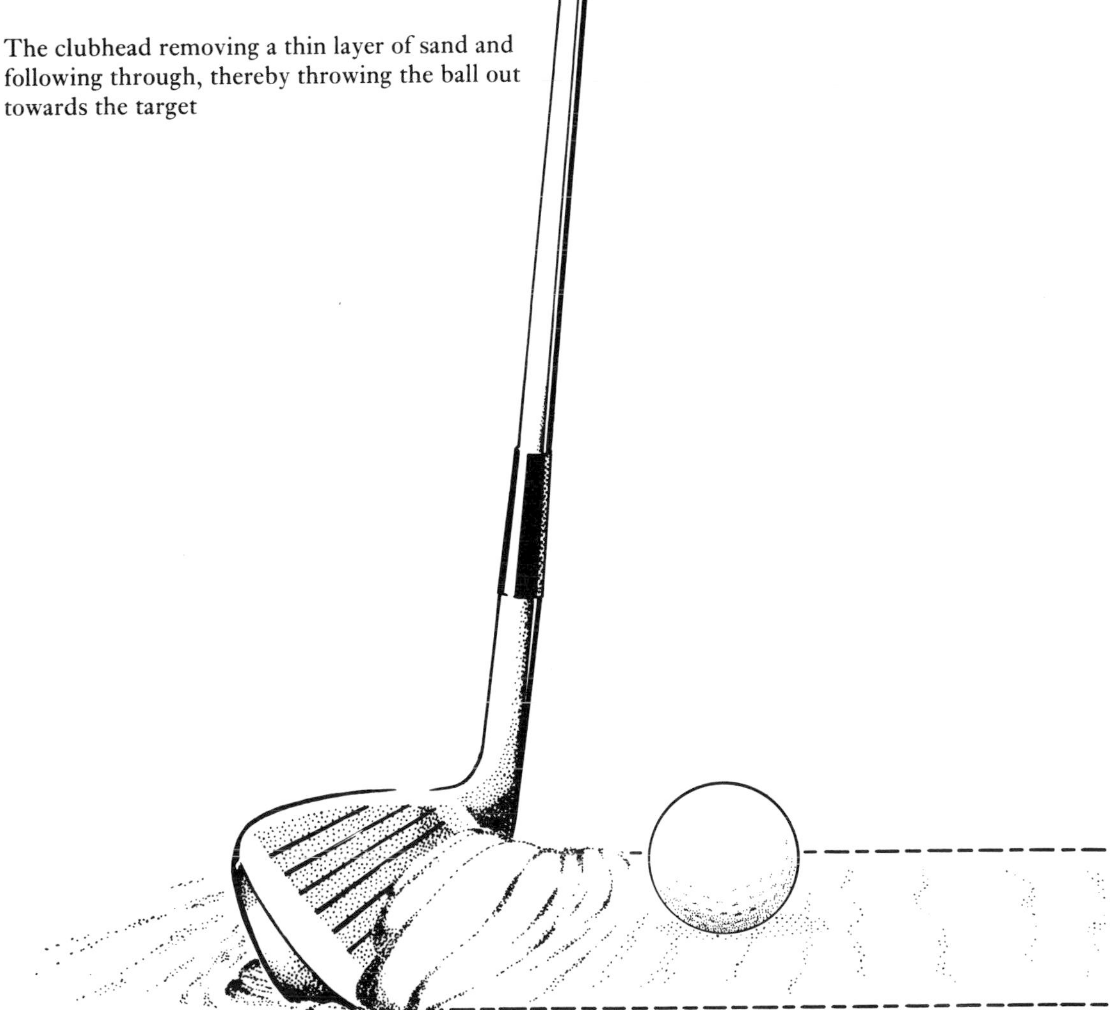

The clubhead removing a thin layer of sand and following through, thereby throwing the ball out towards the target

Nevertheless, I would be the first to admit that putting is the most individual part of our game of golf. There have been great putters who have broken this basic rule. Willie Park, for instance, believed that every putt should be sliced. He believed that this helped to hold the ball on line. One of our great moderns, Billy Casper, used a very wristy method; if you putt with your wrists hingeing you must lift the clubhead as you swing away from the ball. Alf Padgham suddenly had the thought that the putt is the golf swing in miniature and therefore putted with the ball much farther away from him than normal. For a while, around 1936, he carried all before him, so much so that he was considered superior to Henry Cotton and people began comparing him with Harry Vardon.

But these players, for a time, were geniuses on the greens. By the law of averages, you are unlikely to be, so follow the method that is tested by time and keep your clubhead close to the ground and in line with the hole.

Bunkered!

There are few things more annoying to the long-handicap golfer, or indeed to one with no handicap at all, than to be told that bunker shots are the easiest in golf. To get the ball close to the hole from a greenside bunker is a matter of both touch and artistry. Simply to get it out and onto the green is easy, however.

This is how you do it. For once I am going to allow you to lift the clubhead and on the outside rather than straight back or inside. Set the face of your club at least a little open. Now forget about the ball. Instead, concentrate about 2 inches behind the ball on that point in the sand where your clubhead will strike. In your mind's eye have the picture of removing a thin layer of sand which, just incidentally, happens to include a golf ball. What you should be thinking of is splashing sand onto the green.

You will need some experience of this basic shot so that you know how firmly to swing. Obviously the distance the sand and ball will go will depend on the speed of your swing.

Recovering from fairway bunkers is a different matter. You can still use your standard 2-inches-behind-the-ball shot to get out, but if your ball sitting cleanly on sand is hindered by the bunker face, you may wish to attempt a shot of some distance. In this case it is very much like striking a ball from turf. The problem is that there is almost no room for error. Hit the ball above centre and you will cause it to burrow into the sand. Hit a fraction behind the ball and the power of your swing will be lost. In either case, the likelihood is that you will see the ball still in the bunker and will have to try again.

A little experience should teach you what you can reasonably attempt. Remember, however, that even if you decide you are striking very exactly on a particular day there may be a bunker face in front of you. If it's 2 feet high and 2 feet in front of your ball you are going to need quite a lofted club to clear it. Otherwise, there is no objection to using, say, a 4 wood or a medium iron from a bunker if no real height on the ball is needed.

In the Rough

The most difficult club to use from the rough is a long iron, as I mentioned earlier. From the rough, use the easiest clubs in your bag, the short irons and lofted woods. If there is a lot of grass between the clubhead and the ball, the wedge or even the sand wedge are likely to be your best answer, and you should also be thinking in terms of the shortest route back to the fairway – even if it's only a very few yards away. Otherwise, a lofted wood is likely to be best because it will brush through the grass rather than have to cut its way through as an iron must do.

There is another advantage. A mediocre shot with a wood will travel much farther than a less-than-perfect iron shot. My advice to you is first to think 4 wood and then, if your lie is horrid, to switch to a lofted iron, nothing straighter in the blade than a 7 iron. Above all, leave the long irons safely in your bag.

As a postscript to this chapter, I should just like to add that, whatever your handicap or level of play, it is essential that you recognize your limitations and play to your strengths. Do make sure, too, that you understand the basic rules of the game, books on which are available at most golf clubs and centres.

Audrey, can you really get through those trees?

Fancy trying to hit a 3 wood from that lie!

Now, Audrey, you can't possibly carry all that water

Roddy, why not settle for a 1-stroke penalty instead of a possible 9?

It's not a sin to use a putter

3 On the Practice Ground

Practice is *not* a matter of going out with a bag of balls and hitting away until they are all used up, you exhausted and your hands well and truly blistered. That is no good at all for your golf. Mindless practice is something my father taught me to avoid years ago. 'Peter,' he said, 'you can learn more from hitting just twelve golf balls if you think about each shot and make each one count. Take time between each shot, as long as you like, and try to play a specific shot.' How right he was!

Hitting away at golf balls without pausing to think can only do any good when a player is in top form. He will have an aim even then: to keep the feel and rhythm going; but there will inevitably be faults that will still need attention.

Even the greatest players were, and are, not strong in every department of their game. Bobby Jones confessed to being weak with a niblick. Arnold Palmer has always been relatively inferior as a wedge player. Jack Nicklaus, so Lee Trevino has declared, was born without a sand wedge in the bag. My great friend David Thomas, who twice came so very near to winning the Open Championship, was the worst short pitcher and chipper I have ever seen for a player of his class. My own failings as a short putter I have recounted elsewhere. All these players have put in hours of practice to try to eradicate a weakness. Although practice may not always make perfect, great improvement can be expected.

Alas, many club golfers find this boring. If they are good drivers, they like to get out there and watch the ball fly up and away. I can hardly blame them, but if you have a weakness in your game it will find you out again and again as you go through your golfing year. If you are frightened of bunkers, fate will frequently put you in one. Whatever kind of shot, if you step up to it feeling that disaster lies ahead, disaster will result, flukes apart.

Henry Cotton training a pupil to use his wrists on the 'Cotton' tyre

The need for experiment

It pays dividends if you take time to build confidence – or at least banish fear. The place to do it is on the practice ground. And always choose a good piece of ground to play from. If the ground is very bad, use a tee peg.

Let's suppose your wedge play is giving you cause for concern. Faced with a shot of, let's say, 80 yards to the flag, you have no idea how far the ball will fly. Sometimes it climbs skywards and falls well short, at others it bores quite low through the air and you finish through the green. You realize that this is no good at all. Consistent length with the wedge is vital.

For the time being, you would be wise to leave it at home and play easier, more gentle shots with your 9 iron instead, or perhaps a push with an 8. But this is not the answer if you are one of the many who find it difficult to play half and three-quarter shots. Your lack of confidence with the wedge becomes a serious chink in your golf armoury.

Go to your practice area and experiment. The cause of your variety of high and low shots, as I have mentioned in chapter 2, is almost certainly that sometimes you get your hands in front of the clubhead at impact, while at other times they are behind. The first means low shots; the second means high. You may find that hitting a dozen

An easy backswing, a gentle follow-through, arms, hands and club together

or so shots free from pressure gives you the feel of the club and, suddenly, the problem disappears. If not, a change of ball position might well help. Move the ball back in your stance towards the right foot, just a touch for a start. If that doesn't work, take it farther back. Eventually, the very high shots will disappear and you can then modify your ball position until you get a reasonably consistent height of shot. In the end, you don't want to be hitting very low wedge shots – you might as well be using a 7 or an 8 iron if that's the case.

Always remember in your experimenting that the few basic essentials must be right before you draw the club back. Wherever you place the ball for wedge play matters very little if you have a quick, jerky backswing and no rhythm and balance into the ball.

Let's move on to another example, driving. The driver is one of the most difficult clubs to use for most players for the simple reasons that the shaft is the longest and the clubhead has the least loft of any club, putter excepted. The greater length of shaft makes it more difficult for you to control the clubhead and the straighter face increases any tendency you may have to hook or slice.

Well, for a start, I am not sure that you should be practising with your driver at all; certainly not until you're a fair to good player from the tee with a 3 wood. Almost every beginner and even moderately good club golfer will get better *average* length with this club and hit far more fairways.

Are you, I wonder, one of those many players who always starts a round using a fairway wood and then, if all is going very well, switches to the driver? You would be far better off to stay with the 3 wood, thinking not of the occasional long one but of the far better average you'll strike with it.

Whatever club you are practising with, always take your time. Think what you're trying to achieve with each shot and aim at a target. Practice facilities at many of our clubs are by no means what they should be. Perhaps there aren't any markers to aim at. If not, you will have to make do with aiming at a fold or a rise in the ground, a clump of grass or a shadow, so far as distance is concerned. For direction, there must surely be something – tree, chimneypot, pylon, telegraph pole – to align yourself with.

After each shot, stop to consider it. If it was good, why was this so? Don't hurry to try to repeat the performance but instead fix the feeling of that successful shot in your memory. How often you will find that it was rhythm and balance that did the trick. Hardly ever will a full-out flail at the ball deserve the credit.

When Not to Practise

Perhaps, dare I say it, you shouldn't be practising at all. Does this sound sacrilege after what I've been preaching? The fact of the matter is that you may be practising *faults*. If the whole of your golf game is in a hopeless state, you'll not have enough confidence to hit relaxed shots even on the practice ground, where there's no competitive pressure at all. You will merely be anxious and filled with self-doubt. Of course, you need help. If possible, go back to the professional who started you off in the game. He'll know your swing. If you're lucky, he may be able to spot a simple but basic fault that has developed without your being aware of it. Let me give you an example from the career of perhaps the greatest of them all, Bobby Jones, who wrote in the 1920s at the peak of his abilities:

> I've studied the irons a lot, and listened to many a lecture. The last one I listened to was the shortest, and it seems to have done the trick – for the time being, at any rate.
>
> I got away fairly well in Britain [a trip during which Jones won our 1926 Open Championship] with iron play that was never really satisfactory . . . I wasn't satisfied with the somewhat compromised style in which I was hitting the irons, and when I got home to Atlanta after the big journey of 1926 I went out and had a little talk with Stewart Maiden, who to me will always be the first Doctor of Golf. I suppose I did a little confessing.
>
> Stewart said, 'Let's see you hit a few.'
>
> I hit a few. Stewart seemed to be watching my right side. He is a man of few words.
>
> 'Square yourself round a bit,' said he.
>
> I had been playing a long time with a slightly open stance, my right foot and shoulder nearer the line of the shot than the left side.
>
> 'Move that right foot and shoulder back a bit,' said Stewart.

I did so, taking what is called a square stance.
'Now what do I do?' I asked Stewart.
'Knock the hell out of it!' said he concisely.
I did. The ball went like a ruled line.
That is Stewart Maiden's method of teaching or coaching. In this imperfect and complicated world I have encountered nothing else as simple and direct. Stewart saw that my swing was bringing the club on the ball from outside the line of play. He didn't bother with explanations or theories – he never does. He settled on one single thing by way of adjustment. It worked. That is a prime feature of his adjustments.

Of course, Bobby Jones was a genius. He had still been playing magnificently, subconsciously using his hands to compensate for the fact that he was swinging across the ball. All Stewart Maiden from Carnoustie had to do was to set his man up correctly. Certainly, for good players, bad alignment is the most common fault they have, when playing below their best.

Your professional may be able to do the same for you, though the results will hardly make you a Bobby Jones. Nevertheless, it is surprising how many simple faults there are which the golfer cannot see and feel for himself. Bad alignment is one example. Or perhaps the ball is too far forward (or back) in the stance. You've been in the wrong position for so many months or even years that it's come to feel, and look, normal. You need someone who knows what he's talking about to say something as simple as, 'Move the ball back 6 inches. Square your hips and shoulders to the target. Look at it over your left shoulder.'

These are just a few examples of simple faults your professional may notice immediately:

Your backswing is as fast as your downswing.
You're lifting the club up, not swinging it.
Your knees are as stiff as a guardsman at attention.
You're hardly turning the shoulders at all.
You're starting back to the ball before you've completed your backswing. It's all far too hurried and snatchy.
You're not using your right hand at impact. It's dead.
Your right hand is overpowering your left.
You're turning your shoulders away from the target as soon as you begin the downswing.
Your head and body are lifting up to follow the ball before you've even hit it.
You're trying to scoop the ball up into the air. Let the club do it for you and hit down and through the ball.

All these points are very simple. Yet how many golfers will not accept a particular point until someone they believe in tells them!

But don't just have a lesson when you're playing badly. There is a very good case for increasing your practice and taking lessons when you are playing well. If you are doing most things right, your professional can pick out far more confidently the one or two errors that remain. Perhaps he has a video machine and you will be able to see for yourself what is right and wrong. Remember, the right is just as important as the wrong! Far too many players think only in terms of why they are hitting bad shots. When they are playing well, they tend to think they are just playing their 'normal' game.

When your professional has made his point, this is the time to go off to the practice ground to work on what has been said while his words are fresh in your memory. If you are on form, you will have only one or two things to work on. This makes your task much simpler as you will not be burdened with too much detail. Work on these points and, again, do things slowly. Think. Hit a few, not a few hundred, balls. Pause after each shot to consider the result and analyse the causes.

In The Bunker

Bunker practice can cause the club golfer great difficulties. The reason is simple. The club does not allow practice in on-course bunkers, which is fair enough – we don't want our greens covered in sand. Alas, however, so many clubs fail to provide a practice bunker. Even if there is one, it's very unlikely to be adequately maintained. But scruffy as it may be, you'll have to make do or find a beach or a sandy stretch of ground.

Most high handicappers are frightened of the bunker shot because they remember previous failures from sand. Confidence is totally lacking; fear predominates.

The curse for the long hitter is that the fairways get narrower

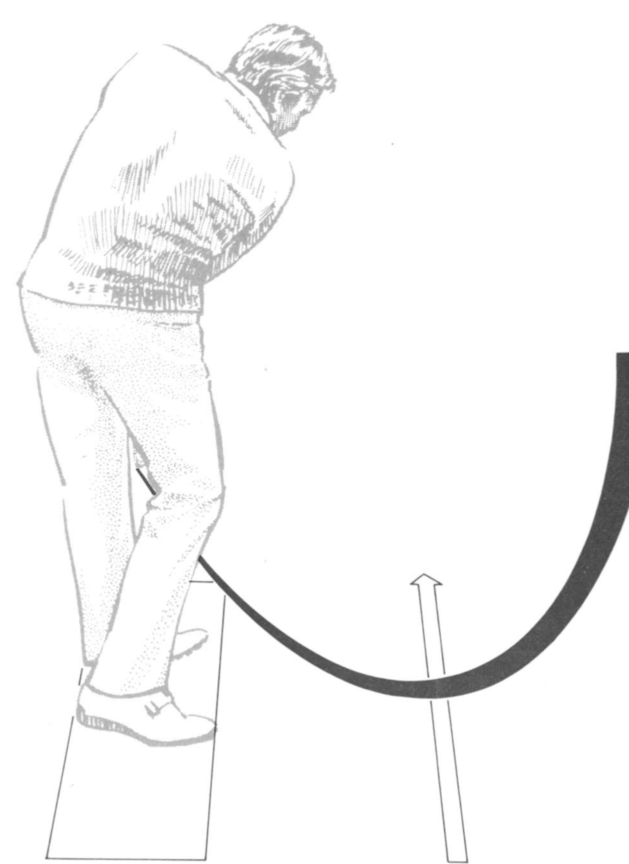

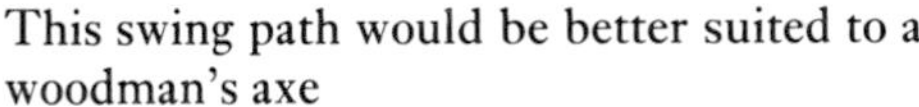

This swing path would be better suited to a woodman's axe

Yet if you practise bunker shots just a little you will rapidly lose most of if not all your fear. The sand shot is possibly the simplest in golf and the sand iron is the easiest club to use, designed with a single purpose in mind – to get you out of that bunker.

I don't, of course, mean that if you have a few sand shots you will, in the twinkling of an eye, become a maestro of the calibre of Gary Player or Isao Aoki. What I can promise you, however, is that you will soon learn to play the uncomplicated bunker shot with confidence. You will soon find that there is really not all that much to it. Just hit a couple of inches of so behind the ball and keep the clubhead going. In a trice both your ball and the sand beneath it will be on the imaginary green. In no time, you will learn to get the ball out with very fair consistency. Getting out of a bunker does not require a great golf swing; what you need is the ability to strike accurately at a particular spot in the sand. And confidence. Once you have that essential confidence, you are well placed to get distance from fairway bunkers and precision from greenside ones.

Pitching

Unless your club has a practice green to pitch to – alas, quite rare – pitching can be misleading on an ordinary practice ground. On landing, the ball will not behave as it would on a closely mown, well-prepared green. Instead, you will have to aim at a marker and note how near to it your ball lands. As the ground will almost invariably be uneven, the ball will not pitch and stop predictably as it would on a receptive green. However, your batch of balls should all end up in as tight an area as possible, with no wild strays. Remember, though, that the short pitch is per-

How much better this swing is!

haps the weakest shot of all in most club golfers' repertoires. It really ought to be possible for you, from 50 to 80 yards, for example, to knock the ball up in the air and pitch it in somewhere near the flag. Yet how few can do this consistently. It most certainly is an area of your golf where you can hope to improve enormously with practice. In the average fourball, the man who can play this shot well prospers and will collect most of the sidestakes.

Chipping

Chipping does not need a splendid swing. Mainly, you need the ability, which should come from experience, to judge the run of the ball in the prevailing conditions; and you also need *confidence*. You must feel sure that you can strike the ball as you intend so that you can concentrate on the pace of your miniature swing rather than worry whether you are about to top the ball or scuff the ground in front of it. Here you can usually practise in ideal conditions: from just off the edge of your club's putting green. You will benefit more from using it in this way than from practising your putting there. Yet very few golfers chip to their putting green. It's usually somewhere where they take out their putters.

There are two schools of thought as to which clubs should be used for chipping (remember, this is a running shot with little height where most of the travel is over turf, not in the air). Some say that a golfer should be able to chip with every club from a 4 iron to a sand wedge. Others, Neil Coles, for example, prefer to use the same club all the time, in his case a sand iron. Whatever the club, the aim in chipping is to send the ball onto the closely mown surface of the green and then let it run towards the hole. On average you will do better if you specialize in, at the most, three clubs – the 9, the 7 and the 5, or some similar variation. The greatest chipper I have ever known, Charlie Ward, concentrated on the wedge and the 4 iron; they suited him best. It's up to you to decide which clubs you feel most confident with. And don't forget the putter. If you are a good long putter and a rather poor chipper, you could do worse, especially when the ground is either frozen or soft, than use the putter from, say, 10 yards off the green. You may well be able to judge the run of the shot better. I know some club golfers who choose to putt from the semi-rough. It works (more or less) for them because they have that essential ingredient of confidence when using the club.

Putting

Now it's about time to finish off with a little putting. Again, as always, think about what you are trying to achieve. Don't just go out there and knock balls about.

Long putting is a matter of touch, judgement of distance and striking the ball in the sweet spot. Short putting, except for the occasional little curly ones, demands that you should be able to knock the ball a short distance dead straight, with rhythm and tempo. For both lengths, you need good nerves and confidence, and I'm afraid I have no magic words or pills for either. Your own confidence will have to be the answer and, to a greater or lesser degree, that will come from practice, from knowing that you can do it because you've done it many times before.

Many of us are very unsteady from 3 or 4 feet. Even without thousands of pounds or dollars at stake, we may well be appalled at the thought that something so obviously easy can, as Babe Zaharias once said, be so 'fouled up by the mechanics'. And nerves or, more exactly, the fear of looking a fool. In fact, there is no golfer on earth who wouldn't hasten to pay you good money for a guaranteed method of pushing the rather short ones into the hole, T. S. Watson and J. W. Nicklaus included.

Once again, confidence is the first requirement and you can build it in the following way. Start from somewhere around the 1-foot mark and bang them in. You can now begin to introduce a drill that is extremely boring but effective. Insist to yourself that you must hole every ball from 1 foot. Then you go on to, let's say, six balls from $1\frac{1}{2}$ feet – and so on. But if one misses, then it's back to the beginning again. Charlie Ward used to throw down twenty balls just off the practice putting green at Little Aston. If he could not get each down in 2, with a chip and a putt, he started again. You need to be programmed to know and feel that a short putt is easy (although, of course, some will unaccountably miss).

It is also interesting to notice just how hard you can strike the ball at this range before it jumps out of the hole. Nick Faldo always seems to hit his short ones in very firmly indeed. No doubt his reason is that spike marks and other little imperfections in the putting surface around the hole will have less effect on the run of a fast-moving ball; they most certainly do interrupt the run of one that is dying into the hole.

When practising your long putting, pay relatively little attention to line. Most players fail to get these putts close to the hole (within 3 feet) because they have failed to judge the strength of their putt or have mishit. Bad judgement can cause you to be either too long or too short. A mishit one will always be too short.

Experience will improve your judgement. I doubt that all the prowling and plumb-bobbing indulged in by today's stars make very much difference. Experience enables you to judge, after little more than a quick glance, the pace of a green. I know from my own experience that much of my best long putting came in exhibition games. With no real pressure involved, I would walk up to the ball, look carefully but quickly along the line and then send it away. It was surprising how often it went in.

Nerves apart, poor striking is the root cause of most bad putting, especially from long distance. Yet may club golfers fail to notice when they strike a putt badly. They think their ball is well short because they didn't read the green correctly or they think, 'Damn, I didn't give it enough.' Well, the putt was made with the right strength, but perhaps because of body movement the sweet spot on the blade has not met the middle of the ball.

Obviously you must know where the sweet

spot is. Don't assume it's exactly midway between the toe and the heel of the club, though it may well be. Sometimes, however, it's nearer the heel (seldom the toe). To find out, bounce a ball gently on the face of the club. You will know by the feel of the bounce when you have found it. You can then make a small mark or perhaps use a letter of the maker's or model's name as a guide.

It is also useful to ask someone to check that your line into the ball is correct. Jabbing down is a common error. It may have worked wonderfully well for Gary Player; it doesn't for the rest of us. It is possible to putt very well indeed like this, *à la* Isao Aoki or the young Dai Rees of the 1930s, who used to slice everything into the hole. But it takes a rare touch. Why make the putting game more difficult for yourself? Bobby Locke believed that this was the worst fault of all.

Remember, whatever method you eventually find that suits you best, it must enable you to strike the ball well consistently. This is just as important as a method that enables you to putt on the line you've chosen.

Practice need not be a drudgery. If you set yourself reasonable aims and achieve them, you will get enormous satisfaction – and practice does improve your game.

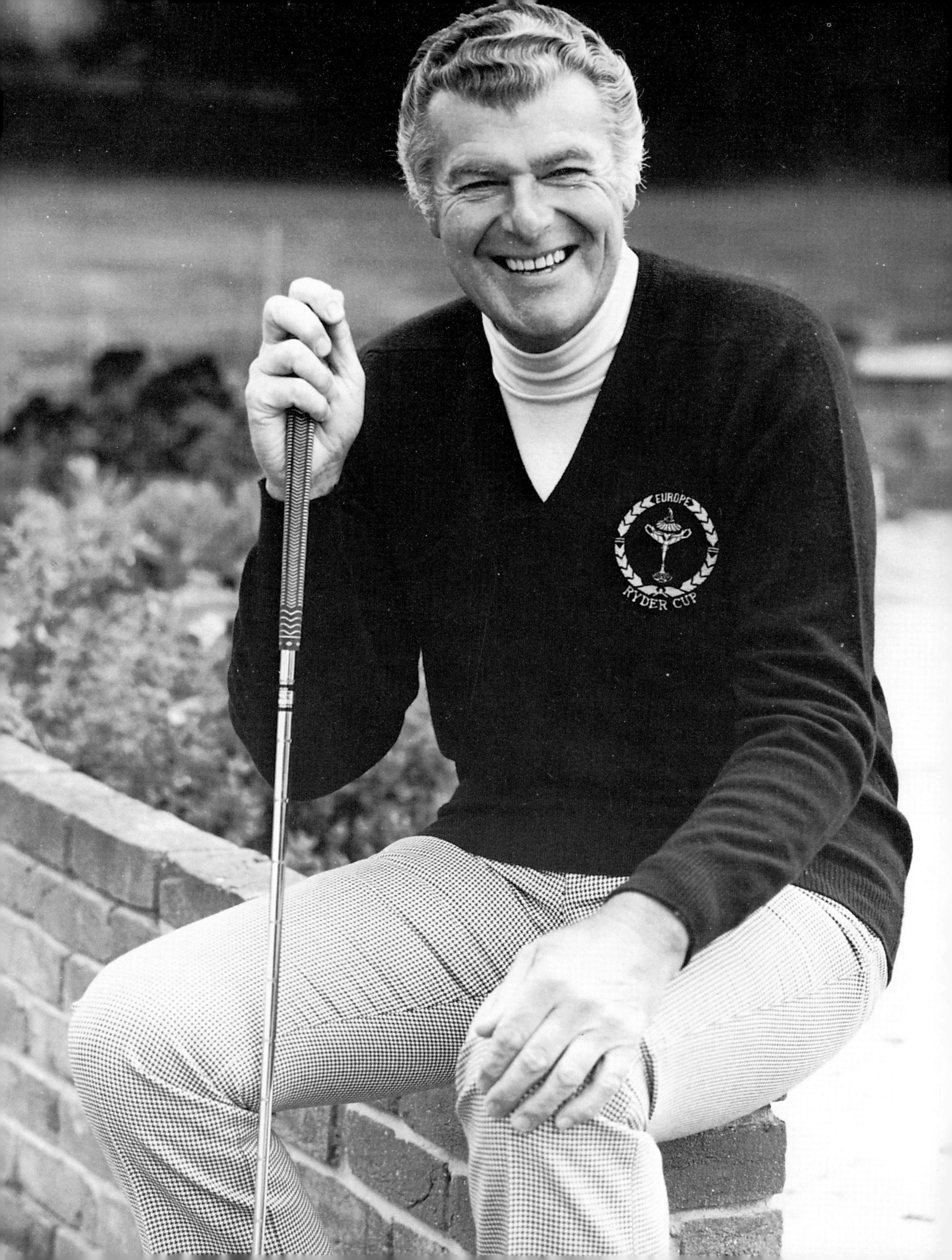
EUROPE
RYDER CUP

4 Tips from the Top

Golfers are used to reading advice on how to play the game from the great players of the day – the Nicklauses, Watsons and Ballesteroses of modern golf. Earlier there were the Hogans, Sneads and Cottons. All have dispensed their philosophies, hoping the books would sell and the world be littered with first-class players.

But a club golfer once suggested to me that such mighty men don't have the slightest idea of what it's really like to be less than talented. 'Look,' the high-handicapper said, 'these fellows are actually superbly gifted athletes. I'm not. Their advice to me is about as much use as Daley Thompson writing a book about how an ordinary chap with a nine to five job can win the decathlon. It just ain't on. I'll never be able to thunder a drive 300 yards, force a 1 iron from a bare downhill lie with just that right touch of fade to feather it in at the pin. I don't even have much feel for the little chips and putts either.'

He had a point. What he seemed to want was a book or series of articles written by a man or woman who was no more than a 'respectable' golfer. He wanted advice that was not too ambitious.

I'm responding with this chapter title. 'Top' does not refer to the superstars of golf but to those who have achieved fame in other walks of life. The sort of people, in fact, who appear on our BBC 'Pro-Celebrity' series.

This has run since 1974 and we've seen countless celebrities at both Turnberry and Gleneagles. They make a very good cross-section of the world of golf. Yet, make no mistake about it, some are very good indeed. As far as striking the ball, two have stood out: Sir Garfield Sobers and Ted Dexter, both cricketers supreme. They had the balance, rhythm and timing to be exciting strikers of a cricket ball and it's not surprising that they can deal with a golf ball just as effectively.

Ted Dexter, right at the top of my list of exciting, elegant batsmen, produced drives at Gleneagles of a length that amazed not only me but Lee Trevino also. But because of his better touch, I'd rank Sobers the higher of the two.

What marks out these men, and nearly all the others who have appeared in our programmes, is their competitiveness. Whether they have reached the top as singer, sportsman, comic, actor – no matter what – they have the desire to succeed. It shows through in their golf. The majority don't have impressive golf swings but do remarkably well at making the best of what they have. Of course, they all dream of being so much better, but, in the meantime, they battle on.

Of them all, perhaps the racing drivers have impressed me the most. To someone who can accelerate up towards the 200 m.p.h. mark along the Mulsanne straight, and corner flat out on 'dry' tyres when it's pouring with rain, a little golf ball shouldn't be all that frightening. Yet when they stand on the first tee, with the cameras turning and 2000 people looking on critically, it's entirely different from a private game at a golf club. No one likes looking a fool and golf is not their business.

Although the racing drivers seem to make the most of their abilities, the others are not far behind. Take Henry Cooper, for example. He'd be the first to admit his swing is not elegant. His

John Jacobs – a dear friend and the world's leading coach

body is all over the place and he looks very stiff for a man who moved so lightly around the boxing ring and punched with such speed, timing and precision. Even so, the results he gets from his swing are not at all bad. His putting action also looks rather rigid, but it's an asset in his armoury. He's a good holer-out and gets the long ones close.

When the day's filming is over, golf is usually the main topic of conversation. Many's the tip, over the years, I've heard from these celebrities, keen handicap golfers to a man. Of course, they concentrate on something that has been useful for their own games. Many have contributed their thoughts to what follows; they include Jackie Stewart, James Hunt, Nigel Mansell, Alex Higgins, Ray Reardon, Cliff Thorburn, Gary Sobers, Ted Dexter, Colin Cowdrey, Gareth Edwards, Sean Connery, James Bolam, Richie Benaud, Cliff Michelmore, Henry Cooper, Jimmy Tarbuck, Dickie Henderson, Ronnie Corbett, Brian Close, Howard Keel, Eric Sykes, Val Doonican, Terry Wogan, Bing Crosby, Michael Bonallack, Hugh Scanlon, Harry Carpenter, Michael Parkinson – indeed, Uncle Tom Cobleigh and all.

To their thoughts can be added those of the top professionals who have appeared in the series. They too have each tried a gimmick for a while before eventually it lost its magic. This might be a key thought about their swing, a pressure point on one finger, a weight adjustment. The list is endless.

I've grouped the tips I've collected over the years under a few headings. When your game is off, leaf through. You may pick out and try a couple of suggestions, and suddenly, hey presto, you've found the secret!

There are many different ways of playing golf well. Equally, there are different ways of saying the same thing. So don't blame me if some of the tips don't work and, let me be the first to point out, some contradict each other. However, let's begin with putting.

Henry Cooper displaying good firm wrists

Putting

There've been more tips by far about putting than about any other part of golf. Although there are accepted ways of doing it, there's no accounting for genius. Looking back, Bobby Jones used a very light blade – 'Calamity Jane' he called it – standing with feet very close together. On the other hand, his great contemporary, Walter Hagen, stood with feet wide apart. In more recent times, Jack Nicklaus has stood hunched over the ball, his right arm acting like a piston; Ben Crenshaw with both arms acting in unison; Bobby Locke swinging the club around his right ankle; Peter Thomson with a very long backswing and almost no follow-through at all; Seve Ballesteros getting lower and lower over the ball with the toe of the club getting higher – not quite to the extent of Isao Aoki but coming closer.

Yet the accepted classical styles remain good examples. Amongst these, I would rank the shoulder movement of Bob Charles, the forearm action of Tom Watson, and the wristiness of Billy Casper. Three great putters and three very different ways of doing it. Perhaps, in the end, if you can keep your body still and time your swing with a rhythmical back and forward movement, and send the ball at the hole at the right pace, you really ought to be a better putter than most.

So let's go through our tips. They are general pointers that have brought success over the years to not a few.

1 When lining up from whatever distance, pick a spot, say, 6 to 9 inches from your clubhead and on line to the target. Decide your strength and then roll the ball over your selected spot.

2 Keep your putter low to the ground on the backswing. (Yes, I know Peter Thomson picked the club almost straight up in the air!)

3 Keep your head still. Don't look up quickly to see if you've holed it. Hit and listen for the sound of the ball tumbling into the cup, like Harry Bradshaw. Arnold Palmer always thought a still head and body of vital importance and that's why he settled into a locked and knock-kneed stance.

Just a small selection of the stars who have appeared on BBC's 'Pro-Celebrity' golf over the past ten years

4 Think of your wrists as a hinge on back and forward swing. Your putterhead will naturally return square to the ball. In essence this was Casper's method and also Kel Nagle's, winner of the Open Championship in 1960. This Australian imagined his action as being like the opening and closing of a gate.

5 On the other hand, don't break the wrists at all. Think of the putting stroke as an arm and shoulder movement from the base of the neck.

6 Choose a heavy putter. You won't have to hit the ball as hard. This may prove useful to those who play on the slower greens of parkland courses and in the winter.

7 Try a light putter. You may feel free to strike the ball more positively. The lightness may help on fast links greens in particular.

8 Find a putter that suits you and stay loyal to it. When you putt badly, blame your touch or alignment, not the putter.

9 When your putting goes off, try another club.

10 For long putts, concentrate on strength alone and let direction come naturally. Try for a strength that will get your ball into the 3-foot range.

11 For short putts, push your bottom hand through at the hole. Aim at a particular spot on the edge, not vaguely at the whole target.

12 Take the putter back with your left arm and strike the ball with your right hand.

13 Think of the putt as a backhand stroke. Your right hand just steadies the club.

14 Always be comfortable.

15 Always have your eyes over the top of the ball, preferably just behind it.

16 Try different stances – closed, square and open.

17 Try different ball positions, from in front of the left toe to near the back foot.

18 Try different grips – all fingers on the club, the Vardon, the reverse overlap and hands spread apart.

19 Vary the distribution of your weight.

20 Point your left foot at the hole or, alternatively, keep it exactly square.

The Full Swing

1 Keep your elbows in time with your hips. Tom Watson aroused great interest, during filming of the BBC 'Pro-Celebrity' series in 1983 at Gleneagles, when he said this was what he always looked for in his own swing.

2 'No one ever swung a golf club too slowly.' This was said by Bobby Jones and featured in his own swing, which had an almost drowsy rhythm. Similarly, the great English amateur Leonard Crawley swung lazily. He didn't seem to accelerate, even in the hitting area. However, it is possible to swing the club *back* too slowly. The whole thing can become too ponderous and rhythm can be lost.

3 Correct alignment of the body along the target line and correct ball placement is half the game of golf. I believe it's easily the most common area of trouble. Good players often find they gradually come to aim too far to the right and poorer ones set up to the left.

4 Try to feel 'oily' in your swing. This key word may help you to be relaxed and fluent.

5 Freewheel *through* the ball. Don't swing *at* it.

6 Think of the golf swing as a windmill. Your body is the tower and your arms the sails. The great difficulty in golf is to synchronize the body turn with the arm swing.

7 Good leg action is the foundation of the golf swing. Leg action is essential for rhythm and balance and helps keep the club going along the target line. I am amongst those who think, however, that leg action is not by any means as important a source of power as some have argued. Seve Ballesteros can hit a golf ball 250 yards, either seated on a shooting stick or on his knees, while Bob Toski can manage 230 yards on one leg. The great Jack Nicklaus has become an 'arms and hands' man, whereas he used to believe much of his power came from the legs.

8 Good golf is played with the hands and arms. Bad golf is played with the body. Don't hit at the ball with your navel or heave with your shoulders.

9 Feel yourself hitting past your chin while your head remains behind the ball.

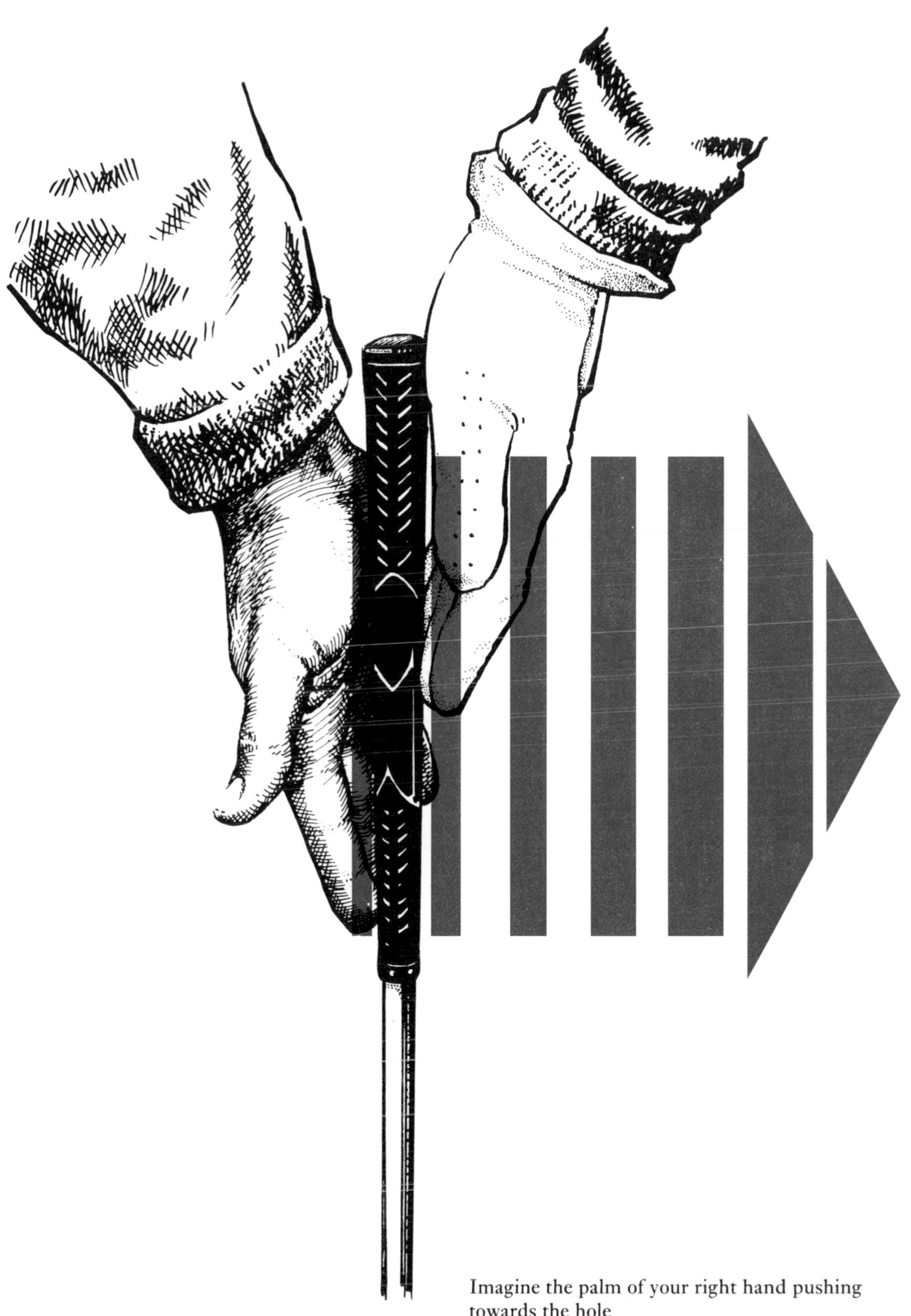

Imagine the palm of your right hand pushing towards the hole

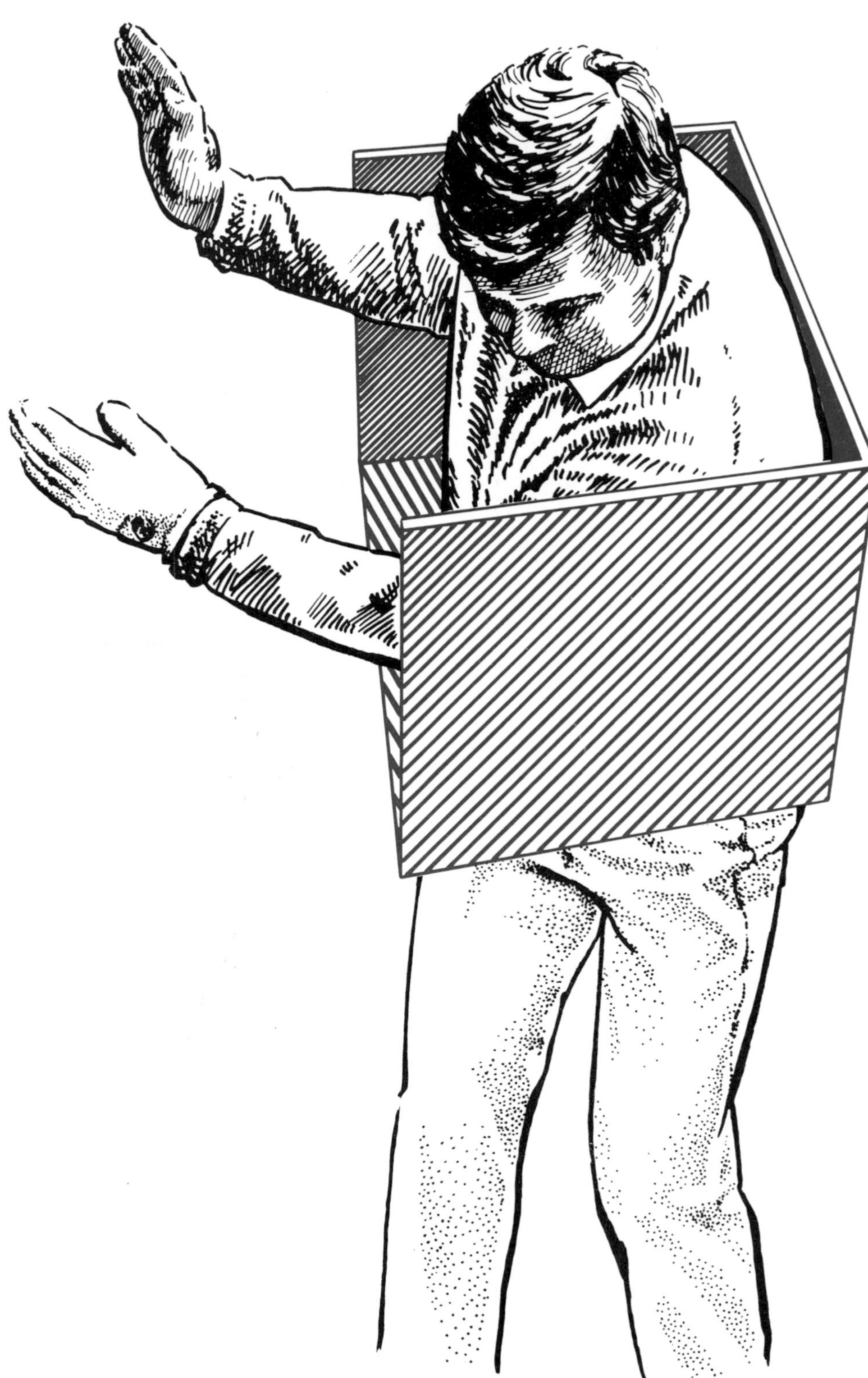

Watson's imaginary box for elbows and hips

10 Feel your feet rocking on the backswing, not lifting. Have your weight on the pad underneath the big toe and rock to the inside of your left foot.

11 Swing against a firm left side and throw the clubhead towards the target.

12 Nothing should resist your follow-through. Slide your knees towards the target. Perhaps Byron Nelson was the first great player with this philosophy, while Henry Cotton was the most important advocate of the firm-left-side theory.

13 If you get blisters and sore places on your hands, your grip on the club must be faulty, allowing movement. Practise without a left-hand glove to check. Indeed, don't slavishly wear a left-hand glove. Most players, however, apparently find that wearing a glove is helpful and it serves as a reminder that golf is a left-sided game. Max Faulkner, 1951 Open Champion, used to argue that if using a glove on the left hand gave a more secure grip then surely wearing one on the right hand would be equally beneficial!

14 Keep the club low to the ground as long as is comfortable on the backswing. It helps to stop you lifting the club up and stretches the muscles.

15 Make sure your left shoulder swings back at least so far that your back is square to the target.

16 Don't break your wrists early. This will help you to make a good shoulder turn.

17 Break your wrists early. This helps set the angle of the backswing and you can then go on with the body wind-up. When I won the Italian, Spanish and Portuguese titles in a row in 1958 the one thing I thought about, after I'd taken aim, was breaking the right wrist as I moved the clubhead away from the ball. I then kept it in that position and drove through the ball to a good finish. It was terrific. I couldn't miss. I was disappointed when the season ended and I had to wait until March for action to begin again. Alas, I then found I'd lost most of the magic.

Chipping

1 Set your weight towards the left side and have your hands well ahead of the ball at both address and impact. This is illustrated by both Gary Player, who produces a chip that runs and checks (rather than floats and checks), and Lee Trevino, who allows very little follow-through.

2 Imagine you're bowling the ball towards the flag with your right hand. The clubhead should feel an extension of that hand as you float your palm towards the hole.

3 Feel you are striking the ball with the back of your left hand. This helps to keep your hands ahead of the clubhead, vital in good chipping, and is Lee Trevino's method.

4 Pick the spot where you want your ball to land, just on the green, and select your club accordingly.

5 Concentrate on becoming confident with just two or three clubs. Some players use only the one and vary the kind of shots they play with it, opening and closing the face and varying the height by the angle of their swing into the ball.

6 Chip with a club that'll give little backspin, the 6 and 7 irons especially. The more lofted clubs can confound even a good shot when the ball checks unexpectedly.

7 Get used to every club in the bag for chipping. It's perhaps a rather old-fashioned concept, but Henry Cotton once said he used his 1 iron more from around 30 yards than for full shots.

8 Keep your wrists out of your chipping stroke. This is likely to suit those who putt with a shoulder movement.

9 For short chips, try using your usual putting grip. Many top players use their reverse overlap grip and it's at least worth a try. But don't be greedy and use it from farther and farther away from the green. It won't work for ever.

The Short Pitch

1 Make your sand iron your friend and practise with it. As it has the most loft, it will give you the most backspin and you may have the feeling of placing the ball very near where you want it to finish. You'll have to move the ball back in your stance, however, so that the leading edge of the club is nearer the ground than the rear flange.

2 Or the reverse. Play with the ball positioned well forward in your stance and the blade of your

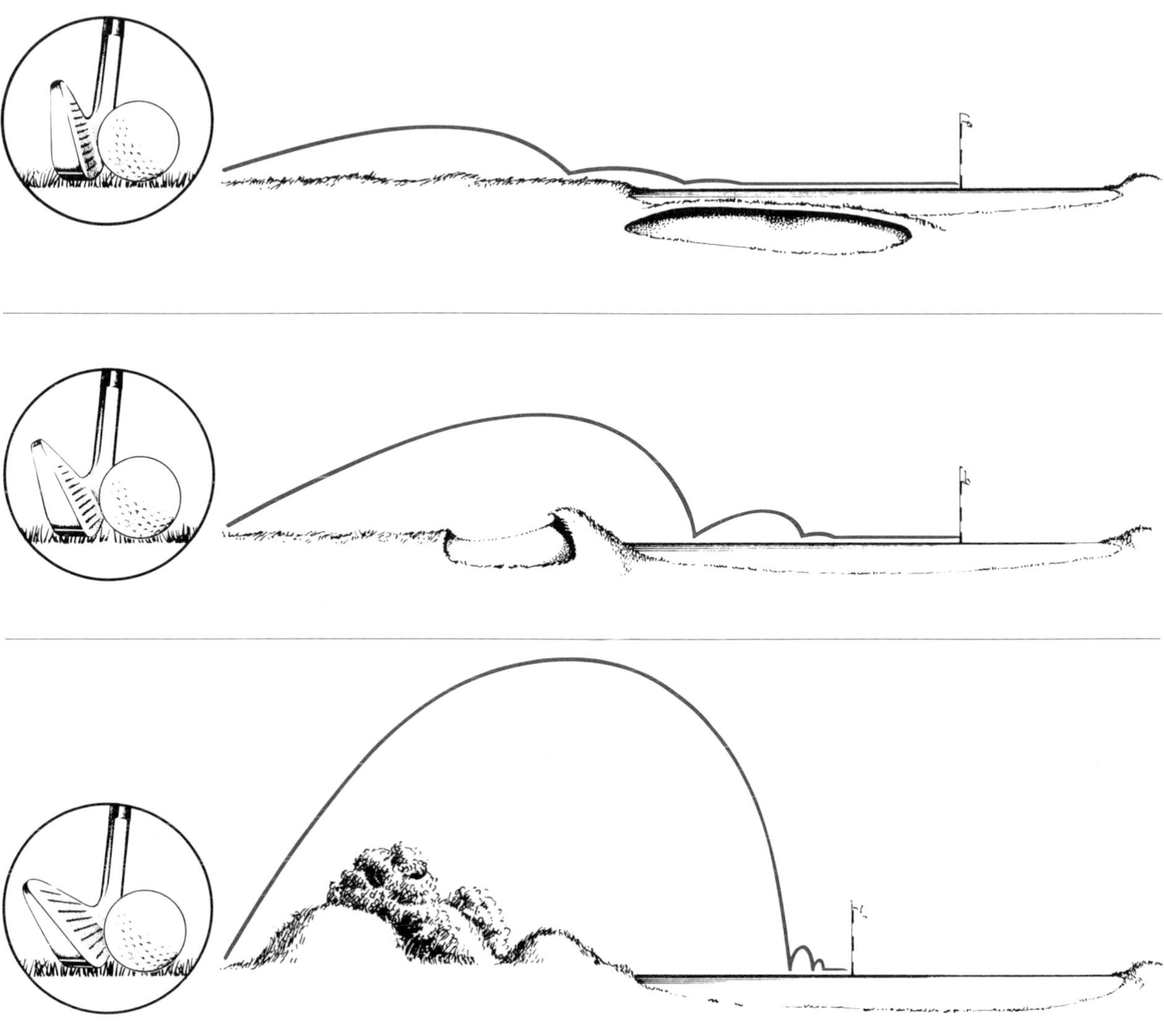

These three illustrations show how under various conditions you should try to imagine the pitch and run of the ball to the target

club open. Have both feet turned slightly towards the hole with about 70 per cent of your weight on the front foot. Hands must be kept ahead of the clubhead.

3 Imagine you are playing off a pane of glass or marble. Better still, actually do so. If you can flick the ball off the surface you'll be well on the way to excellence.

Bunker Shots

1 Think in terms of throwing the sand underneath your ball, as well as the ball itself, onto the green.

2 To vary the length of shot, hit into the sand nearer and nearer to the ball, thus increasing your distance. Start about 3 inches away.

3 Always play from sand with a firm grip and keep the clubhead moving through the sand.

4 Switch to your wedge or 9 iron when the sand is hard and wet. Your sand iron may well bounce.

5 Make sure you have a sand iron that suits both you and the bunkers of your home course. In general, for soft seaside sand a heavy club with a deep flange or low rear edge is best. A thinner flange may be better on clayey inland

courses as the shot becomes more of a pitch. If you find the right club, keep it when you part-exchange your irons for a new matched set.

6 Slide the clubhead under the ball from right to left and keep the clubhead moving towards a full follow-through.

7 When the ball is buried in soft sand, consider realistically what the alternatives are. You may well be better off playing out sideways. There are two ways of playing the shot when all is not impossible. One is the Chi Chi Rodriguez method, as I call it. Open the blade of your club, keep your hands well forward, break your wrists and drive the clubhead into the sand behind the ball and keep it going deeper and deeper in the general direction of Australia. The shock waves will remove your ball, with some height. The other method, which will work if the bunker's face is not too high, is to close the club face and strike the sand between 1 and 2 inches behind the ball; keep the clubhead moving to a full follow-through.

8 Most bunker shots fail because the player doesn't hit firmly enough. Practise a little and you'll find that you can hit full out and the ball won't go very far if your club enters the sand well before the ball. A snatchy, twitchy stroke is death to good bunker play.

Well, there's my brief selection of tips. When you come across one that works for you, be sure to make a note of it. Many of the great players have learned that the memory can play us tricks. Even if the magic fails totally in 1985, if you've written it down, it might well come in useful in 1995.

A good finish to a greenside bunker shot

5 The Mental Game

The right mental approach begins long before you get to your golf club. It starts with your equipment. Are your grips dry? Have you cleaned them recently to get back the tackiness and remove the shine? What are your shoes like? Have you dried them out in a cool, dry place (not on a radiator!) if they were soaked through last time out? Are spikes missing or too worn down to grip? If so, get to your pro's shop early and have replacements fitted.

A look at the faces of your irons is always worth the trouble. Are the grooves filled with hard dried mud and grass? Although this makes little difference to backspin, everyone *feels* more of a golfer when using a new ball and setting a gleaming clubface against it. It helps to give you confidence, the lack of which is a prime cause of many bad rounds.

Finally, think about your clothing. See what the weathermen have to say and plan your day's outfit so that you can keep yourself and your clubs dry. Both winter and summer, temperatures can change a great deal and winds suddenly rise or fall. No professional worth his salt sets out in a tournament without a spare sweater or two, an umbrella and a reliable set of waterproofs. Some kind of headgear is also essential. None of us likes the feeling of rain trickling down the neck from a rain-soaked head.

Of course, temperatures can also rise, storm clouds give way to hot, humid afternoons. You should always be able to strip down to something both comfortable and acceptable to your club – perhaps a cotton shirt.

Gary Player – determined concentration

These minor, but highly important, things accomplished, you are ready to set out. I hope you've allowed yourself plenty of time. It doesn't help produce a relaxed swing on the first tee if you have had to fight a losing battle on the way, with every traffic light set on red and every car in front of you apparently on a leisurely sightseeing excursion. It is much better to arrive for a game with a reasonable amount of time to spare. If you are playing at your home club, this need only be ten minutes or so. If, however, you are due at a strange venue, bear in mind that most golf clubs are not well signposted. You may have to stop a couple of times to ask directions, and you will also need time to solve the geography of the clubhouse once you have arrived.

All right, let's suppose your achievements have been 100 per cent by the time you reach the first tee.

You are now about to play one of the most important shots of your golfing day. Not many courses start with a par 3, so you will probably need to use a wooden club for your first shot. Success or failure at this point can have a very strong influence on your confidence in the rest of the round. So give yourself every chance and use a club you trust. If it's your driver, fine, but if you feel safer with a 3 or 4 wood (even a 5 iron), use that. For most of us, the choice will probably be a wood with some loft on the face. If in the end you hit a shot with some slice or hook on it, the loft will help to prevent a disaster.

For this first shot of the round, be sure that you *complete* your backswing (nothing hurried and jerky please!) and that you swing freely through the ball, your main thought being to make solid contact. If you manage these two things, your chances of making a successful shot

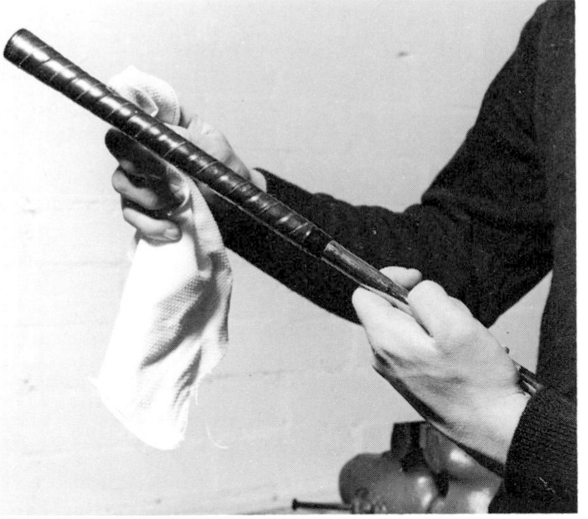

I know it's a bore, but golf equipment is expensive so why not spend a moment or two looking after it?

are quite high; slim or none if you jerk the club quickly away, hurry it back down and are all anxiety in the hitting area, ready to look up to see what disaster has befallen you.

Good, that wasn't bad at all, was it? You carried out my basic demands well enough. Perhaps the clubface was a little open or shut, but your ball is on the fairway, a respectable distance away.

Let's suppose you are now faced with a second shot to a flag some 180 yards away in the middle of a green. Even if you are a fair long-iron player, now is not the time to take one out of your bag unless you've given yourself some time on the practice ground and are full of confidence. Far better to use a club with which you don't need to hit flat out, so you can concentrate on swinging easily but firmly and getting the clubhead to meet the back of the ball.

'I'll be through the back of the green,' did I hear you say? Well, possibly, but it's early in your round and your muscles won't have loosened up, so that's unlikely. Even if you do go through, consider how much trouble there is on the approach. Most golf holes are designed with bunkers to catch and slopes to divert inaccurate approach shots. Sometimes going through a green gives less of a penalty than being short. However, ignore my advice about over-clubbing if there's river, ravine or impenetrable bushes immediately behind!

Ah, you struck that one moderately well, though nothing fancy. It was a little off line but almost exactly the right length. You've a 20-foot putt from the left edge.

So far, your confidence ought to be building nicely. You have attempted nothing spectacular (your opponent, who tried to boom a drive off the first tee, half-topped it and then tried to crack a 3 iron out of the rough, has just reached the green in 4) and you've done nothing very wrong.

You are now faced with another of golf's frighteners: the first putt. Weigh this one up carefully, though there is no need to take an age about it. Try to feel in your hands and arms just how hard you are going to strike it so that you get the right length. Delightful, should you happen to hole it. But I'm more concerned that you shouldn't rap it 6 feet past or dribble it the same amount short – and then miss the next. So concentrate on length and strength and let direction take care of itself – it usually does.

Well, not bad, you gave the hole a chance but you're 3 feet past. But, alas, 3 feet is still a little longer than most of us like for the first 'easy' putt of the day. It will be no problem if you've given yourself confidence with a few putts on the practice green, but it will look a great deal more difficult if your last putt was a week ago and you missed from that sort of length.

What you must now avoid is being too tense. Most short putts are missed because the player is more afraid of missing than anything else. Simply tell yourself that this is rather early in the round and we all miss a few here and there. So walk up to your ball, make sure you line yourself up well and concentrate on bringing the clubhead smoothly into the ball, striking it solidly.

Whew! Only just, but at least it's in . . .

Well, you've started with a par, and for great and small alike that's never a bad thing.

Now you have a 150-yard par 3 to play. Two or three times a year you hit a 7 iron very sweetly indeed and finish quite close to the hole. You are now in the area where the club golfer's mental approach is at its worst. There by the tee is a box or board that tells you the exact yardage (a problem you don't have to contend with on the par 4s and 5s when playing your shot to the green). You will be apt to think that you 'ought' to play this particular par 3 with a certain club, especially if you are in a fourball and all the others pull out the same club because they are thinking the same thing. But there's at least a club's difference between a shot on a hot day when the air is 'thin' and the same shot when humidity is high. Many players, however, will take out the same club for a winter's day with the air heavy and the ground soggy as they would do in thin air with the ground hard and running. So think about these things and don't allow thoughts of what the other fellow is using or what you 'ought' to be able to reach with to intrude. Even with no wind whatsoever, weather conditions can mean the difference between a 9 or 8 iron and perhaps even a 4.

Above all, remember that the name of the game on a par 3 is putting the ball on the green and, better still, near the hole. What you do it with matters not in the least.

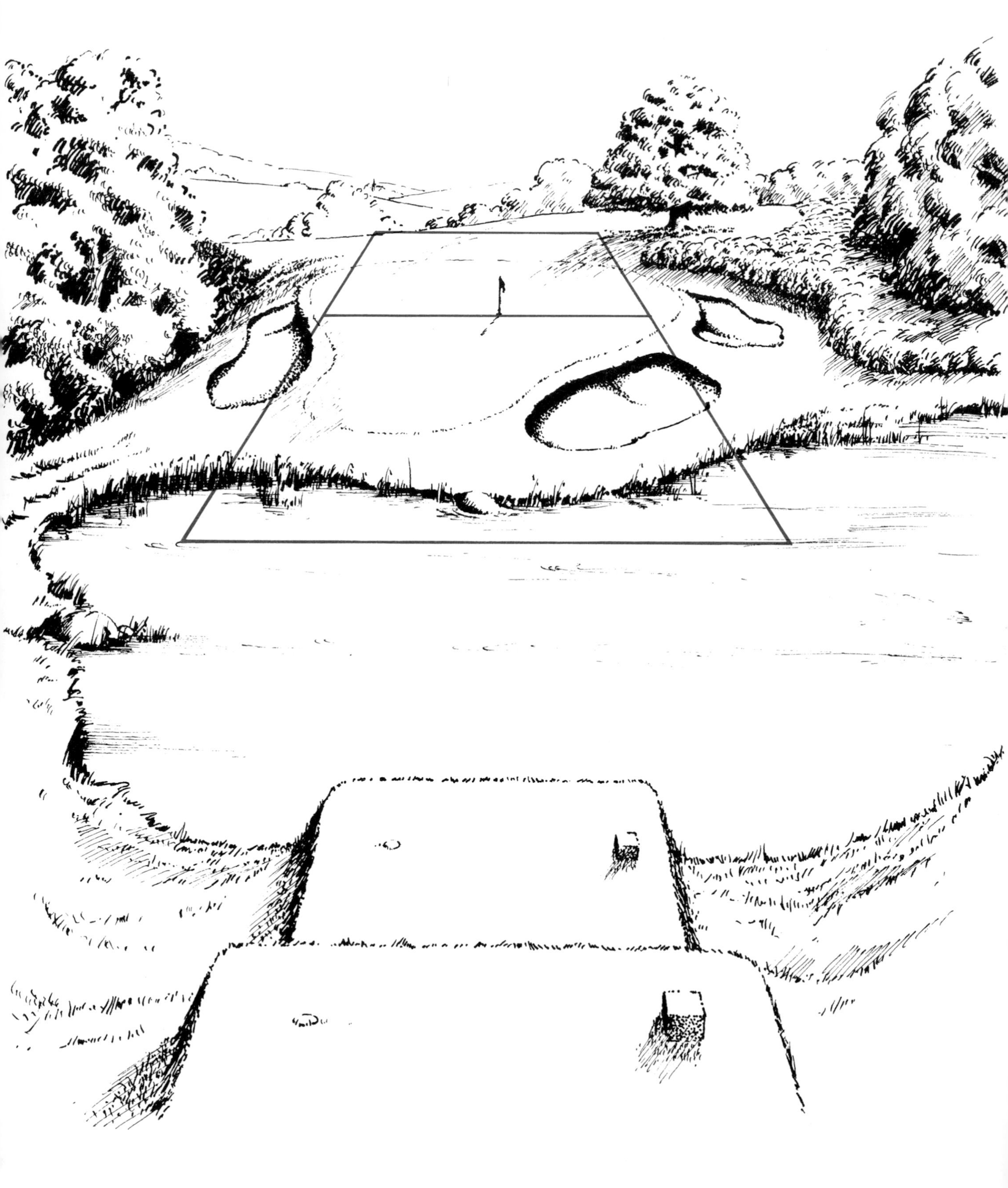

See how much room there is behind the flag at the back of the green and on the apron

Let me illustrate this with a Christy O'Connor story. He was once playing a par 3 with a young muscular up-and-comer. O'Connor coasted in a high, left-to-right drifter quite near the flag. Young up-and-comer responded with a low rasping drawn 8 iron that finished an equal distance away and then asked 'What did you use?' 'A 5,' O'Connor replied. 'Oh, I only needed an 8,' replied the young man, highly pleased with himself and perhaps also feeling that Christy was rather getting on in years, no longer able to crack a ball away with all the exuberance of his youth.

O'Connor decided to give the young man the lesson that a shot to a green is about getting the ball on the green – never mind what club you do it with. He proceeded to tip a collection of golf balls out of his bag and then sent all of them onto the green with every club in the bag, varying his shot-making from a hooded, low wedge to, in the end, a high drifting driver shot. 'That's what it's all about,' said Christy at the end of this demonstration. I don't know if the lesson was learned, but it was certainly well taught.

So my message is: use the club that will get you pin high if you hit it somewhere near the middle with a reasonable swing – not the one that will require a perfect shot.

Good, so far, off your high handicap, you're playing rather better than perfect golf. Your confidence is rising, and confidence is mainly what golf is all about. Any player who believes he is about to hit a good shot, his mind blank to thoughts of failure, is halfway there.

But let's suppose that you have followed my advice as best you could but the results were, well, rather frightening. You took a 4 wood from the first tee, which was very sensible, but hit behind the ball and achieved a distance of about 100 yards. You then took out your 'safest' club, the 5 iron, and half-topped that one another 75 yards. Obviously, whatever confidence you began with will have withered away by now. Yet you must still think positively.

This is the time, in fact, when you ought to remind yourself that golf is quite a difficult game. Those two horrible shots were really only half an inch away from being quite good ones. The next one is quite likely to be much better. I know from experience that so many club golfers virtually abandon the day if they begin badly. But this is rather silly. Better by far to think of the example of Nick Faldo in the 1983 Open, who began with a couple of 6s (4 over par), a start that no club golfer, however high his handicap, could possibly take encouragement from. But Faldo managed to finish in 68. At a very different level, there was a club golfer, playing off a 10 handicap, who began his round on Captain's Day with an 11 on the first hole, a par 3. Eight of his strokes had gone in the first five minutes. Yet Alan Telford (the 10 handicapper's name) had the rare ability to look at each shot as a separate matter. Of course, he wasn't in the least pleased by his 11, but at the second he was able to put the disaster out of his mind. He birdied the hole, made few errors in the rest of his round, and eventually finished with a net 67, good enough to win the competition.

Most club golfers are a little more dogged and persistent in match play than they are in a stroke competition. But there are situations in which nearly all of us would give up. A friend of mine, Michael Hobbs, has bored me more than once with a blow-by-blow account of a singles match he played in his club knockout nearly thirty years ago. It went something like this, as I remember.

Going to the eleventh tee, Michael was 8 down with eight holes left to play. He had not been playing particularly badly, but his opponent was way above his normal game. Then came a remarkable swing as the form of the two players went into reverse. Michael began to get all the pars and birdies, while his opponent played steadily enough off his 16 handicap but dropped a shot a hole, or matched his par against a Hobbs birdie.

Well, they finished all square on the eighteenth and there was no club rule governing procedure for the competition. Should they play sudden death or come back and fight another day over a full round? Of course, Michael was bursting with confidence, whereas his opponent's game had fallen to pieces as the unthinkable had come nearer and nearer to reality. Foolishly, Michael agreed to a rematch, when his psychological advantage in sudden death would have been overwhelming.

However, what happened later (he lost!) is beside the point. The lesson is that very strange turn-arounds can happen at golf. Never give up.

The look on the faces tells it all: Eric Brown . . .

Let me give you an example from my own career.

Strangely enough, though I won more than twenty major events, I never managed to win the Matchplay Championship (sponsored for many years by the *News of the World*), which was lower in status only than the Open Championship. But in the Ryder Cup I learned a great deal about the matchplay mental game and the importance of not giving up.

It took very many years to live down my nervous start in the 1953 Ryder Cup when I took 4 to get down from a little way off the last green in my singles against Jim Turnesa and lost when it looked for all the world that I would halve. Nevertheless, I was bitterly disappointed to be omitted from the team in 1955. I was, however, back again in 1957 and eager to do well. Our cause looked hopeless after the first day's play at Lindrick, when we trailed by three matches to one. Yet what a turn-around there was on the second and final day for the eight singles as American after American went down. Great Britain and Ireland won. Young Peter Alliss was the only member of the team to lose his singles – 2 up and 1 to play – against Fred Hawkins, not one of the leading lights of the US side. At this point, my Ryder Cup record read: matches played four, lost four. I wondered if matchplay wasn't for me . . .

By this time, I had played in several *News of the World* Matchplay Championships. I don't think I'd got past the third or fourth round. People always seemed to raise their game when they played against me, rather like a Third Division side when confronted by the Liverpools and Manchester Uniteds of the football world. I was getting my fair share of publicity at the time; I was a powerful player and was looked upon as the main British hope for the future in golf.

Of course, I didn't consider giving up matchplay and the Ryder Cup stirred my emotions far more than any other kind of competition. I suppose I wanted to 'do it for Britain'.

At last the tide turned in 1959. In the Ryder Cup foursomes, I teamed up with Christy O'Connor and we were the only winners. In the singles, five of the eight matches were lost and Eric Brown was the only victor. I had a tremendous battle over thirty-six holes with Jay Hebert (pronounced 'Aybear'), who was PGA champion that year, at the El Dorado Golf Club, a course just outside Palm Springs. Even that early in my career my putting was relatively poor, but I had found the magic weapon, a hickory-shafted Otis Chrissman model, rather whippy of shaft. With it, I adopted a style I hadn't tried before: wide stance well away from the ball, and flicking at it. The greens were very quick and grainy but the method worked. Most of the short ones went in. I halved my match and the tremendous burden of failure was lifted.

In 1961 in the Ryder Cup at Royal Lytham came one of my most emotional experiences. Christy and I won one and lost one of the eighteen hole foursomes on the first day. On the morning of the second day I found myself facing Arnold Palmer, then at the very peak of his career and fresh from having won our Open at Royal Birkdale. No one wanted to play Palmer. He was thought of as invincible, 'King Golf'. Strong and swashbuckling, he was everybody's hero. I can remember it very clearly. I have a photo in front of me showing Alliss in a pair of trousers containing about 9 yards of material, looking very sombre indeed. I was frankly terrified that Palmer was going to beat me 9 and 8!

Seve Ballesteros...

... and Jack Nicklaus

Yet I matched him shot for shot and Palmer had most of the luck that was going, holing out three times from off the green, with two chips and a bunker shot.

Nevertheless, we came to the eighteenth tee all square, at which point I pulled my tee shot and could not quite get up in 2. Palmer hit a very good drive and his second was 20 feet or so from the hole. I remember looking at the massed crowds and seeing my father looking down from a clubhouse window. I gave myself a quick talking to. 'Don't be a complete twerp,' I said. 'You're one of the best chippers in the business. Roll this one up nicely to the holeside.'

I remembered everything that Ken Bousfield had instilled in me about rhythm and control. Glory be, I ran the ball up to the hole and on, about $2\frac{1}{2}$ feet past. Palmer had a real go at his putt and went past the hole, just a touch farther than I had.

Palmer looked at my putt and at his. I was fiddling in my pocket for a coin to mark my ball with when he suddenly bent down and picked mine up. I moved away and watched him go through his familiar routine, settling, knees locked, over the ball. I suddenly felt that we'd had a great game and that he had halved with me not I with him. I can hear my voice now saying, 'All right, Arnold, pick it up. Let's call it a half.' He looked up and smiled. It was a fitting end to a terrific game.

In the afternoon, I won my match with Bill Collins with some comfort.

In 1963, at East Lake, Atlanta, I was again drawn against Palmer and was driving very badly indeed. My fade had become a slice and I was reduced to making little choppy strokes down the fairway with a 2 wood, following many yards in Palmer's wake, some 50 or 60 yards, on every hole. I had the crowd to contend with too. There were plenty of wild, red-necked Southerners, well topped up with the odd can of Budweiser or Miller's, shouting and cheering their man on. At the seventeenth, a crucial hole, I was one up. As usual, I played my second shot first and put it about 12 feet from the hole. Palmer played a magnificent approach to 4 feet. 'Go get him, Arnie!' the cries rang out. I knocked mine plumb into the middle of the hole for a birdie. Arnold had to hole his to stay in the match. He did so.

The last was a long short hole, played over a ravine. My tee shot was just on the green but well right. Arnold went straight at the pin, but much too far, finishing some 15 yards and more past. I had a frightening putt across the slope to contend with but judged it to perfection, finishing stone dead. Arnold banged his at the hole, needing a birdie to halve the match, but his ball charged a few yards past. It was all over. I was more than happy enough to put my result down as a one-hole victory when in all probability I would have won by two up if we had both had to play our next strokes. What the hell, I had beaten the great man on his home ground – and good putting had helped me do it when my quite famed driving had been little more than an embarrassment.

My Ryder Cup career eventually came to an end. In it I had played some of my finest golf, exalted by the occasion, the flag-raising ceremony with the bands playing, we Davids against the Goliaths. So, although I never won the Matchplay Championship, after a poor start, I lost my fear of match golf. Today, I consider it the finest form of the game, though many professionals dislike it. They hate the finality of being beaten in the first round and prefer strokeplay events where, after a fairly poor start, they can still produce a string of 66s and take the prize.

You may not be able to do the 66s or beat Palmer, but with the right mental approach you will have a full measure of success at club level, in both medal and matchplay.

One of my favourite photos. I wonder why I couldn't swing like this all the time

6 A Round with Alliss

Sunningdale Golf Club, 27 March 1984. In my opinion there's no finer place to play golf. The weather was no more than adequate: a fresh breeze with occasional sunshine and, as is frequently the lot of the British golfer, the odd shower of pelting rain.

Sadly, I myself wasn't able to play. Just before Christmas I'd been a little too energetic in handling some heavy boxes and sprained my right thumb. Despite the best efforts of the medical profession and cortisone injections, I had to cry off, an operation in prospect a few days later.

However, two contestants remained: Roddy Bloomfield, my publisher, and Alec Bedser. Alec, perhaps the finest fast medium bowler the world has ever seen, first played golf in 1946 as an artisan at New Zealand Golf Club in Surrey as a winter member. For many years he has been a member at West Hill, that splendid course cut through heather and pine, achieving a lowest handicap of 5. At the age of sixty-five, he still plays golf off 7 and is a good striker with plenty of power. There are faults in his game, of course, and these will appear as my tale unfolds.

Roddy had the advantage of local knowledge as a Sunningdale member and also enjoys his golf at Le Vaudreuil Golf Club in Normandy, close to the home of his wife's family. He started golf eighteen years ago after participating in many active sports, particularly cricket and tennis, but he doesn't get the time to play as often as he'd like. Roddy's handicap is 11, so he was receiving 3 strokes. His game looks a little manufactured at times, but he's both cunning and shrewd.

The wounded Alliss with Bloomfield and Bedser

I decided that my role would be as a kind of caddie-cum-coach-cum-adviser – though fortunately that didn't include carrying their golf bags. I was hoping to improve their scoring by making points about managing their golf games rather than attempting to remould swings so well established over the years.

And so to the first tee.

The first at Sunningdale is a generous opening hole. There is an out-of-bounds and trees along the right-hand side but the fairway is wide. Away on the left there are one or two large bunkers. Without wind to contend with, it's far safer for the handicap golfer to choose a 3 wood to make sure of getting the ball away. Alec, in fact, is one of those regrettably rare club golfers who always likes to hit a few balls before playing – not so few in Alec's case. He reckons on about forty before going out for a round, as he often does with his identical twin Eric.

Both men played the first hole splendidly, getting good tee shots right down the middle, followed by good fairway-wood seconds. Both had short pitches left to this 494-yard hole and both got them to within some 8 or 9 feet. Splendid shots, but neither then holed for birdies.

So far there had been little need for Alliss's advice. The second is a par 4 of 456 yards and a bogey 5. Retaining a bogey score is a feature of Sunningdale. Altogether there are four holes with a bogey as well as a par rating. The bogey derived from the mythical Colonel Bogey, a fellow who could be relied on to hit straight and never one- or three-putt. His problems came at the long par 4s, where he could not get up in 2 strokes. The American use of the word bogey, to mean 1 over par, has now sadly taken over almost universally.

Both Roddy and Alec had the length to get up in 2. Roddy's drive carried a nasty little bank on the left and he put his second just short of the green. Alec hit a magnificent 4 wood for his second about 12 yards past the hole. Alas, he misjudged his first putt uphill and took 2 more to get down for his 5. Alec has an unusual habit in putting that might be worth a try. Just before he begins his stroke he turns his head to the right. It is a gimmick to make sure that he keeps his head behind the ball, and is reminiscent of Jack Nicklaus, who does it on full shots to avoid pulling his head back and away as he reaches the top of the backswing. The game is full of gimmicks to keep you going from day to day.

Roddy ran his ball some way past but holed his next. First blood to Roddy and one up.

The third is a very short par 4 at under 300 yards, but it makes you think all the time. There are several bunkers up the right-hand side of the wide fairway – a peril to many a handicap golfer's fade (dare I say slice?). On the left there is heather in plenty plus a small gully and bank. I advised both men, as they could not hope to smash one to the green, to play a positional tee shot, hoping to pitch and one-putt for a birdie. Alas, it didn't work out quite like that.

Roddy hit his drive thin and left. Alec was right up the middle with just a touch of fade, an ideal safe tee shot. However, Alec then rather came off his pitch shot, a near shank, and was bunkered short and right of the green. I had told him to walk forward to get the feel of the weight of shot required and to go boldly for the flag, for this green is always holding in early spring, but the best-laid plans can sometimes go awry. He really played the cricketer's forward defensive stroke. Eventually both took 5 on this 'easy' hole after Roddy was too long and three-putted.

The first of Sunningdale's par 3s came next. It is vital to get your 3s in a round of golf. If you can get four of them it helps to keep your scorecard in good shape. With four 3s and four 5s written down, the par 4s will do you less damage.

With the honour, Roddy struck a good 6 iron, rather to the right, but he was in luck. His ball stopped just 2 feet from a big fall-away to the right. Alec played what he called a 'chopped' 6 and was a little short of the green. However, he ran it up well and the putt was conceded by Roddy, rather generously, I thought, as there was a couple of feet to go downhill with borrow. A long way from the hole, with a big swing, Roddy was always likely to three-putt and did, after he had sent his first 4 yards or so past. He couldn't have been helped by rain pelting down at this point. All square.

Alec tried to be too greedy with this shot from the rough at the fifth . . .

The fifth, 400 yards, is one of Sunningdale's most famous holes. The prospect is certainly pleasing from the elevated tee, but there are heather, trees and a ditch to the left and bunkers along the right. I said, 'Professionals consider this one of the most dangerous drives on the course, especially in any sort of a wind. Play for position.' As if on cue, both found trouble. Alec hit a cracking drive down the left but this time

. . . and ended in here!

his fade didn't 'take'. He was in the little ditch on the left. Roddy pushed into a bunker on the right, well up towards the steep face.

Well, I'm still learning about the game of golf and I picked up a good tip on this tee. A very simple one it was. Alec told me that the best thing for drying your hands and club grips is a generous-size piece of chamois leather. I tried it and, my word, it certainly works far better than any towelling. I now keep some in my golf bag because it really is a boon.

Roddy was now faced with a bunker shot over the pond to the front right of the green. 'Don't try it,' I told him and he played sensibly out to the fairway, almost sideways. For Alec, disaster followed the tee shot which had almost been a very good one. His club twisted as he came into the ball and it flew off the toe into the pond. I told him he had been attempting too much. He should have been content to punch it along some 60 yards or so.

In the end both took 6, but Roddy, receiving a stroke here, won the hole. But troubles lay ahead. He was to drop 8 strokes on the next four holes.

At this point I was reflecting how both might well have avoided trouble by using a 3-wood. The saying 'You drive for show and putt for dough' is not true. You can't be a very good player if you can't drive straight. On the other hand, too many glory too much in the length they get with their drivers. 'Remember,' I said, 'all your tee shots just get you into position to continue with the game. Good scoring comes

Roddy at the sixth attempts the near impossible – perhaps he should have called it unplayable

mainly from accurate iron play and steady putting, but you can't do that unless you can get your tee shots on the fairway. Most of the great players have been only modest hitters.'

Both played the sixth badly. Alec drove well but then got his shoulders in too early with a 5 iron and saw his ball drift right into a greenside bunker. He got it out, but off the socket, so was still not on the green. Roddy's second shot had finished well right of the green at the edge of the woods and he found a twig hard up against the back of the ball. If he had tried to move that movable object, his ball would have rolled. 'Try a 7 iron,' I said. 'Hit the twig quite firmly with the aim of bumping your ball up the slope and onto the green.' Roddy caught the twig too thinly and skimmed his ball over the bank and across the green. He followed with another thinned one, back more or less to where he'd come from, and then a socket. The thing was getting infectious. Hole to Mr Bedser, match all square.

Roddy's troubles continued on the next hole, where he skied his drive, pushed his second into the gorse bushes, but then played a very good run-up shot. However, it was still a 5 to Alec's par. Nevertheless, I was pleased with the way Roddy had landed the run-up exactly where I had told him. 'Good riding to orders,' I said. 'Always look around when playing a running shot. There's often a slope or a hollow you can use.'

Roddy now hit an excellent 5 iron to the short eighth, but luck was against him at this point. It was too well struck and he was through the green and bunkered. After Roddy had thinned his bunker shot across the green and up into the bushes, Alec made sure of the hole with a good first putt. He was taking command of the match.

The ninth, well under 300 yards, has often been driven. As Roddy was now two down, I advised him to try to stay out of trouble and take a 3 wood. But no, as I said at the time, 'Carefully ignoring my advice, which comes from years of experience, a true handicap golfer is now going to smash this one into trouble with his driver.' Sure enough, he pulled it into a bunker on the left and that cost him the hole to Alec's par. He was now three down. Against a par of 35, Bedser had taken 41 and Bloomfield 47. Not scintillating stuff, but I hoped they were learning. The match was in Alec Bedser's mighty grasp.

Playing the famous long par-4 tenth hole, there is just about the whole of Surrey to aim at along the left. Roddy pushed his drive into the first shallow bunker on the right. When we got there, we found that the ball had rolled in just a couple of inches. As there was no lip I said, 'Use your 4 iron and try to hit the top half of the ball and it'll run 80 or so yards.' Roddy followed orders to perfection and did just that. 'The best shot of the day from Mr Bloomfield,' I declared. He smiled.

This was the beginning of one of those sudden swings of fortune so common in singles play. Alec pushed his shot to the green into a bunker, got out well, but three-putted, while Roddy sank a very long putt for par to get back to two down.

Looking back from the seventh green

The eleventh is the last of Sunningdale's short 4s with a blind tee shot. Roddy was once more bunkered from the tee and needed a very good putt for a 5. Alec split the fairway with a superb drive, got his par and returned to three up.

Alec again drove very well indeed at the twelfth but his 4 iron was heavy and he was aiming too far left. I decided to tackle him about ball position. 'Look, you've got it way outside your left foot. Bring it back to just inside the left heel. That will stop you reaching into the ball with your right shoulder and let you swing your arms and hands through.' Both took 5s, Roddy with a stroke to get back to two down.

At the par-3 thirteenth Mr Bloomfield suffered one of the perils of the handicap golfer, the sudden perfectly struck shot that flies on and on – and through the green. However, he ran it back well and got his par. I had spent quite some time on the tee getting Alec squared up to the line with the ball just inside the left heel and this time it achieved the desired effect. 'I do believe I detect a yard of draw,' I cried. Alas, though, it had taken him just left of the green but pin high. Alas, also, Alec fluffed his delicate little pitch and his lead was cut to one hole only.

Roddy's last stroke came on the fourteenth, a par 5. Both drove well and hit good fairway woods, though Roddy's was eventually lost in casual water in mid-fairway some 80 yards from the green. No penalty for that, if the players are agreed on where the ball finished. Both got their 5s. Match all square. Roddy had won three holes in a row, two of them using his strokes.

A fine view down the tenth – Alec looking good

Roddy's ball already on its way to the right-hand bunkers

The fifteenth is a long par 3 of well over 200 yards, a bit of a monster for the handicap player. Roddy sent his 5 wood to the green, but my coaching did Alec no good at all for his tee shot. He had the ball nicely inside his left heel and struck right on the button. His newfound draw took it into a bunker to the left of the green and in an awkward corner. He got out well, as usual. (Alec tells me he has no problem in simply getting out of bunkers, but finds distance harder to manage. All his bunker shots go some 6 to 10 yards. Both two-putted and Roddy was in the lead for the first time since the sixth tee.

The finish at Sunningdale is three excellent par 4s, all over 400 yards. Any professional is very pleased with himself if he can finish even par over this stretch.

At this point, Alec seemed to lose his rhythm. He started to aim left again, picked up the club and chopped down on and across the ball. He had three miscues in a row on the sixteenth and had a horrid 7 to Roddy's 5.

Again things went very wrong for Alec on the seventeenth. He heaved at the ball from the tee and was bunkered, and followed by taking too much sand, his ball coming to rest under the face. This was a difficult bunker shot for Alec to play because he squares the face of his sand iron to the line and loses the quick height that the open face would give him. Eventually, he reached the green in 5 – all because of a poor pushed tee shot.

So that was that. Match to Roddy, 3 and 1. However, they played out the last hole and, as if to emphasize his increasing confidence, Roddy hit his best drive of the day and followed up with one of those 'handicap golfer' shots I mentioned earlier – a 6 iron struck, I thought, too well. However, this time his ball had enough bite to stop quickly, right at the back of the green. He judged the pace on his first putt very well and got his par 4.

The second-half strokeplay scores show why Roddy swung the match around. He was home in 39 against Alec's 48, which included 7 strokes dropped on the last three holes. Roddy was well below his handicap on the inward half.

As I mentioned earlier, a singles match can swing round far more drastically than is likely in fourball play. Roddy, for example, went from three down at the twelfth tee to three up after the seventeenth. He had taken six holes in a row! I think Roddy had been almost resigned to defeat, his concentration poor. Suddenly he produced a very good bunker shot and holed a whopping putt. The world became a friendlier place.

There are some lessons that I hope they will learn and work on. At the age of sixty-five, Alec is a very good player and very competitive. In the match he suffered the handicap of trying to adjust the ball position in his stance, something

Bedser ahead of the ball and out of position – result, ball pushed right

Looking down the hill to the short thirteenth

No penalty for a ball lost in casual water as long as all players agree that that is where it is

OLD COURSE SUNNINGDALE S.S.S. 70

Date 27th MARCH 1984 Handicap 7

Event Blood Match A.B v. R.B Name of Player Alec Bedser

Hole	Marker's Score	White Tees	Par/Bogey	Stroke Index	Player's Score	Points + − 0	Hole	Marker's Score	White Tees	Par/Bogey	Stroke Index	Player's Score	Points + − 0
1	5	494	5	9	5	−	10	4	463	4/5	7	6	−2
2	4	456	4/5	4	5	+1	11	5	299	4	15	4	−3
3	5	296	4	14	5	+1	12	5	423	4/5	~~1~~	5	−2
4	4	161	3	16	3	−	13	3	178	3	17	5	−1
5	6	400	~~4~~	2	6	+1	14	5	477	5	~~3~~	5	—
6	7	388	4	11	6	−	15	3	226	3	12	4	+1
7	5	383	4	6	4	−1	16	5	423	4/5	10	7	+2
8	6	172	3	18	3	−2	17	5	421	4	5	7	+3
9	5	267	4	8	4	−3	18	4	414	4	13	5	
OUT	47	3017	35/36		41		IN	39	3324	35/38		48	
							OUT	47	3017	35/36		41	
							TOTAL	86	6341	70/74		89	

Marker's Signature Roddy Bloomfield

Player's Signature

Handicap 7

NET SCORE

R.B WINS 3/1

G2394

The comforting clubhouse at Sunningdale

far better done on the practice ground, where he can try to work into the stance and the feel of the shot gradually. I hope I convinced him that it's necessary, however, because, to amateurs and professionals alike, wrong ball position can come to feel right. Remember, though, just about anyone can help you get this right, but you must choose someone whom you trust.

Oddly, Roddy Bloomfield has the same fault in reverse: the ball is too far back, sometimes past halfway. This leads to a steep arc on the backswing and the strong tendency Roddy has to pull and push his tee shots alternately, depending on the position of his body at impact. As we've seen, both dropped a high proportion of their shots as a result of hitting a tee shot off line. They would have scored a great deal better with less ambition and more thought. A positional 3 wood here and there would have done them no harm at all. Play short of trouble sometimes, aiming for the broadest stretch of fairway or away from the worst hazards. The real game of golf begins after you've set yourself up to play the rest of the hole.

RYDER CUP
1979

7 Etiquette

Fear not, this chapter is not about the right way to hold your knife or how to eat peas or whether you should click your heels when being introduced to the secretary or captain. No, etiquette in golf is about being sensible and gentle – gentle both to the courses you play on and to the people you play with.

Perhaps the clearest way to describe how you ought to behave when starting out in the game is to take you through an ordinary round of golf with three other players, in fact an everyday fourball so much enjoyed by most golfers.

On the First Tee

Make sure you take all your warm-up swings away from the teeing ground. Far too often we see experienced golfers, even professionals in front of the public eye in tournaments, take one, two, even three swings before the real thing. Sometimes accidentally and sometimes on purpose, the turf flies. Remember that the tee areas are the most heavily used part of any golf course. It is difficult enough keeping them in good condition.

Make sure also that you know at all times where other golfers are standing. There have probably been more serious accidents on the golf course as a result of someone being struck by a clubhead or flying stones during practice swings than from golf balls in flight. Never swing towards anyone.

At the start of a round there are usually local customs concerning order of play. This will present you with no problem so long as you don't march on first. Wait and see what the home club players do.

Trevino – always courteous and seldom, if ever, bad-tempered on the course

Look at all the trolleys at the tee – another lecture coming up!

After you have played and, let's say, taken a divot, this is the one place where you do not replace it. Later players may slip on a loose one when playing their shot.

Having played, you need to know where to stand while your companions follow you on the tee. Well, obviously not in front of them, unless you are seeking a quick exit from the world. The general rule is that you stand facing the player as he lines up to play so that if he looks directly up he will see you some 4 or so yards away.

Pay attention, be courteous, don't talk, and remember that you should always stand facing the players, particularly in the case of left-handers

There is an exception, however. If the sun is going to be shining in the player's eyes as he looks up to follow the flight of the ball, it is sensible for someone to stand behind the line of flight to watch for him. So offer to watch; the decision is up to him, but you will have done everything correctly.

Above all, *always stand still.*

The Second Shot

In due course, all four of you will have played and we come to the etiquette of the second shots. Here, the player farthest from the hole plays first. However, most golfers are none too willing to believe that their drive was necessarily the shortest. It is tactful to suggest that you think yours was the shortest; 'Is it my turn to play?' is a question that few will quarrel with, even when their tee shot is in fact rather shorter than yours. Such gentle conduct will earn you no enemies at all.

What you have to watch out for is the man over-obsessed with being the longest driver. If you have hit one respectably but firmly straight up the fairway, whereas he has lashed one farther but less in the general direction of the green, you may espy him waiting for you to play first. Do so. It does no harm and playing first to the green always is an advantage.

I have said little about where to stand for the second shot. If the balls are close together what I have already told you as regards behaviour on the tee will still apply.

The clatter of clubs at the wrong time (when another player is looking for an excuse for his bad shot) should always be avoided. If you use a trolley, make sure the wheels don't squeak while preparations for a shot or backswing are in motion. If you are equipped with a battery-driven trolley or caddie car, likewise keep it under control when players are most likely to be distracted.

Raking bunkers

Let us now take two instances of what is likely to happen at a par 4 or 5 after the tee shot. The first is when you are in a fairway bunker. How you should attempt to play out is nothing to do

When a rake is there, use it

Give the girl a chance!

with the content of this chapter, but what you do after is. If there is a rake, use it to restore the sand to pristine condition. If not, do not scrape your club vaguely around in a pretence of tidying up when really you are furious that an attempted 4 wood to the green from a shallow scrape has gone badly. If there is no rake, use your feet, rather than waving your club about.

The approved method for smoothing over with the feet is quite simple. Just retrace your plodding steps from the point of entry to exit, lightly erasing traces of your progress by sweeping over the marks with delicate wafts of your feet.

You may protest that you have seen tournament players on TV stride out of bunkers with little or even no attempt to smooth the sand. This indeed is so – but, remember, they have caddies and one of the things a caddie is paid to do is this particular little chore.

Replacing divots

Of course, more likely than not, your ball finished on the fairway. With your second shot you probably took a divot. This must always be replaced. Think how embarrassed you would be if one of your companions had curtly to remind you to do your duty. Even worse if a cry echoes out to the same effect from a neighbouring fairway and it turns out to be the secretary or the chairman of the Greens Committee.

Remember also that if you've taken a practice swing or two and disturbed the turf, there will be more for you to replace.

On the Green

Eventually you all arrive at the green. Here the rules for where you should stand are quite different from those for the tee area. Once again, you should keep well away from the putter and not to the rear or in front of the line of putt.

Silence is just as important. There should be no talking, absent-minded (or deliberate!) hissing through the teeth, rattling of coins in the pocket, lighting of cigarettes, ripping open of velcro glove fasteners, indeed any noise at all – while a player is preparing to putt or is actually putting. If you transgress you are likely to receive a baleful glare and may be roundly cursed if a poor putt ensues. You may even make an enemy for life. It can be serious stuff, this golf.

The order of putting is exactly the same as for play through the green: the farthest away from the hole goes first. There is, however, one exception. If three players are on the green but all some distance from the flag and the fourth is bunkered or chipping from the fringe but closer in, it is usual for him to play first although the rules indicate differently. It's a matter of common sense. An explosive shot from sand can be played with considerable force and if the ball is hit thin it can fairly whistle across the green.

Repairing pitch marks

Just as you must avoid unnecessary damage to teeing areas, you must try to cause none at all on the greens. If you have hit a good approach shot there will certainly be a pitch mark unless the surface is very hard. It is up to you to repair it. You can usually buy from the pro's shop a little plastic or metal fork with two prongs designed to lift the indentation the ball has made. The blade of a penknife will also do the job. When you have restored the surface to its original height, smooth everything down by tapping lightly with your putter sole.

If you can't find your own mark, repair another one instead – there'll be plenty, I'm afraid. Indeed, why not decide right at the outset of your golfing life to be a public-spirited member of your club and always look round when you reach a green for two or three pitch marks to repair. If every good member did this it would largely make up for the omissions of the remainder. So don't just be good, be a saint!

Here are some other 'don'ts' on the green:

Don't throw the flagstick down. Place it.

Don't scuff your feet carelessly as you walk.

Get your feet away from the hole, Michael

Don't swivel about on your feet, however agonized you may be, when your putt fails to drop.

Don't, when attending the flag, stand too close to the hole. This is the part of the green that receives most wear and is the most vital; a ball can be thrown off its line by little spike marks when it's moving slowly as it nears the hole.

Don't stand on the line of someone else's putt. This is not against the rules of golf, but it does offend against etiquette and you are highly likely to be blamed when someone else's putt misses.

Don't bang your putter on the green in anger when your putt just misses.

Don't lean on your putter when bending over to pick your ball from the hole. All your weight will be concentrated in the slim putter blade and a dent in the surface is inevitable. This is a very common sight amongst even top players, though I've noticed that Gary Player makes a great effort not to offend.

Showing the yellow card for a trolley on the green

Don't wheel your trolley over any part of the green or the closely mown fringes.

Don't let your bag fall on the green or, worse still, drop it or throw it down. When I was a lad we always used to place our bags on the green before putting, but it has since become good golfing manners to leave one's equipment, be it trolley or carrying bag, a little away from the green and usually, to save time, en route for the next tee. If you don't know where the next tee is, watch where your companions place theirs.

Don't try to flick the ball out of the hole with your putter head. Although it is possible to do this without causing damage, the inch or so of soil above the metal cup is easily damaged and cannot be repaired.

At most of our golf clubs nowadays, courses are far more heavily played than in years gone by.

The way *not* to get your ball out of the hole

This means far more wear and tear. It is up to every golfer – professional, low handicapper, high handicapper, or with no handicap at all – to avoid doing damage. Be gentle with your golf course. Remember, as a member it's your greatest asset.

The Next Tee: Order of Play

Order of play from the next tee depends on what has just happened. In a fourball or foursome, the winners of the hole have the honour. In a singles match the same applies. In a threeball there is a variety of possible games: two-way matchplay, strokeplay, Stableford, bogey, Bowmaker, Chairman of the Board. Normally, whatever the form of game, the lowest scorer has the honour. If you don't know, ask. No one will mind telling you. What you must not do is charge off first when it is not your honour. It is bad manners and you may be required to replay your shot. This will only happen if you have hit rather a good one and can be most annoying.

Bad Temper on the Course

People get cross in every game and maybe in golf most of all. In theory it is all so simple. There is nothing to prevent you sending a reasonably straight drive a respectable distance, hitting a short pitch somewhere near the hole and getting a 4-foot putt into the bottom of the hole. All of us get cross with ourselves when we fail in the attempt, but we must practise self-control.

Take Jack Nicklaus, for example. No one in golf's history has come close to his record of nineteen victories in major championships, but it's worth remembering that no one else has also *lost* so many. There have been times when the trophy has almost been in Jack's hands (that chip-in by Tom Watson on the seventy-first hole in the 1982 US Open, for example) and yet he has come second. There must have been many time when he felt angry or disappointed but he manages to produce a rueful smile instead of the McEnroe scowl. But make no mistake about it, the anger is there all the same. I recall Jack's reaction when he hooked out of bounds in the 1968 Open at Carnoustie when in hot pursuit of Gary Player, the eventual winner. He kicked his golf bag as hard as anyone I've seen. But that was the last time, to my knowledge, that the mask slipped.

Minor bad temper is very common on most golf courses. Let me tell you a little tale that illustrates this. A club golfer was out with his son, a ten-year-old playing only his third game. At the second hole, young Matthew thinned his iron shot to the green, threw his club away and then immediately strolled over and picked it up.

Stern father: 'Now look here, Matthew, I don't ever want to see you do that again. You'll just have to learn to control your temper if you want to play this game. One more bit of anger and you're straight off the course.'

Matthew: 'What do you mean, Dad? I'm not angry. I thought you were supposed to do that when you played a bad shot.'

Stern father: 'What makes you think that?'

Matthew: 'Well, I've seen a lot of people throwing clubs. You did it yourself last time.'

Matthew learned a lesson there – but so did his father.

Slow Play, Safe Play

A major cause of irritation on the golf course is slow play. If the group you are playing in is caught up by another, why not stand aside and allow them to play through, unless you are held up only temporarily, perhaps looking for a golf ball. They will enjoy their game more, and so will you.

Searching for golf balls brings me to another piece of golfing etiquette which is often not understood and just as often ignored. The rules of golf state that you are allowed to look for five minutes before, in competition, a ball must be regarded as lost. But this does not mean that you're allowed five minutes before you wave the game behind through. In fact, you should allow *no time at all to elapse*. The rules of etiquette are as simple as that: you must not hold up another game while you look for a ball. However, perhaps this is a touch too strict and few will object if you spend half a minute, but it really should be no longer than that. Play must be kept moving.

If you find the ball immediately you have waved players through, you are not permitted to play on while they are still on the tee. However,

The businesslike face of Mr Trevino

at some golf clubs this seems to be regarded as acceptable, but, of course, you must be sure about the customs of your particular golfing tribe. Otherwise a letter to the secretary objecting to your behaviour may well follow.

There are certain points that you will have to observe if your own game is being held up. The most important is that however just your feelings may be about the dastardly characters in front who are paying no attention whatsoever to good golfing etiquette, you must not hit towards them until they are out of range. The risk of injuring someone must be eliminated. Save a verbal lashing for the clubhouse bar afterwards. Remember also that if you are standing on the tee of a short hole, you should not play until all players ahead are *well* clear of the green.

At all times you should take note of matches playing other holes, perhaps coming along a parallel fairway. Do not play until you are sure you will not strike them, and, of course, always shout 'Fore!' if you hit an erratic shot in an unlikely direction. Surprisingly, some people seem afraid of the sound of their own voice.

Dress

I have already outlined the minimum requirements for suitable clothing on the course. The rules of etiquette for on-course wear are not rigorous, but here are a few 'don'ts'.

Don't wear disreputable clothing such as a tee shirt with a Mickey Mouse emblem on the front or, worse still, a string vest. Clothing is not a subject about which one can be entirely precise but it is a fairly simple matter not to offend against golfing etiquette in this respect. Just about any pair of slacks, shirt and sweater will do, but you will look more of a golfer if your clothes are well coordinated in terms of colour and pattern.

Don't play in shorts unless you have a pair of knee-length stockings to go with them. Almost all clubs allow play in shorts; a few stipulate that stockings, not socks, must be worn. Oddly, they usually fail to take note of the player who prefers neither or the man who likes an occasional outing in bare feet. The great Sam Snead, who was partial to the feel of turf under the naked foot, was once told this was not acceptable at Augusta National in the U S Masters. I wonder how many championships Sam would have won if golf shoes had not been invented.

Don't play in normal walking shoes. Your balance may be superb and you may never slip during your golf swing, but you will certainly sooner or later take a tumble when going down a grassy bank. Many clubs insist that spiked golf shoes be worn. Some have banned shoes with rubber studs, a fairly recent invention, under the impression that they cause more damage to the greens that metal spikes do (actually this isn't true, as the USGA have proved by research). Obviously, though, it is sensible, when buying your first pair of golf shoes, to inquire what type is acceptable at your club.

Remember that tucking trousers into socks was very sensible for Lord Raglan's men in the Crimea or Kitchener in the Sudan. After all, there were scorpions, mosquitoes and myriad other threats from the insect world to keep at bay. On a British golf course, however, it looks decidedly out of place, sensible though it may be on a muddy winter course. 'But,' you may ask, 'what about Ray Floyd at the Ryder Cup at Walton Heath in 1981?' What indeed? The answer to that is, alas, Raymond did not look entirely a pretty sight. I used to *turn* my trousers up many years ago, and even created something of a fashion, but this was rapidly killed stone dead when 23-inch bottoms came in and I flapped around the course like a sailor in Portsmouth High Street in search of a pint.

Perhaps the answer is to consider the conditions in which you play golf. If you appear on only the balmiest summer days, complete with caddie or golf trolley, you can encase your mortal flesh in the finest silks and cashmeres. For an all-the-year-round golfer, however, a decent pair of fellwalker's stockings and plus-twos may be the answer in cold weather. Many of us who walk with feet splayed at ten to two seem to catch our heels on our trouser cuffs. With plus-twos, this hazard is avoided. You will be warmer into the bargain with the calf sheathed in fine Cumbrian wool. Perhaps you are embarrassed at the thought of running short of petrol and being giggled at by the girl at your local filling station when she catches sight of your noble calf muscles rippling under the Cumbrian stockings. But this too can be avoided. Arrive at your club in what you will and change into the plus-twos before the game and out of them after.

All in all, you really need little more than a clean shirt, clean shoes, clean trousers and clean sweater. In the immortal words of Hugh (now Lord) Scanlon when he appeared in 'Around with Alliss', 'There's nothing wrong with clean poverty.'

8 Preparing for Golf

General Fitness

In 1958 I was in the England team of two for the Canada (now World) Cup, held that year at the Club de Golf Mexico at an altitude of more than 7000 feet. I, together with the representatives of the other countries of Great Britain and Ireland, was invited to a reception at the British Embassy in Mexico City. The Duke of Edinburgh was present and in due course the conversation turned to the difficulties of playing at such a height. He looked at the assembled golfers and said, 'Well, never mind. None of you should have any difficulty. You're all trained athletes, aren't you?'

I think that this was said a little tongue in cheek for there was evidence of bulging waistlines here and there. Nowadays we hear that young heroes such as Nick Faldo and Sandy Lyle do fair stints of running in the quest for fitness, something almost unknown in my day, although Dai Rees, Charlie Ward, Ken Bousfield and Max Faulkner were exceptions. It was generally felt that if your hands were strong and your legs would carry you round thirty-six holes in a day, that was quite enough for golfing fitness. At that time such powerful players as Arnold Palmer and Jack Nicklaus did little other than play golf to maintain their strength.

Indeed, the most rotund in that gathering of golfers in Mexico City was Harry Bradshaw, who, together with Christy O'Connor, took Ireland to overall team victory. Harry, with a four-round total of 286, tied for the individual title with Angel Miguel from Spain, only to lose narrowly in the play-off. I am sure dear old Harry, now playing his share of golf as the retired professional at Portmarnock, will not mind my saying that he was most certainly not a finely tuned athlete, yet he was one of the finest golfers of that time. He coped very well with overweight, rather flat feet and a horrendous nose bleed, caused by the altitude, which went on for many hours.

Sensible Eating

Have no fear. I'm not about to try to put you on a stern regime of no alcohol and a lettuce salad garnished with the occasional small nut. Indeed, I have had problems with my own weight. Ideally, I'd like to weigh 14 stone, but have not achieved that for three years, but I do take action when the scales begin to tip at 15 stone 6 pound, which happened at the end of 1983. I had to cut out alcohol and go on a relatively strict diet.

My main problem over food is that I like stuffing down bread and potatoes, and many's the time I've been caught in the act of sneaking out of the larder with a couple of fresh bread rolls in my hot little fingers. They may not be exotic, but they are undeniably fattening. When my wife, Jackie, prepares the children's tea, she cuts the crusts off their sandwiches and I can't resist them. Perhaps it is not sheer greed, but the legacy of a wartime upbringing when we threw nothing away and were sharply told to think of the starving people of Europe and to remember the relative good fortune we enjoyed in England.

My wife doesn't use slimming recipes as such, but if she feels that one of our favourite dishes is very fattening she modifies it so that it will be less damaging to my weight. She believes that it is vital to cut out fried foods completely and to concentrate on fresh vegetables and fruit instead. For family meals we tend to have a joint, chicken or a roast ham, always served with a salad. For this she uses a huge wooden platter perhaps 24 inches in diameter. On it she places a whole cucumber, quarters of iceberg lettuce, plenty of tomatoes, peppers, celery, sticks of carrot and tinned peaches filled with cottage cheese. It looks most appetizing and the children are particularly fond of it. Potatoes are not needed.

My own feelings about slimming are that you should eat what you like. Keep the calories down by cutting back on quantity. That way you can still enjoy adventurous foods, but avoid gluttony! There are certain foods we cut out completely – chips, for example – and it is sensible to try to do without puddings and sweets; have fresh fruit instead.

Slimming should not have to be a matter of the occasional rather painful crash programme, or perhaps a stay on a health farm and periods of intense exercise, but, if all else fails and the extra ounces have become too many to be contemplated, it is essential to consult your doctor before embarking of any kind of dramatic crash diet. Normally it is safe enough to cut out sugar, starch and sweets, but extreme diets can be dangerous. These may consist of eating nothing but hard-boiled eggs and bread and butter, or sheer starvation. Such diets ensure a startling drop in weight in just a few days, but the question remains; can you keep it up? Many have the ability to make a short sharp effort, but it's far more useful to be able to sustain a prolonged but less drastic attempt. Too much or too little of a particular food can lead to surprising and dangerous results. The Ryder Cup player Harry Weetman at one time in his career had gout, especially in his hands. Gout used to be associated with excessive consumption of port, by no means Harry's tipple. After many tests and lots of questioning, the cause was tracked down. Harry had a passion for vinegar, sprinkling it liberally on almost everything in sight. The result was a build-up of acidity. Once this was pointed out, Harry cut down, albeit reluctantly, and the gout went away.

But for those of us who find it impossible to lose weight, there is a consolation. Plump people often seem happier than the leaner kind, who may become despondent when an extra ounce or so registers on their bathroom scales.

As a final tip, one of my secrets of successful weight reducing is to avoid hunger. A cup of Bovril or something similar in hot water takes away the pangs for a while, but on balance I do better when I rely on the sheer power of the Alliss will. For, really, there is no magic in it. I have got to do it; you have got to do it. No one else can.

Sensible Drinking

Perhaps we should not drink alcohol at all, but I, for one, would find the world a duller place without it; total abstinence would certainly change the quality of my time here. I'd hate to have to do without my gin and tonic or a respectable bottle of wine for the rest of my life. But drinking is really a matter of degree. If you regularly have a few stiff drinks or the best part of the bottle of wine (or both) at lunchtime, and follow that up with a visit to the pub on the way home, wine with dinner and a couple of whiskies afterwards, it is almost impossible for your waistline to hover around the 32-inch mark. The pounds will increase, especially as you stagger into middle age.

One of my weight-cutting stratagems is to banish alcohol completely and try to look as though I am really enjoying those glasses of Perrier water with Angostura bitters or the occasional St Clements, a mixture of bitter lemon and orange juice, or tomato juice at lunchtime. Alas, even total abstinence is now no longer enough, though it was when I was in my early forties. Then a month without alcohol meant a loss of a stone in weight. My friend the eminent surgeon Lionel Gracey tells me that this is a normal experience. It is much more difficult to lose weight once you are past the fifty mark and alcohol remains the main demon; as we grow older, our bodies don't demand large helpings of food as insistently as they used to do. Fortunately, it has become increasingly acceptable socially to decline alcoholic offerings and to opt instead for mineral water or fruit juice.

Giving up drink is a satisfying test of willpower. It's easy enough to kid ourselves that alcohol has no hold over us. Of course we can give it up, we say; the demon is in our control. But the proof is in actually doing it. I have the greatest admiration for those who have had an undisputed drink problem, beaten it, and then resolutely remained off the bottle.

Seemingly, overeating doesn't affect your golf immediately, but excessive drinking does, despite the fact that there are plenty of examples of fluke rounds played by golfers who didn't know what day of the week it was. In my own playing career, I found that I could make do with little sleep, but things were very different if I also had a few drinks and cigarettes.

Most club golf is played at weekends. I'm sure that the pleasure of a vast number of rounds is lost because of too much alcohol the night before. You need good coordination for golf. Alcohol lessens it. If you were drinking heavily the night before, it is not just a hangover that you have to cope with. There is plenty of the stuff still in your system. It's easy enough to fail a breathalyser test in the morning when not a drop has touched your lips for even half a day.

On the first tee the effects of alcohol don't help when you are faced with the problem of getting a respectable drive away. And what of later? There you are, perhaps faced with a long, curling downhiller that you've got to get to the holeside or a delicate little 15-yard pitch over a bunker from a rather bare downhill lie. No, it doesn't bear thinking about! Such shots – indeed, your whole round – will be a good deal easier if there isn't too much of a night before in your quick, jerky backswing.

Not a few club golfers call in at their club bar for a 'putting mixture' or 'heart starter' before they go out to play. One winner of major championships (he shall remain nameless) came to need a shot or two before he could face a golf course in competitive play. He was not an alcoholic, but his nerve endings had become extremely frayed. In the twilight of his competitive career he needed the stuff to calm his nerves and seldom drank much when his round was over.

This has worked for plenty of other golfers. How many of you, I wonder, have had a few drinks while waiting for the rain clouds to pass over or the frost to clear from the greens, and have eventually gone out with quite a carefree attitude. The tension has gone from the swing and the jerk from the putting stroke – though usually for only an hour or two.

On the other hand, there is the example of the great Walter Hagen, who admitted that he eventually gave up competitive golf because of difficulties on the greens. He had been a superb putter, but later found:

> I was having greater difficulty dropping my ball in the hole ... my putting touch was decidedly off. I tried out different stances ... I tried standing with my feet close together ... I tried standing with my feet wide apart. I tried bending over a bit more and I tried standing straight. Actually, my main trouble was just a whisky jerk.

However, perhaps I can assume that I've got you to your club clear-eyed and not grossly overweight. You get out of the car, change in the locker room and go off to the first tee. *Wrong!*

Warming Up

What most club golfers do before beginning to play is to have a few 'practice swings' beside the first tee before it's their turn to set off. I've put the phrase 'practice swings' in quotes because in my opinion they are nothing of the sort. Two vital ingredients are lacking: a golf ball and the feel of striking it with the clubface. Every golf club should have a practice net adjacent to the first tee and another at the tenth if that is an alternative starting place. Not many club golfers seem to have the strength of will to go off to the practice ground (if there is one!) and a net is at least a partial answer. Alas, this facility is either all too rare or very badly maintained. The mat may be worn out, the netting hangs limp and is often in holes so that it's positively dangerous. If practice nets are available, many golfers will make use of them and they are invaluable for warming-up. They get you swinging and, more important, give you the feel of striking a ball. Good players have enough feel in their hands to know what kind of shot they've hit.

My next words are aimed at those willing to make that little extra effort which will help you towards a reasonably successful start to your round.

Try to arrive half an hour or so early (depending on how far your practice area is from your

Starting to get the muscles moving

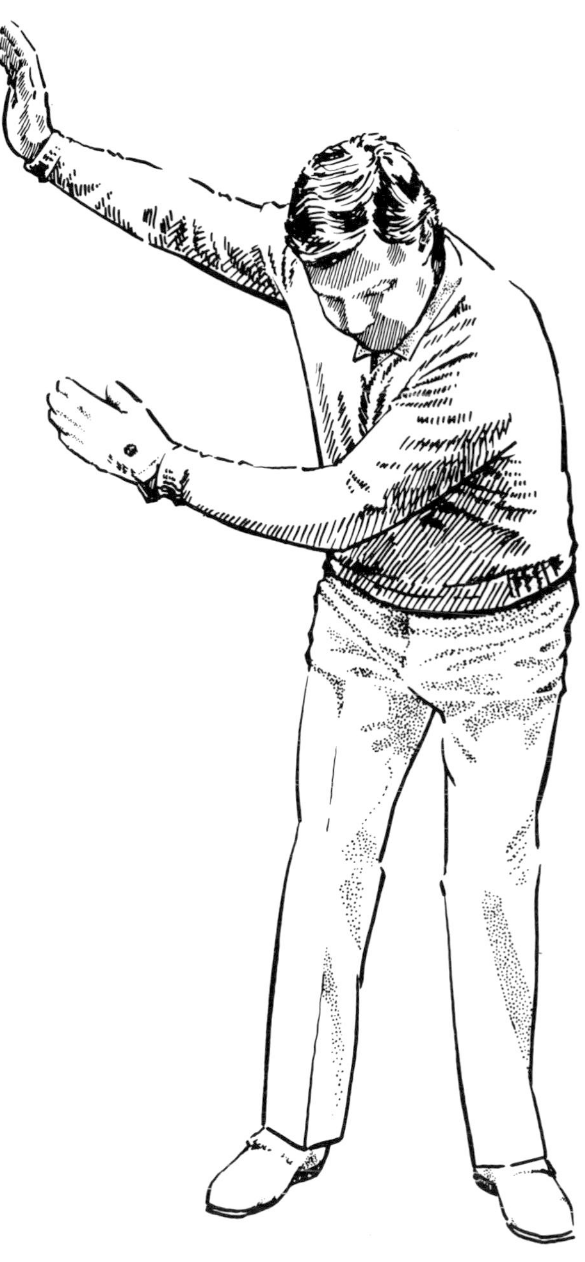

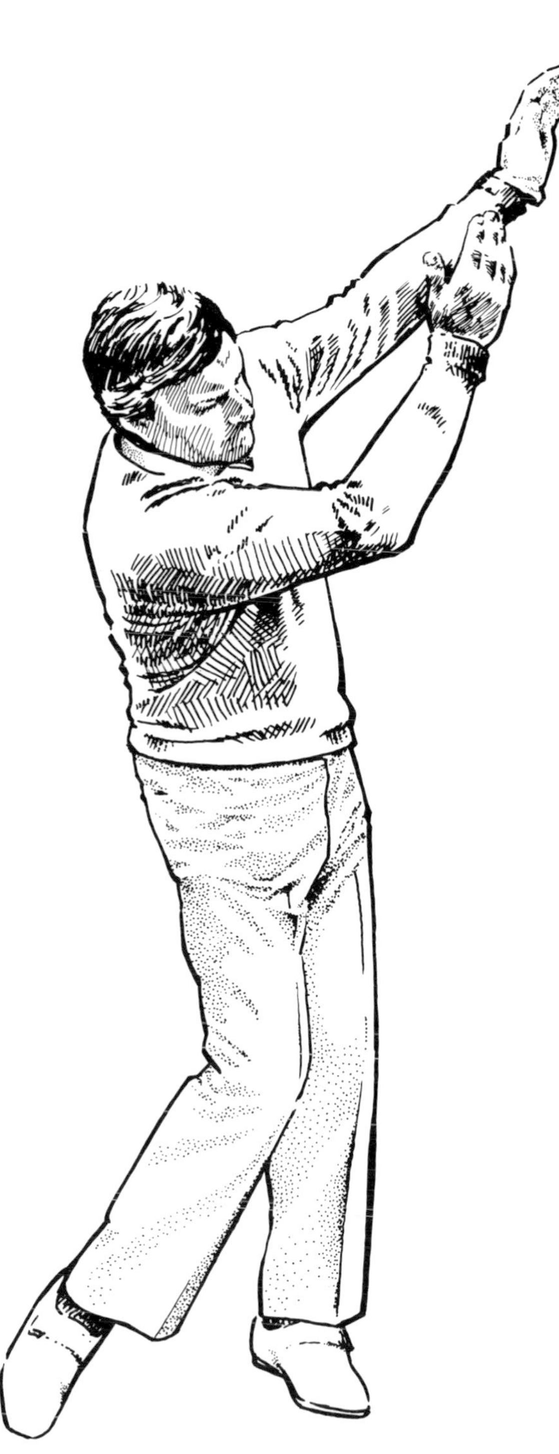

Keep the arms swinging gently . . .

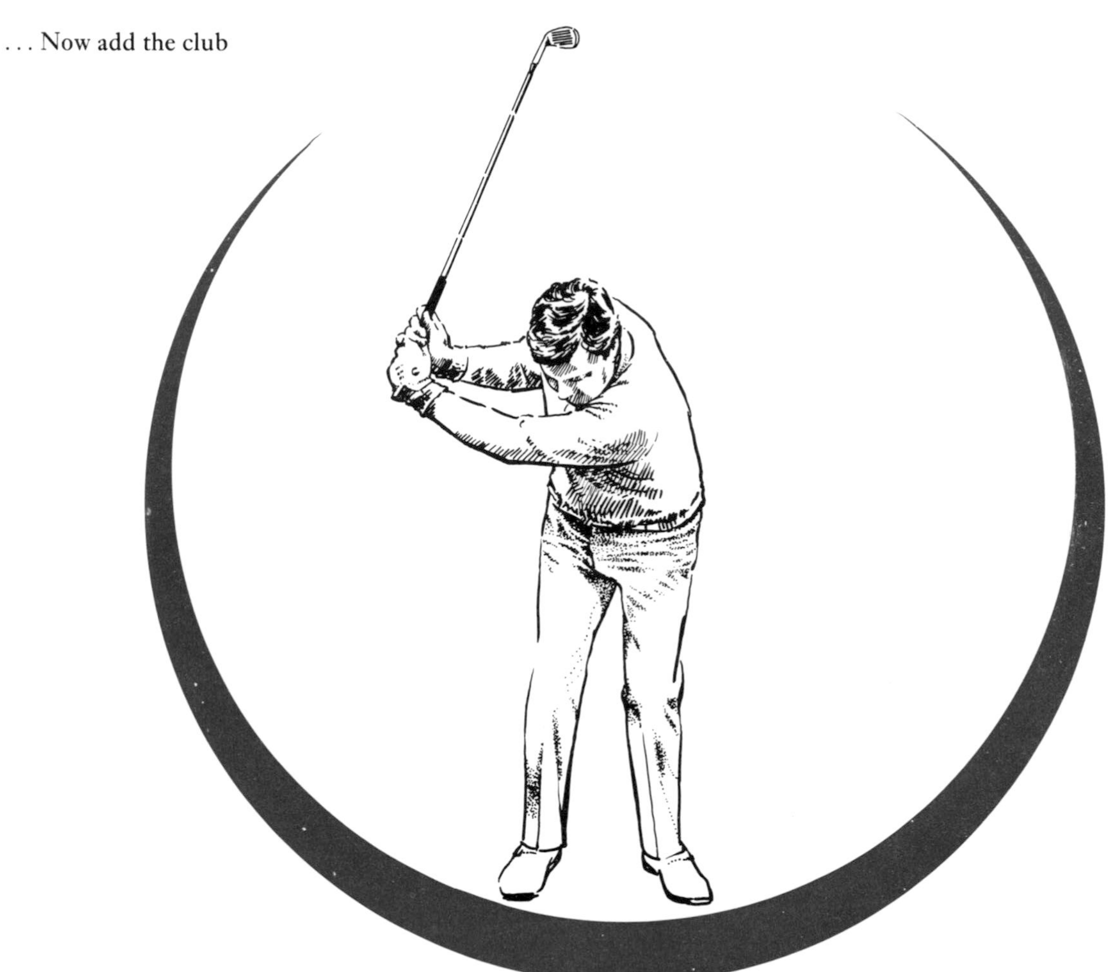
. . . Now add the club

starting point). Don't take a massive bag of golf balls with you. This is a warming-up session, not a full practice programme. Twenty balls should be the maximum, and I would be entirely happy if you took ten or a dozen along.

Once at the practice area, don't immediately reach for your driver. First I want you to get into the golf swing gently and loosen up the joints and muscles with a simple exercise or two which take no more than a couple of minutes.

1 Slip a golf club behind your back and hold it there with the insides of your elbows. Now turn from left to right (gently, gently, gently!) just as you do in a normal golf swing. Make sure you make a really full shoulder turn and get your back facing the imaginary target. Be gentle and work up until you feel you are stretching your muscles and sinews.

2 Now start swinging the arms as well, keeping the full shoulder turn. Avoid doing this violently. Be gentle, trying to feel yourself rhythmically into the swing.

3 My next exercise aims at helping you get the feel of the clubhead. Take the club in your hand and swing it back to about hip height and gently through the hitting area. Concentrate on rhythm and knowing where the clubhead is throughout.

4 Now put it all together, particularly keeping the shoulders turning and feeling where the clubhead is throughout your swing. Don't begin to thrash at your imaginary ball. Aim at a full backswing and gradual acceleration down.

You are now ready to use those ten or a dozen balls. Hit most of them with the pitching clubs, then hit a couple of mid-irons and finally tee one up and give it a crack with a driver or a 3 wood.

Then, if your club has a practice bunker and you are a fairly poor sand player, it will do you no harm to pay a brief visit to show yourself that you can still get out.

Lastly, two or three minutes on the practice green. You should have two main aims. The first is to give yourself confidence in holing the very short ones. Start at little more than a foot away. (You can hardly miss from there!) The sight of a few putts disappearing into the hole will give you confidence if you have to hole a 2- or 3-footer for a half on the first green. Finally, have a few long putts. There is no need to aim at a hole. Just try to get the feel of your fingers coasting the blade into the back of the ball along the chosen line. Aim at striking your ball in the sweet spot.

You are now ready for the first tee.

After these very simple procedures there is no real reason why you should not go out and play the game of your life. You have just gone through most of the things that will be required of you on the course. You will also be looser than your opponent (or most of the rest of the field). I guarantee that you will be feeling very much more confident than most of your fellow players if they have arrived a minute or two before teeing off. You may still not win, but you will have avoided starting with an in-built disadvantage. Good luck.

9 Keeping It Going

People used to think that golf was an old man's game, something to take up when keenness of eye and speed of hand began to wane. Indeed, there is still a bit of truth in this. Not many club golfers begin playing in their teens. However, I am thinking not about how *early* you begin playing but about how long you can continue to enjoy your golf.

The simple answer is: as long as you retain your enthusiasm. As I write, the man I believe to be the greatest British player ever, Henry Cotton, at the age of seventy-seven still has boundless enthusiasm for the game. Of course, on the long shots, Henry, as he puts it, hits a long ball a fairly short distance. By this he means that he is striking the ball out of the middle of the clubhead, that his swing is smooth rather than snatchy, but his physical ability to accelerate a clubhead has lessened drastically. In Henry's opinion, a golfer loses a vital few yards of length every year once he or she has passed the age of fifty.

However, I'm not sure this is totally true. I know of many golfers who have lost little if any length. These are players who, once they can no longer furiously lash at the ball, concentrate on improving their striking.

Undoubtedly, starting late at the game is a disadvantage but one that many have overcome. An outstanding example was Walter Travis. He didn't take up the game until his mid-thirties and in little more than a couple of years was a championship contender. At the age of thirty-eight, he won his first US Amateur and in the next four years won two more US titles and became the first overseas player to take the British Amateur trophy outside these islands. However, he was rather a 'middle-aged' golfer in the way he approached the game. Mr Travis gave the ball little more than a prod up the middle of the fairway and was a champion because he was consistent – and a superb putter.

Ben Crenshaw *almost* in the Bobby Locke position. Will his swing pass the test of time?

An even later starter was the Canadian George Lyon. He did not play until he was thirty-eight and two years later took his national Amateur Championship and repeated that feat another seven times, his last victory coming at the age of fifty-six. George Lyon also reached a final of the US Amateur and won the golf gold medal at the 1904 Olympics. All his achievements in the game date from after he had reached the age of forty.

Of course, both Travis and Lyon almost certainly took to golf late because the game of golf itself was in its infancy in the USA and Canada at the time. Isao Aoki is at the other extreme. I don't know when he first played golf, but it was probably as a caddie in his teens. Aoki turned professional at twenty-two, but was almost thirty by the time he won his first Japanese event. Even so, it was still several years before he established himself as a top player and even longer before he became an international figure. With his wristy backswing and poor balance in the hitting area, very few thought he would achieve the success that was eventually his. Yet despite his many successes in Japan, his best international year was surely 1983, the year he reached the age of forty-one. He became the first Japanese to win a full US Tour event in one of the freakiest finishes to a tournament. Aoki was playing the 539-yard last hole in the Hawaiian Open, knowing he needed a birdie to tie with Jack Renner.

Coles, O'Connor, de Vicenzo, Thompson, Snead and Sarazen – six classic examples of players who have kept on playing

After two strokes, Aoki was about 130 yards from the flag and then holed out with his wedge for an eagle and a 1-stroke victory. Jack Renner was not pleased. (A year later Renner made amends by winning the title.) But Aoki was not finished with firsts. Later in the season he took the European Open at Sunningdale, the first from his country to win a European Tour event. However, despite Aoki's record of more than forty victories in Japan and a run of four out of five Japanese matchplay titles, he had never won the Japanese Open, although he had been runner-up four times. He finally achieved this, his greatest remaining ambition in golf, the same year. Isao Aoki, then, is an outstanding example of a late developer, not becoming a world-class player until past his middle thirties.

And what of Calvin Peete, a very different kind of player from Aoki. The Japanese is one of the most successful putters and bunker players ever; Peete only realized what a good player he was when the US Tour began keeping statistics on the performances of all their players at various aspects of the game – number of putts per round, getting down in 2 from greenside bunkers and, amongst other facts and figures, the most significant for Peete: tee shots on the fairways and greens hit in the right number of shots. It became clear that Peete was just about the best in these two categories (he has been number one in driving accuracy in the 1981–83 period) and made him realize that his putting was letting him down. Peete had won only one event until this dawned on him. In 1982, at the age of thirty-nine, he won four times, netting about three times as much money as in any previous season and finishing fourth in the US money list. Emphatically Peete is another late developer who didn't try his hand at golf until twenty-three and did not qualify for the US Tour until nearing his mid-thirties. Even then he was just a $20,000-a-year man for three seasons, probably not earning enough to cover expenses.

23
Power Bilt
Power Bilt

So far, I have discussed two kinds of golfers: those who have begun late and those who have reached their peak late. But what of those who began early and maintained their form into middle age and indeed later?

Let's take as my first example my old friend and Ryder Cup partner Christy O'Connor. I think Christy began playing at the age of ten but, like Peete and Aoki, was a fairly late developer. He seldom competed in Britain and didn't win his first important British event until past the age of thirty. That hurdle overcome in 1955, he remained one of the top players in Europe for some fifteen years and highly effective for several more. Even now, at the age of 59, he is probably still good enough to earn a respectable living on the European Tour but mainly confines himself to pro-ams and an annual appearance in the Irish Open, in which he finished joint third in 1982. If there were a European Seniors Tour, I feel sure he would do as well as such players as Don January, Arnold Palmer, Miller Barber and Gene Littler do in the US Seniors. Christy has certainly dominated our only important Seniors event, winning the championship six times in the last eight years. In 1983 he returned scores of 72, 69, 68 and 68 at Burnham and Berrow – a formidable test of golf – which was 7 under par, and came home 9 strokes ahead of his nearest rival. Not a few of these were, of course, a good deal younger than Christy.

Christy has his aches and pains, so how is it that his game has lasted so well? What lessons can we learn from his game? Well, of course, Christy is a genius at the game and blessed with an exceptionally relaxed swing. He used to say that he had to limit himself to just a few 'loosener' shots before going out to play a tournament round. If he went through a full practice routine, he became too relaxed and his play suffered. Relaxation in the swing is the key to his continuing success. As we grow older, it is even more important to keep tension out. Inevitably we become less supple and if we are tense as well, our golf swing will soon become short, jerky and snatchy. So try to follow O'Connor. By all means grip the club firmly but not so that your forearm muscles and shoulders feel tight, then swing back easily, making sure you complete the backswing and begin the downswing in as leisurely a way as you can. Make sure you do some simple exercises and movements.

But even Christy O'Connor is a mere stripling compared to Mr Samuel Jackson Snead, who grew up on a chicken farm near Ashwood (population 400) in Virginia. Snead first remembers swinging a golf club at the age of seven. It was rather an unorthodox affair: an old wooden clubhead fixed to a whip. The result of his first shot was rather memorable: he hit a stone straight through the Ashwood church window. Later, Snead made himself an improvised club, a limb of swamp maple, with some bark left on for the grip, and chose to swing at acorns instead of stones. Snead was self-taught, his only model being his brother Homer, who was much older. Yet the lad who went barefoot as often as not grew up to have perhaps the most classically perfect and powerful golf swings ever. He was the first great golfer regularly to drive 300 yards and more and, in 1984, can still play par golf and make money on the US Seniors Tour at the age of seventy-two.

Snead has been helped to last by the fact that he is exceptionally flexible – double-jointed they used to say, although I'm told there is really no such thing. When well past middle age, Snead could do high kicks above his head. Some golfers are not really flexible enough to swing back as far as the horizontal without letting go with either fingers or wrists, but Snead could swing back as far as he liked. Backswing inevitably shortens with age, but this was no problem for Snead: he had suppleness in plenty to spare. He was able to compete effectively on the US Tour for well over forty years. In 1979 he had rounds of 67 and 66 at the age of sixty-seven, was the oldest, at fifty-two, to win a full Tour event, and was joint third in a major championship, the USPGA, at sixty-two.

Roberto de Vicenzo is another example of how a man with a majestic swing can seemingly go on and on. For his age, sixty-one in 1984, he is a most effective competitor on the US Seniors Tour, in which the lion's share of the money goes, as we would expect, to golfers not far past

Sam Snead's putting deserted him, so he changed his method. Here he is with his very personal 'sidewinder' style

their fiftieth birthday, the qualifying mark. Roberto was able to perform well in the British Open when past his mid-fifties. The rapid development of the US Seniors Tour came a little too late for him, though he was able to win the US Seniors Open in 1980 and, competing against men of all ages, tied for the Brazilian Open in 1979. He has always vastly enjoyed practice, the lonely joy of hitting and watching it fly, another vital element in continuing success, at whatever level, in golf for those no longer young. Without enthusiasm you are lost. Many, when they find they are not playing as well as they used to, just give up. I suspect that in a spell of poor form they become confused. They don't realize that it's only a temporary falling off. Instead, they come to believe that the ageing process is to blame, rather than poor technique. It's a time to seek advice, not give up.

Let us now look at the career of one of the great players of all time, Ben Hogan. Born in 1912, Hogan did not become a name player until fairly late – 1940. His career as a winner of major championships was even more delayed. He was thirty-four when he won the first of his nine majors. Unlike Snead and de Vicenzo, Hogan was not a 'natural'. Of course, he always had a great talent for the game and for striking a golf ball, but it took him many years to build a swing on which he could really rely. Hogan himself didn't feel he had found the secret of being able to hit full out without fearing the hook until 1948, when he was thirty-six. He was transformed in confidence and came to believe he could be a champion until the age of fifty, something very few players indeed have really thought. From at one time despairing that he could make even a modest living at tournament golf, at this somewhat late age he set out to prove himself the greatest player who ever lived. Whether the Hogan plan would have succeeded we can never know for he was very badly injured in a motor accident in 1949. He made a fair recovery, even becoming a greater player than before, yet surely those long-term plans had been put beyond his grasp. Hogan, when his days of championship golf were done, remained a superb player through the green. Despite the inevitable aftermath of his injuries, he remained fit enough to compete at the highest level. But, like many before and after him, it was his putting nerve that went. Hogan had to achieve perfection through the green. Once there, he gained nothing, had too many three-putts and was worst at holing out in the vital 3- to 6-foot range.

Ben Hogan – one of the greatest. He has not been a competitor for many years but still hits balls every day

Of course, I know that very many club golfers lack confidence and are nervous when faced with any length of putt, especially those little ones that are missable but ridiculous to miss. This is not because a once iron nerve has finally broken with the wear and tear of the years. If you as a club golfer can develop a good touch and a sound method, there is little reason why you should not keep them the whole of your golfing life.

What we can learn from all these players is that you can continue to play well for as long as you enjoy competing and for as long as you have enthusiasm for playing. Eventually, of course, extreme age will set a limit, but for many long retired from work, a round of golf perhaps a couple of times a week remains an enduring pleasure. There are many indeed who have not taken up the game until this stage in their lives. Before that there were the pressures of work, a family to bring up, the garden to tend. Not until retirement has there been time in plenty to spare. Even this is not too late, particularly, perhaps, for those who have had good ball sense in their youth.

If you start in your sixties, you are unlikely to become a club champion, but with a handicap perhaps in the high teens you will still be able to do what golf is all about: enjoy yourself.

PICCADILLY

10 How My Game Has Changed

I first swung a golf club, so they tell me, at the tender age of twenty months when my father was professional at the Beaconsfield club in Buckinghamshire. My father was not long back from the new Wannsee club in Berlin, where I was born. However, I did not really get 'into' golf until my family moved to Ferndown in Dorset, some six miles north of Bournemouth. There my father remained as professional from 1938 until his retirement more than thirty years later.

It is interesting for what I hopefully call the 'middle-aged' Alliss to look back at those often joyous days of youth and consider how my own approach to the game, both in mind and body, has changed over these many years. I believe there may well be some lessons for you to learn in what I have picked up along the way.

As a teenager, I delighted in smashing the ball as far as I could with the driver. I had much the same aim with all the clubs. I liked, for example, to crack a full 8 iron straight at the flag and delighted in seeing the ball kick, bite and spin back. Not for me the gentler pleasures of pushing in a 6 iron for much the same result, perhaps shaping a low one, with just a bit of fade, working out where to pitch it so that my ball would follow the run of the ground to the flag.

No, for me, for more years than I now care to admit, golf was largely a matter of the flat-out shot. Of course, there were the little pitches and chips, but it was the crack of clubhead against ball and the soaring flight that were the main thrills of my young life.

Arnold Palmer, 1970 vintage

I have told you earlier that I had a horrific grip until I was sixteen. When I hold a club that way today I can't imagine how I managed to play the game as well as I did. With that grip, I was naturally very wild indeed. When I got used to the normal Vardon method, I remained fairly wild, though in a different way. I always took a driver from the tee. I wanted to see how far I could make the ball go and thought very little about the best way to tackle the hole.

I had still much to learn. Not for the young Alliss much thought of playing a fade to the right half of the fairway if there was an out-of-bounds on the left, perhaps with a 3 wood. No, it was out with the driver for maximum distance.

Good sense didn't really prevail until Harry Weetman gave me a $15\frac{1}{2}$-ounce driver with a face a little open. Then followed a great driving time. The extra weight of the club forced me to swing a little slower, which helped my striking, and the open face helped me to develop a reliable fade. This meant that I could virtually ignore all trouble on the left. I could aim to the left and my drives would drift towards the centre or the right half of the fairway.

Before that time, I missed a lot of fairways. As a long hitter you are bound to unless you have a reliable shape of shot, whether fade or draw. I was therefore often in the long grass and heather. But I was lucky to be strong and could shift a 4 or 5 iron a good distance out of quite thick heather or wet, clinging grass. If the ball lay really well down, I was still able to reach for a 6 iron, perhaps, and think in terms of achieving good distance, rather than wedge back sideways on the shortest route back to the fairway.

Of course, this was well before I became a

Alliss then and now: can you spot the difference?

fully-fledged tournament player. I was still in my teens before National Service in the RAF took me away from golf for a couple of years. However, although by this time a scratch golfer, I was by no means scratch in my thinking about the game. As I was still hitting too many wild destructive shots and therefore failing to score as well as I felt I ought to, I consulted my father, a Ryder Cup player, as I was later to be. He told me in no uncertain terms that I should modify my backswing. The clubhead was going back well beyond the horizontal, partly because I was lifting my left heel well clear of the ground. Sometimes I was even on tiptoe! 'Keep that left heel on the ground,' he said. 'Don't take the club back so far. You've power to spare but you'll not progress until you can be consistent.'

I followed his advice a little reluctantly because I wanted to hit the ball the maximum distance possible. As time passed, though, I found the ball did indeed go just about as far if I gripped half an inch or so down the shaft and shortened the backswing. Using a three-quarter swing as preached by Open Champion Henry Cotton, there were days when I felt that I'd never again miss a green with a 4 iron. It all seemed so much easier if I didn't lash at the ball and thought much less about how far I could hit and a lot more about compiling a score and keeping the bad shots out of a round.

It reminds me of a famous Henry Cotton remark. As the acknowledged maestro of British golf for some thirty years, he was always having people come up to him full of enthusiasm about some bright new prospect. The lad had a super swing and could hit the ball a country mile. (How many proud fathers have come up to me in later years and said much the same thing. Surely their sons should turn professional and make their fortunes.) Cotton's standard reply usually went something like this: 'Oh yes, you say he hits the ball well, eh. That's all well and good, but can he *play*?'

Henry was quite ready to accept that the young player might indeed be able to propel a golf ball many a mile, hit the greens with his irons and even putt well to boot. He wanted to know whether or not that young man could put it all together out on the course in competition. What, Henry would have been wondering, was the young fellow like at thinking his way around a golf course, at deciding when to take a safe line from the tee or aim for the safe side of a green – or did he always fail to pause for thought but pull out the club and give the ball a crack? What was his nerve like when victory was in sight, with, perhaps, par for the last three holes needed to get home by a stroke? Had he learned the most important lesson of all in golf, that playing no really bad, destructive shots in a round is very much more important than playing exceptionally good ones, even if there are a good number in a round. A mixture of splendid shots and foolish errors never leads to good scoring.

So, after I left the RAF in 1951, I immediately went on the tournament trail and grew more successful the more I *played* golf rather than just hit the ball well. It still took a few years before the tournament wins began to accumulate and all the time my game was changing. Learning a consistent fade from the tee was perhaps the most important thing of all. I certainly believe it is more reliable than drawing the ball. Here a quick hook is likely to occur but even with very good drives you cannot predict where the ball will finish with great accuracy. A draw runs. All well and good if it goes on and on down the middle of the fairway but no good at all if it runs into bunkers and rough. The faded ball stays pretty much where you put it.

Of course, I am not recommending that you try to acquire a banana slice. You want the ball to start off straight, hold on line and then merely drift from left to right towards the end of its flight. Most golfers are better off if they begin as natural hookers, often the product of a good swing, and then learn to fade the ball.

Most of all, however, it was my short game that changed as the learning process went on. Like many another long hitter, my main strengths lay in the full shots and in putting. I was far less competent when, perhaps, a deft, floating pitch from, say, 50 yards, was needed. I was fortunate indeed that Ken Bousfield, who at the time had the best all-round short game in British golf, took me under his wing. What he most emphasized, and what I now pass on to you, is that a *long* – or at least long enough – backswing is essential. 'Give yourself room,' he would say, 'and then float your blade into the

The flight pattern of a drive fading left to right and holding on a right-to-left-sloping fairway

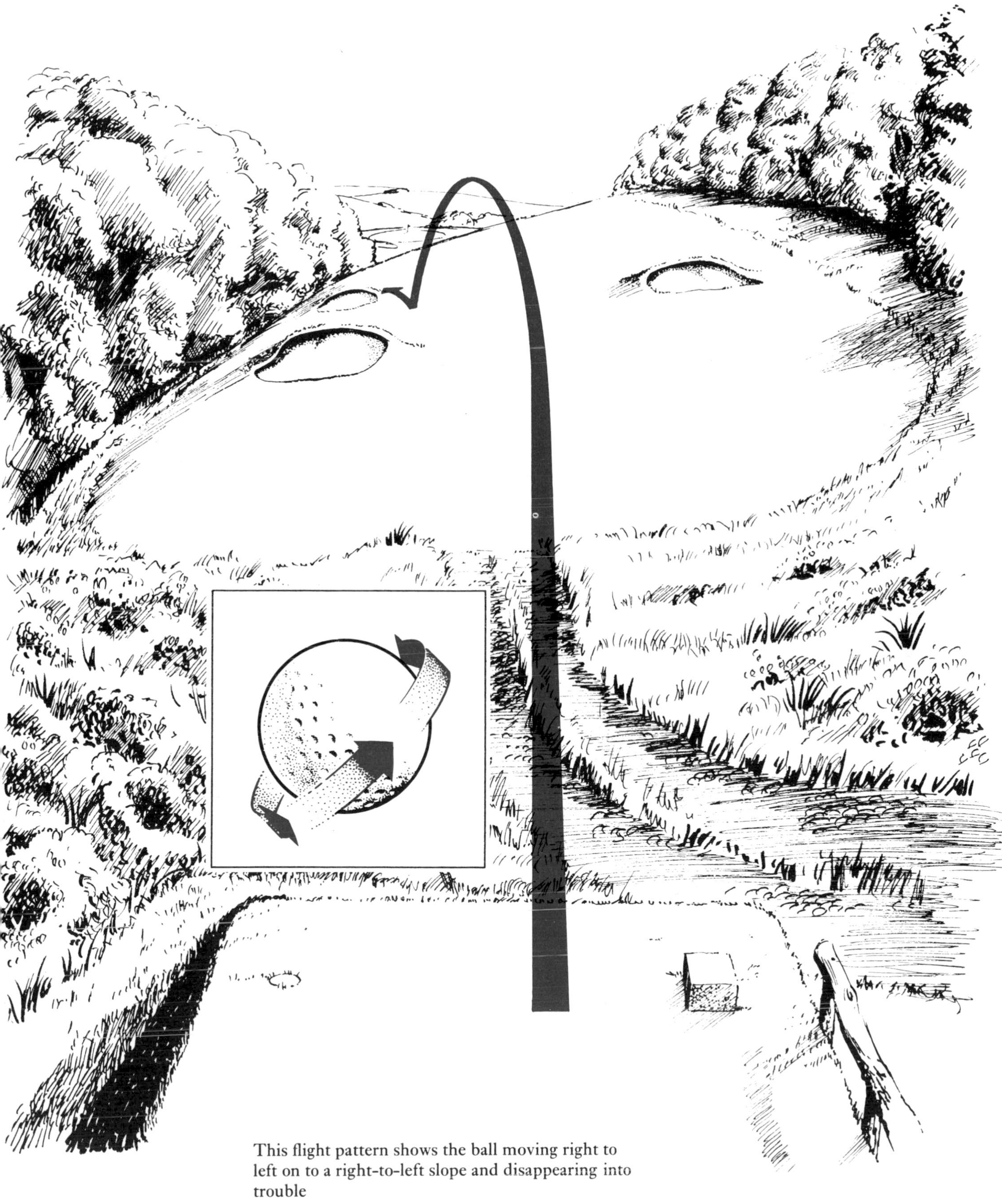

This flight pattern shows the ball moving right to left on to a right-to-left slope and disappearing into trouble

Arnie, 1984 vintage, still giving it hell

ball.' I learned to give myself room and to vary distance by learning to feel the pace of the clubhead into the ball. This is the opposite of what you can see on your own golf course any day of the week: a short takeaway that hardly reaches knee height. With so little room to work in, the player then has almost to shove the clubhead jerkily at the ball with his hands. He has no feeling in the shot at all.

It's funny really. You won't see too many golfers looking delighted if there's a branch in the way of their backswing. They realize that they haven't enough space to develop the swing properly. Yet on the little shots they seem to feel safer if they jab at the ball. No, although you will not need a full swing, make sure, as I learned, to take the club back far enough. As a guide, think of these short approaches as needing a golf swing in miniature. You won't go far wrong, but remember that you must still accelerate the clubhead into the ball, even if quite gently. Don't quit on the shot.

For some great players the concept of the miniature swing applied even to putting. Bobby Jones, Sam Snead and Alf Padgham (our Open Champion in 1936) all saw medium-length and long putts as requiring a good swing back of the club and did not mind body movement. Oddly, Bobby Locke had body movement on even short putts. It worked very well for him but I don't recommend this to you.

So, swing the club into the ball, always feeling the pace and position of the clubhead. Never push it.

So my victories gradually mounted up towards the score. My golf improved in most departments, except a vital one – putting. This problem grew worse as the years passed, and holding the nerves and stroke steady from this distance sometimes made golf purgatory.

In 1969 I played in my eighth and last Ryder Cup at Royal Birkdale and also had my last major win. It came at Sandwich when I beat George Will in the final of the Piccadilly Medal, having beaten that year's Open Champion, Tony Jacklin, in the semifinals. I then decided not to play full-time tournament golf any longer. I thought I would continue to appear fairly frequently but, as other horizons beckoned and began to occupy my time, this was not so, though I continued to play in the Open Championship every year up to 1974.

I am now much nearer to the club golfer. I enjoy my golf rather than worry about it. I am still learning. Above all, I've learned that golf is different – but no less enjoyable – for those whose sheer physical strength has grown less as the years have passed. This does not mean that at thirty, forty, fifty or even sixty you become relatively weak. There is certainly less power, however, and you have to adapt your game. It's a challenge and an enjoyable one.

Nowadays, if I see my ball in rather a tight fairway lie, I no longer reach automatically for the 2 iron with a couple of hundred yards to go. Instead, I'll probably reach for the trusty 4 wood, although that club gives me more than

200 yards. However, I won't be thinking of a full shot. I'll have in my mind's eye an image of a high, fading shot alighting softly a little to the left of the flag and then rolling on, carried by the sidespin. I'm the first to admit that it doesn't always work, but it's more reliable than forcing a 2 iron from a tight lie. Certainly it's great fun when you think out a shot and get the result you intended.

All the time, I try to think of the *kind* of shot needed. Should it, I ask myself, be moving from right to left, or from left to right? Should it be low or high, a runner or full at the flag? What is the condition of the ground?

I have also had to learn, getting far less practice than I used to, that slight mishits are far more likely. A 400-yard hole that was once a drive and a 9 iron in good conditions might now find me hitting a drive a little out of the heel and a 4 or 5 iron to the green.

I have also learned that over-clubbing is far better than using the one that will just get you there, provided you keep an easy rhythm and control the pace of the clubhead through the ball.

Just watch any fourball play a par 3, on any course (unless there is a lake to carry from the tee!). You will find the average result, even if they are good players, is two balls short of the green and the other two on the green but still short of the flag. All of them have looked at the tee marker and said to themselves something like, 'Ah yes, 140 yards. I can get there with an 8 iron if I catch it just right.' Well, they don't – or not often. So why not choose the club that will get you the distance when you hit your good average shot?

My own attitude is far more: 'Yes, I'll get there with a cracking 8 iron, but the flag is 20 yards from the back of the green with no real trouble behind. I'll use a 6, firm but not full out. I'll play it off a tee peg and have the feeling of floating it to the target. I shan't be much past even if it leaps off the clubhead and I won't be too far away after a poorish strike.' I get as many 2s with that kind of thinking as when I used to take a 9 iron, perhaps even a wedge, for that distance.

How often have you played with someone who can't drive much more than 200 yards and then finds himself confronted with a 195-yard par 3. You'd think he'd use a 3 or 4 wood, wouldn't you? Not a bit of it. He'll almost certainly reach for an iron. He won't reach on the best day he ever had. Those tee markers on the par 3s have a remarkable effect. The male golfer (the ladies tend to be more sensible) seems to feel less of a man if he shows all and sundry that he needs a wood for this kind of distance. He ought to prefer not to sacrifice his score to vanity, but it could be that he's never learned that his 3 iron will just not get him the distance. Know your own game and capabilities. You'll enjoy yourself more and score lower.

There are some things I can no longer do anyway. My wrists, for instance, are at least three-quarters of an inch less in circumference than when I was in tournament practice. This has affected my length from the tee very little, but I can't force balls from poor lies in the rough with a fairly long iron as I used to. So I have to take a short route back to the fairway with a lofted iron or, if the lie is not too impossible, reach for a lofted wood with a little head that will sweep through the grass.

As I grow older, how often I play is, of course, very important. I cannot play nearly as often as I would like – who of us can? Muscle tone cannot be as good. But players I grew up with such as Arthur Lees and Ken Bousfield have retained their enthusiasm and remained very good indeed. So too did Dai Rees until his death in 1983. They are all much, much older than I am. Ben Hogan still goes down to the Shady Oaks club just outside Fort Worth in Texas and heads for the practice ground. They tell me he strikes the ball as well as ever. Henry Cotton, past his mid-seventies, remains a total enthusiast and an experimenter with clubs, balls and shafts. He still likes to take on the young bucks at the course where he is in charge of golf, Penina in Portugal. Henry needs no handicap as regards his striking and touch, but is, of course, a fairly short hitter at his age. Accordingly, he plays off the ladies' tees.

None of the golfers I've mentioned are as good as in their prime years. Yet they do still play very well and – most important of all – enjoy golf enormously.

And that's what we're after, isn't it?

Bobby Locke, affectionately known as Old Muffin Face, celebrating his last championship victory on the verandah at St Andrews in 1957

Bad luck, Doug, but that's golf!

My son Gary checking my card at the Strongs Tournament at Stoneham, 1966

Henry Longhurst at St Andrews for the championship in 1955 in what today would be considered very primitive conditions

11 A Chapter of Memories

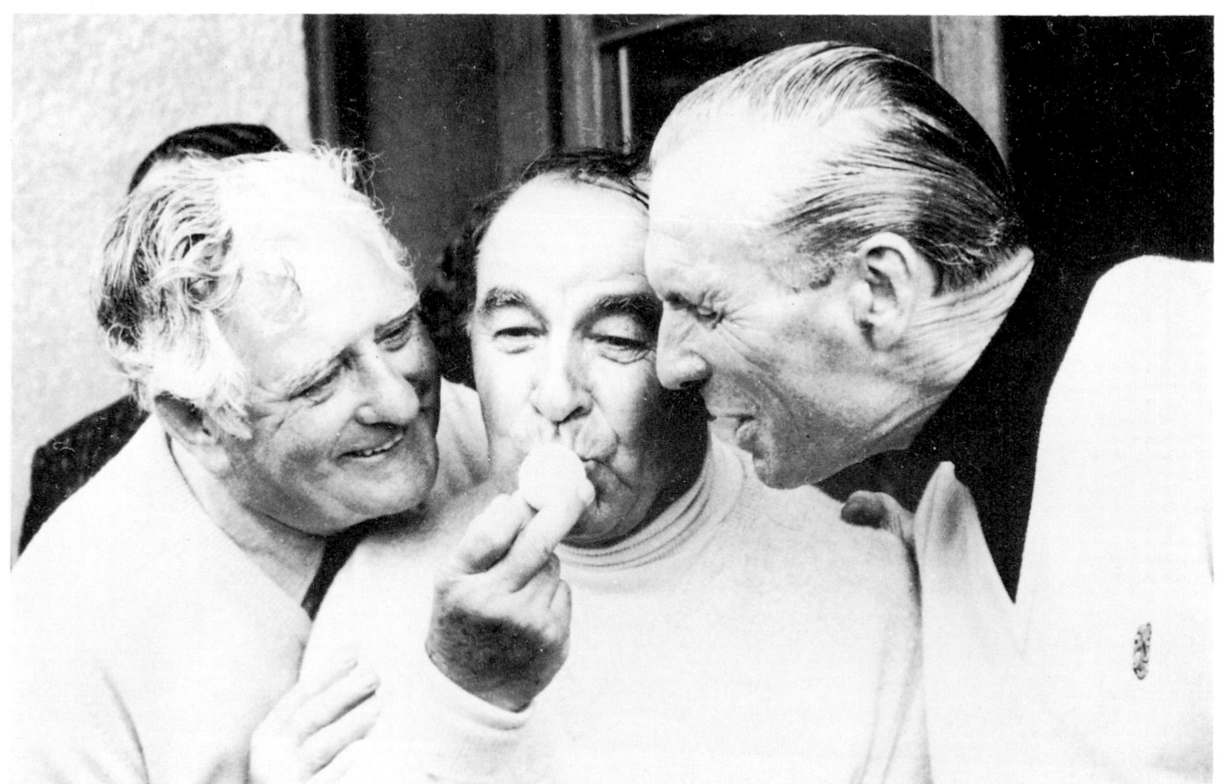

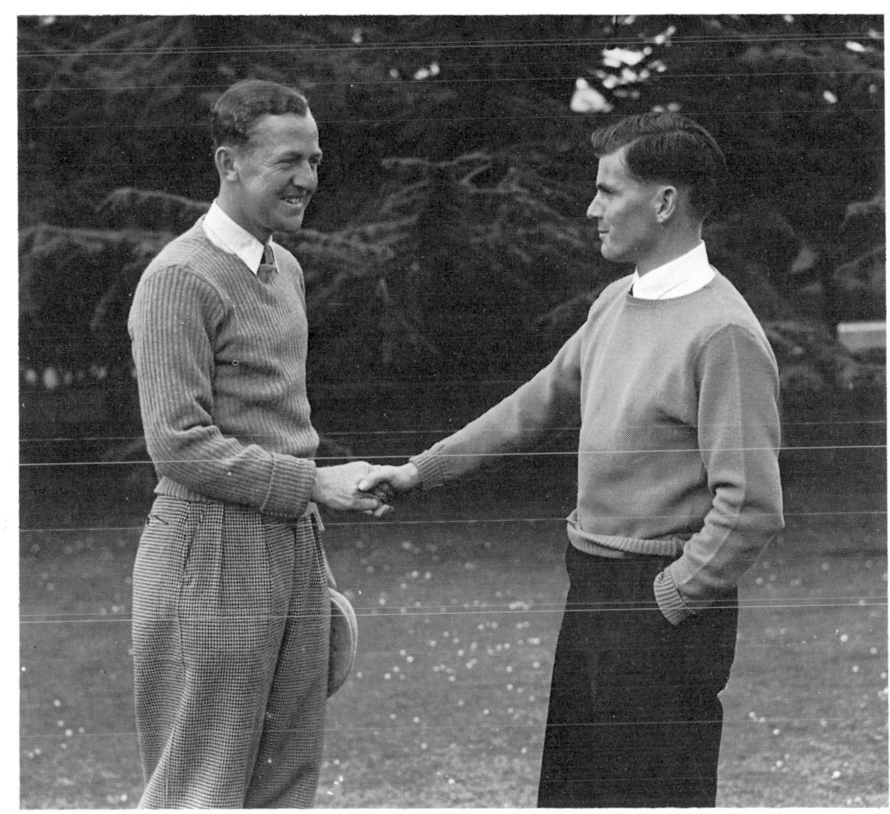

Fred Daly and Max Faulkner congratulating Gene Sarazen on his hole in 1 at the eighth at Troon, 1973. They have all kept on playing

The Whitcombes – a most extraordinary golfing family: the three brothers on the right, Reggie, Ernest and Charles. Ernest's son Eddie, on the left, waiting to be demobbed

With Lady Heathcote-Amery, *née* Joyce Wethered, at Wentworth, 1980

Can that really be Bobby Locke and Dai Rees? Yes, it really is Bobby Locke and Dai Rees

JACK
NICKLAUS
Slazenger

PETER ALLISS

Jack Nicklaus with his faithful caddie Jimmy Dickinson – a great combination

My eldest son's godfather Leonard Crawley, for many years correspondent of the *Daily Telegraph*, playing with guess who?

Jimmy Cousens and I – not a bad combination for over ten years

Jack Newton and Tom Watson after their play-off at the 1975 Open Championship

My final professional victory: the Piccadilly Medal, 1969 – yet another scintillating speech

With Ziggy and putter – at least one of them was my friend

My one and only appearance in the Seniors, here with (from left to right) John Panton, Christy O'Connor, Peter Butler, Bernard Hunt, P. A., Dai Rees and Ken Bousfield

Taking Jackie, my wife, to Ascot for the day

12 Holiday Golf

Golf holidays are as varied as any other holidays. If you study the adverts you will find that you can spend a week or so, including flights, on the Costa del Sol or the Costa Brava for £200 or £300. A weekend break for a couple of days' golf in Britain is likely to cost in the region of £50 inclusive. On the other hand, you can journey to the Mecca of golf, Dornoch, well beyond Inverness, and enjoy one of the world's top-rated courses for not much more than £100 a week. A package golf holiday need be not much more expensive than any other kind of holiday. At the top end of the market, if your pocket can stand it, they can cost £1000, but there are many that are much cheaper.

What I have tried to do in this chapter is suggest a variety of areas where, come rain, searching wind, or the kindly old sun beaming down, it's a delight to play golf. We are very fortunate in this country in having so many attractive courses. Hardly anywhere is without one. I have selected six areas which are close to my heart, having been associated with my teenage years or my career as both a club and a tournament professional. More recently, television work and other travels have enlarged my experience, but one of my regrets is that I had no real amateur career. The amateur, if in funds, has the world as his oyster.

In my recommendations for holidays, I have left the choice of accommodation up to you. You can reach for the phone, having discovered which is the most expensive hotel in the area, or can go up to the attic to see if the mice have made inroads into the tent. One thing well worth considering is a caravan, if you are part of a fourball, for example. When the company is good, all that is really necessary is a roof over your head. The great advantage is that you have total control over what you spend. Excluding travelling, you can live and play on not much more than £10 a day.

I have also kept in mind the importance of ease of travel, and for that reason have excluded London and other densely populated urban areas. For my six suggested holidays, you should have few travel problems once you have arrived in the locality.

Before you set out, however, there is, as for any holiday, a little preparation to do. Public courses do not insist that you be a member of a golf club, but many private ones do. Make sure, therefore, that you get some evidence from your own club that you belong – a handicap certificate or a certificate of membership. Better still, ask your secretary for a letter of introduction. This should state that you are a member in good standing at your club, give your handicap and request playing privileges on your behalf. A few clubs require a secretary's letter in advance, in a sense making an appointment for you. For the clubs I have included, this is usually not the case, but I have noted where it is necessary.

The other task is to make sure that your equipment is in order, especially the grips. Think also about clothing and be prepared for wet weather. Take plenty of spare slacks and sweaters and, even more important, shoes. Clothes can be dried quickly overnight, but good leather shoes must be allowed to dry out slowly. So play safe and take too much rather than too little. It is also worth investing in good waterproofs and an

St Andrews

umbrella. Many top players rely on just an umbrella and waterproof trousers. The umbrella will cope with the heaviest rain on a reasonably still day, but you will be lost if a stiff wind gets up. Look after your waterproofs. Hang them up when not in use and give them an occasional brush down. Don't stuff them in an odd corner of the car boot, damp and smelly. Finally, for men, take a jacket and tie to wear in the clubhouse. Most golf clubs have become far more relaxed about clubhouse dress, but the rules vary considerably. However, the main requirement is that people should look neat and tidy both on and off the course. So leave the old jeans at home and change your clothing after you have played.

One thing to bear in mind is that playing strange courses is more difficult than playing your home course, with which you are familiar. But you will never be much of a golfer unless you enlarge your golfing experience. Golf is not just a matter of evolving a super swing. You must develop your judgement as well, and playing on unfamiliar courses is the way to do that - and have fun as well.

Addresses, telephone numbers, course lengths, and travel directions for each club are listed in alphabetical order at the end of this chapter.

Are you ready? Well, let's go.

The Bournemouth Area

Because this is a holiday area, avoid the high season and go for spring, early summer or autumn. The queues can build up at the first tee in July and August. But April, May and June are a delight, and September and October can be glorious months.

Where better to begin than Ferndown, in Dorset, where I took my first steps on a golf course and where I played from the age of eight after my father left his club professional's job in Yorkshire and moved south a year or so before the war.

If I had to play all my golf on just one course, it would be a difficult choice, but **Ferndown** would certainly be in my top five. There are no uphill slogs, but there is no flat either, which can be boring in a golf course. There are plenty of pine and silver birch, excellent greens and everything is always neat and tidy.

The most interesting hole for me is the twelfth - one of two holes (the other is the fifteenth) which were designed by my father when the old fourteenth and fifteenth were sold for housing development. The course was originally laid out by Harold Hilton, British Open and British Amateur champion and the only British player to have won the US Amateur title - in 1911.

All the short holes are very good indeed and there is a fine variety of par 4s, with generally wide fairways. To the east of the main course is a nine-hole layout.

My brother Alec and I took over as joint professionals at **Parkstone** on April Fool's Day in 1957 (what better day to start!) and off I went to the PGA Championship at Llandudno, returning with the trophy.

There is a strange mix of long and short holes with five par 3s and five par 5s; the sixth, ninth, eleventh and seventeenth are all over 500 yards. There are also three par 4s which are drivable for some. A possible flaw in the design is that longish hitters don't often need to use a long iron. I never tired of playing at Parkstone, and I am sure part of the reason for this was the heather, pine and silver birch. From the course, particularly from the eighth and thirteenth tees, there are superb views of Poole Harbour and the Purbecks, with Canford Cliffs running alongside the last few holes. I am pleased to say I still hold the course record with 63.

When the first at **Broadstone** (Dorset Golf Club) is played as a par 4, this may well be the most difficult course to play to your handicap in Britain. There are two main reasons: the excellent short holes are both long and demanding and there are many par 4s over 400 yards. There is no poor hole on the course, though you may have your doubts about the second. It's a rather long pull uphill.

The seventh is a long and demanding par 3, especially with the wind in your face; my other favourites are the excellent short eleventh and the twelfth, which is one of the best par 4s anywhere. From the course there are superb views of Poole Harbour and golden sands stretching away to the Isle of Wight.

Wareham is a club fond in my memory. I

Ferndown

recall those far-off days when the little wooden clubhouse still stood and a box was left on the counter for visitors to put their green fee money in. Much the same thing applied to payment for drinks. Visitors and members alike were on trust to put their dues in the box. I am pleased I was alive to see those days. The nine-hole course is heathy in character and relatively undemanding.

Barton-on-sea is not the place for a beginner or high handicapper if the wind is up – from whatever direction. On a still day, Barton is not a severe challenge and perhaps it was in that kind of weather that I once did a 66 there, still the course record, I believe. The twelfth, approaching 600 yards in length, is a particularly long par 5, one of the longest in British golf. Views from the course are as bracing as the weather is likely to be, looking out over the Channel and the Isle of Wight.

Seldom have eighteen holes of golf been provided on so little land as at **Highcliffe Castle** – just 68 acres. Members say that on the cry of 'Fore' the brave duck and cowards throw themselves flat. The course has one superb design feature: at most holes the tee shot placement must be to the correct half of the fairway or the approach shot becomes progressively more difficult. Check that a competition is not being played; it's a very busy club indeed, but a warm welcome is assured.

Brockenhurst Manor is another of my favourites, in a setting of oak, elm and birch on the edge of the New Forest on gravelly moorland turf. The layout is excellent, having three loops of six holes, all finishing at the clubhouse. The short fifth and twelfth are particularly good and perhaps the most difficult is the doglegged seventeenth. I remember it best from days when it

Queen's Park

seemed to be packed with retired military men, doctors and lawyers; and the ladies in those far-off days all seemed to have straight backs, iron-grey hair and just the slightest hint of a blue rinse. It was a quietly sophisticated place.

The **New Forest** club is the creation of Peter Swann, who began as assistant to Reg Whitcombe at Parkstone, Peter and I being lads together. He got permission to carve the course out of the forest. He did it virtually singlehanded and owns the club. It is set quite high up on heathland above the village of Lyndhurst and is super fun for an evening ramble, although there are the unusual natural hazards of New Forest ponies, picnickers, ramblers and courting couples.

A fierce test of golf over undulating terrain awaits you at **Burley**. It is carved out of a sea of gorse, so take plenty of balls if your driving is a little awry. My favourite hole is the seventh, where the tee shot must be very well placed if the second shot is to be not too demanding. It is only nine holes on the edge of the New Forest, with the charming town of Ringwood close at hand, but it is relaxed and enormous fun.

Two eighteen-hole courses are on offer at **Bramshaw** – the Forest and the Manor. The Manor is a parkland course, while the Forest is set over undulating ground right in the heart of the New Forest. On both the walking is easy, and there are streams in plenty that can come into play. All in all, a good day out.

I remember the course at **Stoneham** from days competing in the old Strong's tournament – an event for professionals from the counties where the beer from the brewery based in Romsey was sold. I won a number at Stoneham. One of the few shots I remember clearly as yesterday was at the last hole, a par 5 – a whizzing second shot up to the heart of the green, enabling me to win with a 4.

Most of the holes have an individual character, separated by great clumps of oak and gorse that keep each fairway apart. It is quite a hilly course. The eleventh is a hole to look out for. It features cross bunkers to catch a drive struck not quite cleanly enough, a feature of courses designed by Willie Park, as this one was.

I vividly remember going to **Queen's Park** on my first day of release from the RAF Regiment from National Service on 15 June 1951, to see the Penfold Festival of Britain Tournament. It was the first time I set eyes on Peter Thomson, but a few years away from the first of his five Open victories, on his first visit to Britain. Some consider the course to be the best municipal design in the south of England, and it is certainly a good test, with fast fairways running amidst pine and heather. Perhaps the best hole is the thirteenth, a dogleg right to left, and the tenth is a fine par 5, a double dogleg. There is a run of holes from the third pretty well hard to beat anywhere in the UK.

Meyrick Park is a course with a long history, for it was designed in 1894 by Tom Dunn of Musselburgh. Tom preferred to have cross bunkers for both the tee and second shots, if possible reinforced by ditches as well. What a man! The Robert Trent Jones of his day. The course is parkland type and is quite heavily wooded, with some heather, Scotch pine and silver birch. The fourth is one of the great par 3s of golf and the fourteenth a good 5. The first tee, remarkably, is probably no more than 500 yards from the very centre of Bournemouth, but you feel in the middle of the country.

North Norfolk

Many have heard of the famous courses of this area but few have played them. Like some of the other golfing holidays I have chosen, you do not pass through north Norfolk en route to anywhere else, so a special journey is needed – and why not? You will find a splendid variety of golf here and in the Suffolk area also. The courses would be far better known if the professional golf circus came more often to East Anglia.

Founded in 1890, when the coming of railways to the coasts led to the development of holiday resort towns, **Hunstanton** is a championship course which has hosted many top events. The club has laid claim to being 'the finest test of golf between the Humber and the Thames' and is dominated by sandhills.

Although the course can be crowded in the holiday season, the start helps to alleviate delays, with a short and relatively easy par 4, followed by a long 5 of no great difficulty. The sixth is a splendid hole, just a drive and pitch one might say, at only some 330 yards and the fairway generously wide. But that little pitch is to a green set on a high plateau, well protected by bunkers, with a deep pit cutting into the right-hand side. The eleventh is another excellent hole, with the drive played from an elevated tee with views of the beach running along the right, a long par 4. At the sixteenth, a par 3 of some 180 yards, Robert Taylor, playing in the Eastern Counties Foursomes in 1974, holed in 1 on three successive days, surely a world record. The finish is testing, with the seventeenth a long 4 and the last green needing two good hits to reach it – right in front of the clubhouse windows.

We are back to traditional golf at **Royal West Norfolk** at Brancaster. First there is a drive over a chasm, followed by a long second up into the sandhills, and on the second we first come across a feature of Brancaster, bunkers faced by wooden sleepers. They seem to daunt almost everyone! On the third, a hole of about 400 yards, there is a huge boarded bunker about 50 yards from the green, with the problem of deciding whether to 'go for it' if the drive has been none too good.

The eighth, a par 5, is a most unusual if not unique hole, with arms of the marsh to carry with first and second shots. The ninth is another celebrated hole. Again, the marsh must be driven and then there is another huge sleepered bunker to be carried to reach the green. The fourteenth is a famous hole with a fairway full of humps and hollows, and the fifteenth, a difficult-looking short hole of about 190 yards, has another sleepered cavernous bunker ready to catch a tee shot hit not quite well enough. The last makes a fine finish, for there is another of those sleepered bunkers fronting the green and a second at the back. It must have been a terror in the days of the 'gutty'. Bernard Darwin wrote that when the wind was up it was 'just about the most difficult course in the world'. However, with the modern ball and equipment, it is not a particularly long test and is a place of much beauty on a still summer day.

Sheringham is a downland course, much of which runs close to the cliffs and seems to give golfers the feeling that here they can open their shoulders. But beware, the cliffs are often near to catch the wild shot from the tee.

It was here in 1920 that the young Joyce Wethered, having taken up the game when she was seventeen, two years before, entered 'just for fun' and met in the final the most formidable player of the day, Cecil Leitch, who went to lunch four up and won two more after lunch. Joyce produced a flow of 3s and in the end won by 2 and 1. I believe Sheringham and this epic match was the origin of the famous story that at a crucial moment when she was lining up a putt a very noisy train went by, Joyce holed out, and when congratulated on her concentration said, 'What train?'

There are four clubs in this area with the 'Royal' prefix, perhaps because they are not far from the Sandringham estate. **Royal Cromer** is one of the oldest clubs in East Anglia, dating back to 1888. Then it was a nine-hole course, perched high on the clifftop, some of which has been eroded away. Now, although part of the course still runs along the cliff edge, much of the golf is played farther inland. It is often windy in this exposed position, but the course has frequent changes of direction, so you will not find yourself slogging into the wind all the way to the turn and then being bowled along by it. Gorse, bunkering and, of course, the sea are present in plenty.

Royal Worlington and Newmarket was granted its title by Queen Victoria, and, I must admit, is not in north Norfolk at all. I end this section with it because it is a wonderful place to break your outward or homeward journey. It has the reputation of being the best nine-hole course in the world.

It has been said that this is links golf played inland. Certainly, the greens are fast, even during a wet winter. The start is difficult, a par 5 – where it is possible to have your ball on the road with both first and second shots – followed by a rather cruel hole. This is some 220 yards with a domed green that will throw anything less than a perfect shot into grassy humps or a bunker, while there is a wood immediately to the rear. The third has often been ranked as one of the best short par 4s in the country. The fairway slopes away to a pond and trees on one side and a ditch on the other, and the green is protected by a winding ditch and bunkers. The fifth is a famous short hole, with a narrow green with slopes to sweep anything but a near perfect shot either into a stream and rough on the right or into 'Mugs Hole' on the left.

The eighth is perhaps the best of the remaining holes, although the cross bunkers arranged to catch a poorly hit second should really not come into play. It is said that four Ryder Cup players played an exhibition match here some twenty years ago. The best round amongst them was a 74. I have a horrid feeling I may have been one of those players!

The Northeast of England

Who thinks of going off for a golfing break to this part of the country? Very few, I'll wager. All the better for the holidaying golfer. Except at weekends and in the rush after offices and factories close, you will be able to wander onto any tee and drive straight off.

Banish also the vision that southerners have of satanic mills, decaying pit villages and general industrial decline. True, the urban landscape of this part of England is seldom beguiling, but we have come to play golf. There are some thirty courses within a short drive from the centre of Newcastle. Some are of tournament calibre – Northumberland, Whitley Bay and Brancepeth are examples; there are also unknown gems off the Northumberland coastline such as Warkworth, Dunstanburgh Castle and Bamburgh Castle.

Formalities in this area are at a minimum, so the holidaying golfer can forget the usual fear of 'Shall I be able to get on?'

There is, perhaps, only one snag about golf in the region – the weather. Undeniably, hot summer days are rarer than farther south, and the spring is late, often caused by the easterlies that tend to set in at this time of year, sometimes producing misty conditions for a few miles inland. But this has never prevented the golf fanatic taking his punishment with a smile in eastern Scotland, where the same winds bite far more sharply.

Founded in 1869, **Alnmouth** was one of the earliest clubs in England at the time when the game began to march southwards from its Scottish homeland. The original course has now become the nine-hole home of Alnmouth Village Golf Club and the present course was designed by Mackenzie Ross, architect of Turnberry. Although it borders the sea, it is not always links in character and the graded semi-rough always looks particularly neat.

The par 4s are the most testing feature of the course, two stiff ones being the first and second, and there is another on the way back to the clubhouse that is, or at least used to be, rated as a 5 for bogey competitions. The second half begins with the hardest par on the course, a 4 where few indeed can get up in 2 strokes. Later there are one or two climbs and perhaps a couple of unattractive holes before a pleasant finish of a long downhill par 5, an excellent par 3 and finally a par 4 that requires a precise medium iron to the green.

A mixture of heath and parkland, **Arcot Hall** is an excellent straightforward test of golf, where erratic driving can come in for considerable punishment in the bush clusters that line several fairways. Originally one of the host of courses designed by James Braid, it has few weak holes and one outstanding par 3 shortly after the turn.

Founded not long after the turn of the century, **Bamburgh Castle** is undeniably short, with three or four of the par 4s drivable with a little wind assistance and more than the regulation four short holes. How is it, then, that not a few good judges consider it one of the best fifty courses in Britain? The answer lies in the views of the castle, Budle Bay and the Farne Islands, whose nearest outpost is less than 3 miles away.

The course itself is invariably enjoyed by visitors, even those who normally prefer a long slog. Rocky surrounds to the occasional green are an unusual and disconcerting hazard.

Laid out, in the main, on land that once formed the parkland of Beamish Hall, formerly the home of the family of Bobby Shafto fame, **Beamish Park** plays considerably longer than its yardage. A feature of the course is an attractive stone-banked stream which threatens either drive or second shot on the first, second and seventeenth holes. The fourth, a 450-yarder, is one of the toughest par 4s you will find anywhere. Invariably there is the prevailing westerly in your face as you drive up a gentle slope to be confronted with a second shot that must carry all the way to the green over a deep depression.

The seventh, although a short enough par 4 on the card, is a classic driving hole. If the golfer dares to play close to the trees along the right of the fairway, he will be rewarded with having a straightforward pitch shot left. Sometimes called 'Cotton's Hole' or the 'Ravine', the fifteenth is the most dreaded hole on the course. The drive is to a very narrow fairway, with a steep slope to the right from which a recovery to the green usually proves impossible.

Berwick-upon-Tweed, the only course for many miles around, runs along Cheswick and Goswick Sands, with Lindisfarne (Holy Island) just two or three miles to the southeast. The car driver en route from the south to Scotland will see the course signposted towards the sea, which lies a couple of miles from the A1 at this point, some half a dozen miles to the south of Berwick. A true links course with excellent turf and good greens, it is outstanding for its condition in winter; another of James Braid's designs.

A very pleasant parkland type of course, **Bishop Auckland** begins with a very short par 4 of little more than 280 yards, followed by the oddity of three par 5s in a row. The first of these is the longest in yardage but plays downhill for most of its length, with an intruding gully causing most golfers to play short with their second shots. The third, 529 yards and uphill, is a true three-shotter, but is followed by a par 5 which plays short, allowing hopes of a birdie.

Shortly after, there come two contrasting par 3s, the first blind and about 220 yards, needing a long iron or even a wood, and then the locally celebrated little seventh. The green is small, but some of the sting has been taken out of it now the undergrowth has been cleared and replaced by more civilized bunkers. The first nine finish with a fine dogleg par 5; the final par 5, making a total of five, balanced by the same number of 3s, is the eleventh, again downhill and offering a clear birdie chance. The most difficult holes on the inward half are probably the 221-yard twelfth, with an out-of-bounds close by along the right, and the thirteenth, rated the hardest hole in the stroke index and requiring a good drive if the green is to be reached in 2.

Locally considered the most testing course in the region, not a judgement I would quarrel with, at least for the average club golfer, is **Brancepeth Castle**. This is no course for the topper and scuffer. Disaster is immediately in wait on at least seven of the holes in the form of the ravine that intersects the course. The start is deceptively easy, a short descending par 4, yet there are few birdies on this hole. The first ravine appears at the par-3 second hole, and there follow two long 4s, one of which requires a shot long enough to clear a deep gully. A little later, ravines are a danger at four consecutive holes.

The most attractive hole, known as the 'Garden Hole', the ninth, is a long par 3 requiring both carry over the ravine and backspin to hold the green, with only part of it in full view.

As the second half begins, by when most cards have already been ruined, yet another long 3 with an out-of-bounds to the left is as difficult as what has gone before. Thereafter, steady golf will see you home without alarms. The last nine contain one of the best short par 4s I have come across, testament to the architect Harry Colt's skill at bunker placement. The fourteenth has out-of-bounds close at hand on the right, a narrow fairway and ranks of bunkers along the left. The green is tiny and surrounded by bunkers.

This course is emphatically not for the holiday golfer who has not played for a year or so, or for anyone who is troubled by a widely curving slice or hook. 'Head up' and you're dead.

Wholly unknown to the golf world at large, and little visited even by golfers of the northeast, lies **Dunstanburgh Castle**, a links course ranged alongside Embleton Bay, where you may meet a few knowing ones who have done their research thoroughly. A friend of mine, who has frequently done the pilgrimage to this rather remote spot, tells me that, for example, he has more than once met Americans who have told him they have just done Sunningdale, Wentworth and Ganton and have been advised that here is the place to break the long journey en route to a more lengthy stay amongst the delights of East Lothian.

Embleton, as it is usually called, is playable the year round. It offers all the normal demands of links golf and is particularly exposed to the elements. However, on less threatening days, there is a wealth of good holes, and two rather poor ones, short par 3s.

The start is perhaps a little too severe, with a long par 4, followed by an uphill drive and some length of shot for the green to be in view. Thereafter, Embleton always shows the golfer what he needs to do. Once the course is learned, the main problem is precise placement of the shot to the green when a yard or so to the right or left can mean the difference between a shortish putt for a birdie or a kick-away, leaving much scope for error on the next.

Dominating the course is the gaunt outline of Dunstanburgh Castle, set high on a steep cliff.

Hexham has a gentle start through the parkland, a par 5 that the average golfer might hope to reach in 2 strokes, followed by a straightforward par 3. Then comes the toughest hole on the course, a 400-yard par 4 with an uphill second shot. The drive, though the fairway is broad indeed, must be held to the left, for there will be little chance of reaching the green, or holding it, from the right.

Thereafter, the golf is always picturesque, sometimes with views of the Tyne Valley below. The par 5s are undemanding, but three of the par 4s, the sixth, eighth and seventeenth, take two good blows to get home. As at the first, the last hole offers one of the delights of golf – an elevated tee with a sweep of fairway in view

Hexham

below, with the added incentive that it might be drivable in a stiff following breeze.

A heath and parkland course, **Northumberland** is one of the best-conditioned courses in the region. The course record of 65 is held by Tony Jacklin and Tommy Horton, and it is the most likely choice for a professional tournament in the region. The 1972 Dunlop Masters was won here by Bob Charles, who overtook Tony Jacklin towards the end. In 1980, the Newcastle Brown '900' followed, the tournament that first brought Irishman Des Smyth into the limelight.

The course has an inviting start, with a downhill tee shot, followed by a little pitch to the green. Thereafter, it is mostly stern going, with one par 4 that most of the members have never reached. The par 5s are less severe, with sometimes a clear birdie possibility. The course itself is partly set within Gosforth Park racecourse and the occasional tee shot is played over the course. The finish is a fine one, with a drive from an elevated tee, followed by an uphill second shot where choice of club is crucial, out-of-bounds being just off the green.

Another course that has hosted championship events at amateur level, **Seaton Carew** can be played at not far short of 7000 yards. The oldest club in the region after Alnmouth, it dates back to 1874. It was from this club that James Kay derived. He was the man who, at the 1896 Open Championship at Muirfield, signalled to Harry Vardon that he should not attempt to carry the cross bunkers with his second shot to the seventy-second hole. Vardon took his advice, played safely short, tied with J. H. Taylor and went on to win the thirty-six-hole play-off for the first of his record six victories.

The surroundings are scarcely scenic, for the industrial towers and chimneys of the Andy Capp city of Hartlepool are in sight most of the time. There is, however, nothing wrong with the course itself, an excellent test of links golf at its best, with not a poor hole. The seventeenth, the 'Snag', is particularly worth a mention, as good a par 4 as you will find anywhere. The drive is over dunes, and the second shot to a narrow sloping green, well protected by bunkers, must be both long and precise.

Reputed to be the only club owned by a trade union, **South Moor**, a heath and parkland course, is set in the heart of a former mining area. Though its condition can be variable, it has a high reputation in the region and has been much used for county events. It is no course for a wayward driver; singles matches in the county league have been won and lost as much on the number of balls sent out of bounds as on any other factor.

With associations with early great names of golf and with a Vardon as professional later on, **Tyneside** is the earliest club in the immediate Newcastle area and dates back to 1879. The course is well known for the excellent greens, which seem to vary little in quality, but is a little on the short side by modern standards. No holes should be too difficult to reach in the regulation strokes. There is a very attractive medium-length par 3 played from a tee high above the green; the most difficult hole is usually considered to be the fourteenth, where an accurate iron to the green is called for. The seventeenth needs two firm hits to get up and the eighteenth is a pleasant finishing hole.

Built on land reclaimed after mining, **Whitley Bay** does not suffer from the sparse fairway growth often found on this kind of development. It hosted the Callers of Newcastle Tournament of 1977, won by the South African John Fourie, who set the course record of 66 in doing so. During the event, stewards urged Severiano Ballesteros to drive off at a shortish par 4 before the green was clear, telling him he would not reach it. Ballesteros was doubtful; the stewards were wrong.

The greens are excellent and perhaps more links in character than the course as a whole. The start appears comfortable, with a par 5 of no great difficulty, though beware the pace of this green, the fastest on the course. Later there is the best par 5 in the region, where a stream along the left menaces both drive and second shot, with the player needing to be that side for the best line in to the green. Another par 5 is fairly reachable in 2, if the player takes his life in his hands and tries to find the narrow gap between grassy banks with his tee shot.

Around the Solway Firth

In this section I am going to imagine that you are a southerner and take you on a journey which begins well up in the northwest corner of England but still some 20 miles as the crow flies from the Solway Firth. We begin at Penrith, to the northeast of the Lake District.

A friend of mine was playing at **Penrith** in an annual Open Day competition a few years ago and casually wondered if he might catch sight of the club's most famous member, the Right Hon. William Whitelaw (now Lord Whitelaw), at the time Secretary of State for Northern Ireland. He proved readily recognizable in the far distance, as he plays 12-handicap golf at the top of his voice. Fifty yards or so away, a wayward tee shot clattered into the trees and guns quickly appeared in the hands of the 'caddies', their experience of normal golfing noises obviously limited. 'That's all right,' he shouted, 'no IRA members here today.'

Indeed, at Penrith and thereafter, the troubles of this world always seem far away. The course is set on moorland, with many fine trees and superb views. It is by no means a slog out and back, but frequently changes direction and tee shots can be both up and downhill. There isn't a hole I could pick out as a weak one, and I recall one par 3 requiring a long iron to a small green as being particularly fine.

Set in glorious fell country at some 400 feet above sea level, with superb hillscape views all round, there can hardly be a more beautiful course than **Brampton** in the British Isles. Often called Talkin Tarn, from the lake at one side of the course, the ground is undulating, but few of the climbs are either severe or long and thirty-six holes a day should not prove too exhausting. Although there is no really weak hole on the course, it was, for once, the par 5s that impressed me the most. Early on, there is one that offers a bold or a safe route to the green. The drive needn't be exceptionally long, but must be held away from the trees along the right. The possibility is then open to send a shot soaring over the trees and rough ground beyond and onto the green. The alternative is to play to the end of the stand of trees, which leaves the player a short pitch to the green. Later comes a par 5 played from an elevated tee to a fairway sweeping up a rise with a blind second to be hit over. The toughest hole is a long par 4 near the end, with an out-of-bounds fence and the railway all along the right.

A former home of Syd Scott, my fellow touring professional, once second in the Open, who still holds the course record of 66, **Carlisle** is a grand venue for a day out, parkland golf as good as any you will find. Mackenzie Ross had a hand in the design, though the course has been lengthened quite a bit since his day. Although a full range of strokes is called for, the demands on the visitor's skills are not particularly severe, no bad ingredient for a pleasant day's outing. A stream features in the course and the turf is excellent, but perhaps the greatest appeal lies in the wealth of very fine trees.

Silloth-on-Solway, origin of the famous turf and handicapping system for foursomes competition, is one of the courses that many have heard of but few have played. The holidaying golfer, heading for the courses of the Ayrshire coastline, is perhaps unwilling to wander some 30 miles along the B5305 and B5302 from the M6 just north of Penrith. Yet Silloth is certainly a good enough course to devote a whole holiday to.

Inside the clubhouse, which I think dates back to the founding of the club in 1894, there are reminders of one of the great British women golfers, Cecil Leitch, who four times won the British Ladies Amateur Championship and was the only real rival to Joyce Wethered. She put the name of Silloth well and truly on the map. The story is told that Silloth once fielded five Leitch sisters in a club match against the men of a Scottish club – and won!

The course itself, though not long, is a severe test of golf. It is fully exposed to the winds and the rough is extremely heathery. In modern terms, there are too many blind shots. The second shots at both first and second are semi-blind, with the greens set below fairway level, but the target is clear enough on the next, this time to a plateau green. The fifth, a par 5 of 486 yards, curves along the shoreline of the Solway Firth. The seventh is one of the blind holes, a 400-yarder where the second shot must be hit over a ridge to a small green set in a slight dell.

The tenth is a particularly pretty hole, where the tigers may go for the green, 308 yards away. The thirteenth is a fine par 5 with a second shot to be played between two humps towards a green perched on the shoulder of a ridge above the player's eyeline. All the par 3s at Silloth have their advocates, but the sixteenth is perhaps the best of them, to a plateau green well protected by sand, grass bunkers and, of course, the ever-present heather. For this is a genuine links course, winding amongst a dunescape, where accurate driving is of prime importance and precision iron play well tested by the undulations of the ground.

If you have been following my itinerary, it is now time to set out for the northern shores of the Solway Firth and Scotland, where **Powfoot** is our first stop, some 20 miles or more beyond Carlisle and about 12 miles on from Gretna Green. It is ideal holiday golf, with the going easy underfoot and the golf not too sternly demanding. There are views of the fells of Cumbria, Southerness Point to the southwest and sometimes even the Isle of Man.

There is little walking between green and tee, with the most attractive holes being the second, eighth and eleventh. Thirty-six holes in a day is none too tiring on this course, one designed by the prolific James Braid, who has left behind some of his distinctive trademarks.

After a rather dull first hole at **Dumfries and County**, the course runs through superb parkland. If the weather is wet, the greens staff make strenuous efforts to keep the course open. A friend of mine tells me that he has never before or since seen greens staff spiking fairway puddles to speed up playability. The Dumfries policy is nicely backed up by some framed certificates in the clubhouse testifying to the excellence of the greenkeeping and course condition.

The course itself is undulating – though there are no really steep slopes to climb – and there are a number of blind drives, but shots to the green are usually clear enough. The greens are quite superb and every prospect pleases.

And so from inland Dumfries back to the Solway shores and **Southerness**, a course of true championship standard and a stern test of skill and power in anything above a stiff breeze. Although hundreds of courses have been opened since the Second World War, almost all have been inland ventures. This is a true links. It was the creation of a local major, who brought in Mackenzie Ross to carve out a course from a sea of heather, bracken and gorse.

The first tee is set amongst the gorse and plays into the prevailing wind. However, at just under 400 yards, it is not as stiff a test as the second, again into the wind, but measuring just over 450 yards. At the fifth, you are likely to find the wind behind you. By this time, a feature of the course should be apparent: the par 4s are very long and tough, only one being substantially under 400 yards; three are more than 450. The seventh is a good par 3 of 214 yards, with the shot needing to carry all the way. The twelfth is perhaps the most majestic of the holes. At 419 yards, it is by no means the longest par 4 but it looks it. There are two bunkers which can sometimes be carried in mid-fairway, but they will force most players to aim left, thus turning the hole into a severe dogleg. If the player hits a very good second shot he may still find the pond at the left of the green.

Having perhaps been pleased to escape with a 5, the twelfth is followed immediately by a pair of holes both more than 450 yards and then another long par 3. Relief at Southerness comes at the last. This used to be the longest par 4 on the course, at 470 yards, but became a 5 a few years ago at 485 yards and of no great difficulty, the best chance of the round for a birdie. It is a course Dai Rees talked of as fit to host an Open Championship, but it has not appeared on the tournament circuit, a result of its comparative remoteness and limited accommodation.

The Ayrshire Coast

In this region we are in one of the heartlands of Open Championship golf, with two courses on the current championship rota, Turnberry and Royal Troon, and another, Prestwick, which played host for the first twelve championships and for twenty-four in all.

My first choice, the Ailsa course at **Turnberry Hotel**, was originally developed by the railways and still has that connection – it is now owned by the company that operates the Orient Express. The Second World War was responsible

Turnberry

for the glory that Turnberry has since become, although it was first a golf course early this century. It was used as an RAF Coastal Command base, some of the fairways becoming concrete runways and many sandhills flattened. British Transport Hotels Group, then owners of the vast hotel that dominates the skyline, brought in Mackenzie Ross to design the two courses that became the Arran and the Ailsa. At the latter he set out to produce a course of championship standard, and surely no one would deny that he succeeded. This was first recognized when the Amateur Championship came here in 1961, followed by the Walker Cup a couple of years later. The final seal of approval came from the Royal and Ancient when they allotted the Open Championship of 1977 to Turnberry – and what an occasion that was, with the final two-round confrontation between Tom Watson, who eventually won, and Jack Nicklaus, who finished a stroke behind. The championship returns here in 1986.

The first three holes are good par 4s, but the first real drama comes at the fourth, a par 3 of 160 yards or so to a green cut into the side of a sandhill. The worst trouble, however, comes if you miss on the left. The ground falls sharply away into dense rough and then the beach. Another dramatic par 3 soon follows, the sixth, just a few yards under the limit for a 3, and very well bunkered. The seventh is perhaps the toughest hole on the course, a 4 of 466 yards, with much rough to be carried from the tee to the right-to-left dogleg. The ninth tee is the most photographed in British golf, that little island of green set on a promontory with the often raging sea below. It is a blind drive over the edge of the seashore to a stone cairn to the fairway beyond, and the second shot to a green beyond the lighthouse.

The next two holes play along the coast and you then turn inland. The fifteenth is a very interesting and testing par 3, with the small green set up in sandhills, while the sixteenth is

Prestwick

a quite memorable downhill hole of just under 400 yards. A potential birdie hole, but the second stroke needs courage as there is a stream fronting the green and an upslope beyond.

At the seventeenth, a par 5 played from a slightly elevated tee, Jack Nicklaus virtually lost the 1977 Open when he missed a fairly close putt and failed to match Watson's birdie.

Because of the greater run of the ball on a links course, Turnberry perhaps needs a good blow to protect it – illustrated in the 1972 John Player Classic, when ten players broke 70 in the windless first round, with Brian Huggett managing a magnificent 64. On the last day in a gale a 76 from Bob Charles was good enough to see him home in first place. Twelve of the field could not break 80 and the mighty Gary Player had an 85.

Ayr Belleisle is a splendid municipal parkland course. Though it is not quite of championship standard, it is a course which I well remember from the 1963 Penfold Tournament. Alas, I did not win, for Bernard Hunt was carrying nearly all before him that year. This is a very busy course in high season, so you may have a wait before teeing off, but it will be worth it.

We are on very hallowed ground indeed at **Prestwick**, which, like North Berwick and St Andrews, for instance, has been altered very little to meet the demands of modern golf and different fashions. Not long ago I did a programme for my 'Around with Alliss' television series with the then Royal and Ancient secretary, Keith Mackenzie, as my guest; it was also a must for the 'World of Golf' series, which traced the development of the game back to its beginnings.

In 1860 the first Open Championship was held here over three rounds of a twelve-hole course and the first name to go on the championship belt was that of Willie Park. Prestwick remained on the Open Championship rota until 1925. In that year the Scottish-born Macdonald Smith came to the last day with a 5-stroke lead, and the Scots came out of the hills and danced around their man, taking it for granted he would be champion. They got too close; he got too nervous. Alas, he came in fourth with an 82. That was the end of the Open as far as Prestwick was concerned.

The first hole at Prestwick does not, from a glance at the card, seem much of a test at only 330 yards or so. Yet you will find a railway all along the right. The story is told that it was once done in 2 by a man who was twice out of bounds. His tee shot hit the railway line and rebounded on to the fairway; much the same happened with his second shot, but this time his ball trickled into the hole. Such is the game of golf. The third has one of the famous bunkers of golf lore, the 'Cardinal', which blocks the route onward for a mishit second shot. It really is cavernous and its railway-sleepered face daunts all who come to rest against it.

Soon after we arrive at another famous hole, the 'Himalayas', so called because the tee shot to this par 3 of just over 200 yards must be hit over the Pow Burn and then over the sandhills beyond. The next few holes were not part of the original course and don't have the same sand-dune character. Perhaps the thirteenth 'Sea Hedrig', is the next famous hole, near the maximum length for a par 4 with an upward-sloping green set at an angle to the line of play.

The fourteenth, rather unusually, brings you back to the clubhouse, from where you set out on a finishing loop of par 4s, two of which have been driven on many occasions. Yet the fifteenth has one of the narrowest fairways in golf and the seventeenth, the 'Alps', requires a biggish second shot over a ridge to the hidden green.

Royal Troon has two courses, one being the Portland, no mean layout just short of 6300 yards. The other, of course, is the Old, the championship course, like Prestwick full of history. My memories of it go back to 1962, when I visited it on a sparkling spring day when all was well with the world. By the time we arrived for the Open, however, it was a real terror, a dust bowl where the ball kicked sideways to all points of the compass. This championship saw one of the great performances of championship history by Arnold Palmer, who won by a distance in racing terms. It also saw the first appearance of Jack Nicklaus, who had a 10 on one hole in a round of 80. 'Obviously,' they said, 'this chap will never be any good at links golf.'

The old begins with half a dozen holes running southwards along the shore, the last of which is the long par-5 hole where Bobby Clampett, the young American, scotched his chances of winning the 1982 Open by taking an 8.

The seventh is a very attractive hole. The drive is from a plateau tee over sand and scrub to a narrow fairway which doglegs right to a heavily bunkered green, set in two sandhills. Then comes very nearly the most famous name for a hole in all of golf. Originally, they used to call the eighth hole 'Ailsa', because of the view of Ailsa Craig, but eventually it became the 'Postage Stamp'. At about 125 yards, it is a short par 3 indeed, the shortest in fact on any British championship course. Yet in 1950, a German amateur champion, Herman Tissies, used up 15 strokes, and Palmer saw his prospects fade here in 1973, as had Walter Hagen in 1923, when he took 5. The main problem is that the green is very small and beset by bunkers. At this hole, Gene Sarazen, our Open champion in 1932, holed out in successive rounds in 1973 without using his putter. At the first attempt, his little punched 5-iron shot went into the hole and the next day he bunkered his tee shot, but then holed out with his sand iron for a 2.

Another of Troon's famous holes is the 'Railway', a par 5 that Palmer plundered during the 1962 Open with two birdies and an eagle, and at which Tom Watson played one of the most decisive shots of championship history to begin to swing the event his way in 1982. It was a beautifully struck 3 iron which pulled up very close to the hole and gave him an eagle 3.

Troon is an out-and-back links course, so do beware. If things seem to be going comfortably enough on the outward nine, with the wind favouring and flattering your play, all things may change once you turn back to the clubhouse.

Much less well known than the illustrious near neighbours, **Western Gailes** is nevertheless a course of high standard. It was used for the 1972 Curtis Cup matches and also for the Scottish Professional and Amateur Championships. It would be well to arrive here with a letter of introduction from your secretary. The course starts comfortably enough with a short par 4, but the second, well over 400 yards, is sterner stuff. The par 4s are a strong feature – in fact, there are just two par 5s and three short holes. One of these, the seventh, is a particularly fine one, asking for an accurate tee shot through sandhills, while the thirteenth is guarded by a burn as well as many bunkers. It relents, on occasion, by having a few relatively short 4s, with just a firm drive and a pitch seeing you home. Perhaps the most testing hole is the eleventh, a dogleg of more than 450 yards.

That is the end of my Ayrshire holiday. I am very aware, that it is a rather expensive one as regards course fees. The best must indeed always cost most.

East Lothian

For those who dislike mixing travel with their golf, East Lothian is an ideal choice. In one stretch of 5 miles there is a sequence of seven courses, almost all of championship quality, where you will often be playing in the wake of the great names of golf history.

The last golf course in England and the farthest north is Magdalene Fields near Berwick-upon-Tweed, and through the Borders there is just one on the coast, at Eyemouth. But once we enter East Lothian, they come thick and fast.

The story goes that it was the men of Dunbar who were influential in importing our game to England. Golf has been played on **Dunbar** links perhaps as long as anywhere else in Scotland, and this club dates its foundation as 1794, compared with 1744 for the Honourable Company of Edinburgh Golfers, 1735 for the Royal Burgess Golfing Society of Edinburgh or 1754 for the Royal and Ancient Golf Club of St Andrews.

The course itself has probably been underrated because it is outside that Mecca of golf which centres on Gullane Hill. Yet it is a fine test of golf, with a burn affecting play on some holes. To allow time for the muscles to get working, it begins with a couple of par 5s, the first relatively undemanding. Thereafter, it is classic links golf all the way, with the last a par 4 of 441 yards designed to settle the outcome of any match. All in all, a course fit to whet the appetite for what is to come; not a few will be tempted to stay.

North Berwick is a course which people immediately take to or hate. The West is a championship course, where late on in my career I qualified for the Open. The club dates from 1832, but golf has been played along these links far longer than that. It is an early, very sporting version of a course, with such unusual hazards as a stone wall to be carried across a fairway and another which runs across the approach to a green. There is even a miniature ravine through the sixteenth green.

After a visit to professional David Huish's shop, you begin with a short par 4, where you must decide whether to play short of a little road that crosses the fairway. The second shot is to a plateau green and if your approach is too gentle, back the ball will tumble into the sand. The third has the wall crossing the fairway, and the next two holes follow the shoreline closely, so slicers beware! We then move inland to two excellent short holes, the fourth and the sixth. With the links set so close to the sea and with no protection at all, the wind very often dominates the golf. At the tenth, we turn for home with the sea now on the left with views of Bass Rock, first playing a par 3 to a tightly bunkered green from a high tee. The real fun comes at the thirteenth, where a stone wall dictates play. 'Perfection' follows, the fourteenth, and the name tells us what early golfers thought a par 4 should be like. The second shot is a blind thump over a bunkered ridge to a green right on the shore.

And so we come to the most famous hole on the course, 'Redan', a par 3 of nearly 200 yards to a plateau green that runs across the line of play with deep bunkers in front. The seventeenth shares the first green and needs a very good second shot to get home. The hole is all of 470 yards with a cross bunker about 70 yards short of the green and an uphill approach.

The course is very heavily played in summer – try late spring when it should be at its peak.

With one of the longest histories in all golf, the **Honourable Company of Edinburgh Golfers** can trace its way back to 1744, when one of the members, John Rattray, drew up the first rules of golf that have come down to us, just a simple thirteen of them! The club at that time played over Leith Links, later moved to Musselburgh, and then to the club's present home, Muirfield, in 1891.

The procedure for playing is to get your club secretary to write a letter requesting permission for the named members of your party to play. Once you are allowed to play, on an average day during the week there will be scarcely a soul in sight. Fair is perhaps a key word for Muirfield. It presents its problems openly, hardly a shot being blind. For this and other reasons, Jack Nicklaus considers it the best of our championship courses, and named his course, where the US Memorial Tournament is played, after it.

It is by no means as daunting for the club golfer as might be expected. The first, a long par 4, is a very testing opening hole from which championship contenders are happy to move on with a par. Two shorter par 4s follow. The long fifth has more bunkers than any hole on the course and is not particularly difficult. The eighth perhaps is the first classic hole with a cluster of bunkers in the driving area at the right of the fairway and more beyond, with the dark presence of Archerfield Wood on the left but not really in play. On the right there are the buckthorn trees planted after Walter Hagen deliberately drove into the rough in the 1929 Open and left himself a shortish pitch to the green, with birdies resulting. Most think the ninth a classic par 5, though at 495 yards it is not exceptionally long. The route to the green is threatened by bunkers on the right and an out-of-bounds wall on the other side. The second nine begin with a par 4 of maximum length with a blind tee shot. Arnold Palmer expired here in the left-hand rough during the 1966 Open. The thirteenth is as neat a shortish par 3 as you could hope to find. Charlie Ward holed in 1 here during the 1948 Open with King George VI looking on.

The finish is a fine one with the last two holes full of Open Championship history. On the seventeenth, a par 5, Roberto de Vicenzo holed a 2-iron second shot in 1948, while Lee Trevino in 1972 holed a long chip for a 5, after which Tony Jacklin three-putted for a 6, the whole destiny of the championship changing in a trice. Here also in 1966 Jack Nicklaus got a 4, which eluded other contenders and went on to win.

The eighteenth is one of the great finishing holes of championship golf. There are three bunkers on the left in the driving area and another two to the right, while the green is tightly bunkered. From the bunker in front of the green, Henry Cotton in 1948 shanked his first splash out, but all was well in the end.

Perhaps the first thing to get right about **Gullane** is how to pronounce the name. It's 'Gillan'. There is also the confusing prospect of a choice of three courses. Number 3 has its advocates; it is distinctly short at only a touch more than 5000 yards, yet has plenty of tricks up its sleeve. Number 2 is nearer championship standard, though the start, which involves a blind thrash over a ridge to the green, is not to purists' taste. Thereafter there is a wealth of fine golf, with the eleventh and twelfth having the added attraction of running through a nature reserve.

In 1947, Babe Zaharias, the great American amateur and later professional, caused something of a stir by her play at Gullane Number 1. For a start she was wearing trousers, much frowned on at the time, and also hit a golf ball farther than many thought was quite ladylike. In the first six matches of that British Ladies Championship, she lost only four holes to move on with wide margins of victory. She appeared for the final attired in Bermuda shorts, to the distaste of the organizers, and obeyed their request to revert to her corduroys. In due course, the first American winner of this title was crowned.

Few would dispute that Gullane is more attractive than Muirfield, helped by the rise and fall of the ground and par 4s and 5s that sweep in broad doglegs. Only the second, fifth and sixth, however, make any real demands on climbing prowess, and such holes as the seventh and seventeenth compensate by being exhilaratingly downhill. On the higher parts of the course, golfers are apt to linger at the seventh and the ninth tees for views of Muirfield below to the east and Edinburgh and the Forth bridges to the west.

Longniddry

When the time comes to descend, a hole that remains in the memory is the seventeenth, a 400-yarder which it is possible to drive. Most will finish short, of course, and be faced with three cavernous bunkers barring the way to the green.

Although a golfer of reasonable standard will probably not be turned away at **Luffness New,** it is best to follow the procedures recommended for Muirfield. Many no doubt say, 'why bother when there is a wealth of good golf so near?' However, Luffness will reward the persistent with particularly outstanding greens. The course, though fairly short, has been used for Open Championship qualifying and the section by Aberlady Bay is especially attractive.

Although close to the sea, **Longniddry** is less links in character than the other courses I have mentioned. Some of the holes wind amongst trees and on others the greens are set amongst trees. Many of the holes, particularly towards the end, are fully exposed to the wind. A feature is that there are no par 5s. Instead the golfer is confronted by a number of holes which used to be par 5s, but, with changed methods of rating par, have become 4s. This length of the 4s make Longniddry unrelenting to the medium-length hitter – but it's the same for everybody. There is a most attractive start, with a broad expanse of fairway sweeping away to a green set amongst trees. Later on there is a little par 4 that ought to be easy, but isn't. Best to take a medium iron from the tee, for you will still only have a short iron to the plateau green high above you. The par 3 which follows is very attractive, with play being from an elevated tee to an island green almost entirely surrounded by sand.

Altogether, this is not a course to be missed.

The PGA Seniors has four times been held here between 1970 and 1982, and the World Seniors has also been held here, Sam Snead beating our champion Ken Bousfield by 3 and 2.

One drawback of playing all these courses, except in high summer, is that one must expect to be buffeted by the wind. If this unluckily proves to be the case, it may be as well to retreat temporarily inland to courses at Haddington and Gifford.

Nine-hole courses have become rather unpopular with golfers over the years, though I don't quite see why this should be so. **Gifford** has kept to its nine parkland holes, with alternative tees to give variety. The Lammermuir Hills are close at hand, immediately to the south.

Haddington is another parkland course and a public one, a quick refuge from coastal winds within 7 miles of the courses discussed so far. It makes for pleasant walking and the River Tyne runs through.

We come now to one of the most confusing of golf club names. **Musselburgh** links was one of the homes of golf and six Open Championships were held there until the Honourable Company moved both its club and the championship to Muirfield. The course was for many years hardly a golf course at all, as the clubs which had played there took themselves off to pastures new. In the 1960s it was possible to play the nine holes for a modest shilling and I am not sure it was worth that much, such was the condition.

However, the Musselburgh Golf Club I refer to is known locally as Monkton Hall and was originally designed by James Braid. It is entirely inland in character, although not more than a mile from the sea. It is built on generally open land which has been afforested since the foundation of the club, so that most of the time you are playing through large clutches of pine forest. It is a long course, even from the forward tees, but no real uphill stretches are involved. The greens are excellent and I do not recall a weak hole, something one cannot often say.

Course Details

Alnmouth Golf Club
Foxton Hall, Alnmouth, Northumberland NE66 3BE
Tel. Alnmouth 231
Course length: 6414 yards
Location: 37 miles north of Newcastle upon Tyne, about 5 miles southeast of Alnwick off the A1068

Arcot Hall Golf Club
Dudley, Cramlington, Northumberland NE23 7QP
Tel. Wideopen 362794
Course length: 6256 yards
Location: 8 miles north of Newcastle and 1 mile east of the A1

Ayr Belleisle
Doonfoot Road, Ayr, Ayrshire
Tel. Alloway 41258
Course length: 6540 yards
Location: At the south of Ayr, about 1 mile from the centre

Bamburgh Castle Golf Club
The Wynding, Bamburgh, Northumberland NE69 7DE
Tel. Bamburgh 378
Course length: 5495 yards
Location: 39 miles north of Newcastle and 20 miles south of Berwick-upon-Tweed, leaving the A1 just to the south of Belford along the B1342

Barton-on-Sea Golf Club
Marine Drive, Barton-on-Sea, Hampshire BH25 2DY
Tel. New Milton 615308
Course length: 5632 yards
Location: About 10 miles east of Bournemouth and 1½ miles from New Milton, off the A337

Beamish Park Golf Club
Beamish, Stanley, Durham
Tel. Stanley 32552
Course length: 6013 yards
Location: From the A1 at Chester-le-Street, 7 miles north of Durham and 8 miles south of Newcastle, take the A693 for Stanley, turning right for Beamish Museum

Berwick-upon-Tweed Golf Club
Goswick, Beal, nr Berwick, Northumberland
Tel. Berwick 87256
Course length: 6411 yards
Location: Turn right from the A1 some 23 miles north of Alnwick, 6 miles south of Berwick

Bishop Auckland Golf Club
High Plains, Bishop Auckland, Durham
Tel. Bishop Auckland 602198
Course length: 6340 yards
Location: 1 mile east of Bishop Auckland on the A689 to Durham

Brampton (Talkin Tarn) Golf Club
Talkin Tarn, nr Brampton, Cumbria
Tel. Brampton 2255
Course length: 6426 yards
Location: On the B6413, a mile or so south of Brampton and 10 miles from Carlisle

Bramshaw Golf Club
Brook, Lyndhurst, Hampshire SO4 7HE
Tel. Cadnam 3252
Course lengths: Manor 6257 yards; Forest 5753 yards
Location: Leave the M27 at Cadnam and follow the B3078 northwest. The club is less than a dozen miles from Southampton

Brancepeth Castle Golf Club
Brancepeth, Durham DH7 8EA
Tel. Durham 780075
Course length: 6300 yards
Location: Turn left at the crossroads in the village some 5 miles from Durham along the A690 Durham to Crook road

Broadstone (Dorset Golf Club)
Lower Golf Links Road, Broadstone, Dorset BH18 8BQ
Tel. Broadstone 693363
Course length: 6204 yards
Location: 4 miles north of Poole along the A349 towards Wimborne

Brockenhurst Manor Golf Club
Sway Road, Brockenhurst, Hampshire SO4 7SG
Tel. Lymington 22383
Course length: 6216 yards
Location: About 1 mile south of Brockenhurst on the B3055

Burley Golf Club
Burley, nr Ringwood, Hampshire BH24 4RR
Tel. Burley 2431
Course length: 6140 yards
Location: Some 4 miles northeast of Ringwood on the A31, turning right at Picket Post

Carlisle Golf Club
Aglionby, Carlisle, Cumbria
Tel. Scotby 303
Course length: 6325 yards
Location: 3 miles east of Carlisle off the A69, just a mile from junction 43 on the M6

Dumfries and County Golf Club
Nunfield, Dumfries and Galloway D91 1JX
Tel. Dumfries 3585
Course length: 5908 yards
Location: 1 mile north of the town centre on the A701 Edinburgh road

Dunbar Golf Club
East Links, Dunbar, East Lothian EH42 1LT
Tel. Dunbar 62317
Course length: 6441 yards
Location: Immediately on the 'English' side of Dunbar, about a mile off the A1 and some 29 miles from Edinburgh

Dunstanburgh Castle Golf Club
Embleton, nr Alnwick, Northumberland
Tel. Embleton 672
*Course length:*6308 yards
Location: From the A1 bypass at Alnwick, take the B1340 and follow signs for Embleton for some 7 or 8 miles

Ferndown Golf Club
119 Golf Links Road, Ferndown, Wimborne, Dorset BH22 8BU
Tel. Ferndown 874602
Course length: 6442 yards
Location: 6 miles north of Bournemouth off the A31

Gifford Golf Club
Gifford, East Lothian EH41 4OL
Tel. Gifford 267
Course length: 6138 yards (played twice from alternative tees)
Location: 1 mile southwest of Gifford and 4½ miles south of Haddington

Gullane Golf Club
Gullane, East Lothian EH31 2BB
Tel. Gullane 843115
Course lengths: Number 1 6479 yards; Number 2 6127 yards; Number 3 5012 yards
Location: On the A198 North Berwick to Edinburgh road. The road runs through the courses, which are some 18 miles east of Edinburgh and 5 miles west of North Berwick

Haddington Golf Club
Amisfield Park, Haddington, East Lothian
Tel. Haddington 3627
Course length: 6122 yards
Location: On the A1 about 18 miles east of Edinburgh and just past Haddington to the east

Hexham Golf Club
Spital Park, Hexham, Northumberland NE46 3RZ
Tel. Hexham 602057
Course length: 6272 yards
Location: Immediately off the A69, 1 mile west of Hexham, some 21 miles west of Newcastle

Highcliffe Castle Golf Club
Lymington Road, Christchurch, Dorset BH23 4LA
Tel. Highcliffe 72953
Course length: 4655 yards
Location: 2 miles east of Christchurch on the A337 to Lymington

The Honourable Company of Edinburgh Golfers
Muirfield, Gullane, East Lothian EH31 2EG
Tel. Gullane 842123
Course length: 6601 yards (championship tees 6926 yards)
Location: Off the A198, some 4 miles west of North Berwick and a mile before Gullane

Hunstanton Golf Club
Hunstanton, Norfolk PE36 6JQ
Tel. Hunstanton 2811
Course length: 6670 yards
Location: Half a mile east of the town off the A149 to Sheringham and Cromer

Longniddry Golf Club
Longniddry, East Lothian EH32 0NL
Tel. Longniddry 52141
Course length: 6240 yards
Location: Some 15 miles east of Edinburgh on the A198

Luffness New Golf Club
Aberlady, East Lothian EH32 0QA
Tel. Gullane 843114
Course length: 6100 yards
Location: 1 mile west of Gullane village on the A198

Meyrick Park
Bournemouth, Dorset
Tel. Bournemouth 20871
Course length: 5878 yards
Location: From Bournemouth Square take Bourne Avenue, then Bradley Road and finally Central Drive, a total distance of about half a mile

Musselburgh Golf Club
Monkton Hall, Musselburgh, East Lothian
Tel. Edinburgh 665 2005
Course length: 6623 yards
Location: 1 mile south of the A1 in Musselburgh

New Forest Golf Club
Southampton Road, Lyndhurst, Hampshire SO4 7BU
Tel. Lyndhurst 2450
Course length: 5748 yards
Location: Off the A35 Bournemouth to Southampton road, less than a mile out of Lyndhurst

North Berwick Golf Club
New Clubhouse, Beach Road, North Berwick, East Lothian EH39 4BB
Tel. North Berwick 2135
Course length: 6317 yards
Location: Off the A198 road to Edinburgh, a couple of miles from the town centre and 23 miles from Edinburgh

Northumberland Golf Club
High Gosforth Park, Newcastle upon Tyne NE3 5HT
Tel. Wideopen 2009
Course length: 6643 yards
Location: Follow signs for Gosforth Races along the A1 north of Newcastle. The course lies some 4 miles from the city centre

Parkstone Golf Club
Links Road, Parkstone, Poole, Dorset BH14 98U
Tel. Canford Cliffs 708025
Course length: 6250 yards
Location: About 3 miles west of Bournemouth along the A338. Turn south at St Osmund's Church along St Osmund's Road

Penrith Golf Club
Salkeld Road, Penrith, Cumbria CA11 8SG
Tel. Penrith 62217
Course length: 6026 yards
Location: About three-quarters of a mile northeast of Penrith. Leave the M6 at junction 40

Powfoot Golf Club
Cummertrees, nr Annan, Dumfries and Galloway
Tel. Cummertrees 227
Course length: 6283 yards
Location: Shortly west of Annan along the A75, turn left along the B724 with Powfoot some 3 miles away

Prestwick Golf Club
Links Road, Prestwick, Strathclyde KA9 1QG
Tel. Prestwick 77404
Course length: 6544 yards
Location: About 1 mile from the airport and adjacent to the railway station

Queen's Park
Queen's Park South Drive, Bournemouth (c/o Recreation Officer, Town Hall, Bournemouth, Dorset BH2 6DY)
Tel. Bournemouth 36198
Course length: 6505 yards
Location: On the B3347, 2 miles northeast of Bournemouth Square

Royal Cromer Golf Club
Overstrand Road, Cromer, Norfolk NR27 0JH
Tel. Cromer 512219
Course length: 6636 yards
Location: 1 mile east of Cromer on the B1159

Royal Troon Golf Club
Craigend Road, Troon, Strathclyde KA10 6EP
Tel. Troon 311555
Course length: 6649 yards (over 7000 yards from championship tees)
Location: 3 miles north of Prestwick Airport to the south of Troon

Royal West Norfolk (Brancaster)
Brancaster, King's Lynn, Norfolk PE31 8AX
Tel. Brancaster 223
Course length: 6216 yards
Location: On the A149 Hunstanton to Sheringham Road, 7 miles east of Hunstanton

Royal Worlington and Newmarket Golf Club
Worlington, Bury St Edmund's, Suffolk
Tel. Mildenhall 712216
Course length: 3109 yards (9 holes)
Location: 7 miles northeast of Newmarket off the A11

Seaton Carew Golf Club
Tees Road, Hartlepool, Cleveland TS25 1DE
Tel. Hartlepool 66249
Course length: 6604 or 6876 yards
Location: Off the A178 Hartlepool to Middlesbrough road, some 3 miles south of Hartlepool

Sheringham Golf Club
Weybourne Road, Sheringham, Norfolk NR26 8HG
Tel. Sheringham 822038
Course length: 6430 yards
Location: On the A149, half a mile west of the town centre

Silloth-on-Solway Golf Club
The Clubhouse, Silloth, Cumbria CA4 4DG
Tel. Silloth 31179
Course length: 6343 yards
Location: 23 miles west of Carlisle, leaving the M6 at junction 43 and from Carlisle taking the B5307 for most of the way. There is also an alternative route from Penrith

South Moor Golf Club
The Middles, Craghead, nr Stanley, Durham
Tel. Stanley 32848
Course length: 6445 yards
Location: Take the A693 Chester-le-Street to Stanley and Consett road and at Stanley turn onto the B6313 for a mile or so

Southerness Golf Club
Southerness, nr Dumfries, Dumfries and Galloway DG2 8AZ
Tel. Kirkbean 677
Course length: 6548 yards (can be stretched to more than 7000 yards)
Location: 16 miles southwest of Dumfries on the A710 or some 5 miles southeast of Dalbeattie, also on the A710

Stoneham Golf Club
Bassett Green Road, Southampton, Hampshire SO2 3NE
Tel. Southampton 768151
Course length: 6270 yards
Location: From Southampton along the A33 for Winchester, take the airport turn-off at Chilworth roundabout

Turnberry Hotel: Ailsa
Turnberry Hotel, Turnberry, Strathclyde KA26 9LT
Tel. Turnberry 202
Course length: 6384 yards (championship tees 6948 yards)
Location: 5 miles north of Girvan and 18 miles south of Ayr on the A719

Tyneside Golf Club
Westfield Lane, Ryton-on-Tyne, Tyne and Wear
Tel. Ryton 2177
Course length: 6029 yards
Location: Turn into the village of Ryton from the A695 Gateshead to Hexham road. Ryton is some 7 miles west of Newcastle

Wareham Golf Club
Sandford Road, Wareham, Dorset BH20 4DH
Tel. Wareham 2658
Course length: 5196 yards
Location: At Wareham, near the railway station, on the A351 from Poole

Western Gailes Golf Club
Gailes, nr Irvine, Strathclyde KA11 5AB
Tel. Irvine 311357
Course length: 6614 yards
Location: On the A78, 3 miles north of Troon

Whitley Bay Golf Club
Claremont Road, Whitley Bay, Tyne and Wear NE26 3UF
Tel. Whitley Bay 520180
Course length: 6615 yards
Location: Near the town centre and some 10 miles east of Newcastle

13 Holiday Reading

Golf, like cricket and perhaps boxing, has been fortunate in the writers who have been attracted to the game. So, to close my book, I've chosen some of my favourite golf pieces. All of them, in different ways that I'll leave you to sort out, have connections with ideas I've put forward in this book. I hope you enjoy them as much as I have.

First a brief selection about playing the game.

Swings and Roundabouts

PATRICK CAMPBELL

The thing that astonishes me about golf is that, twenty years after I first began to play it, I still have six separate and distinct methods of producing any given shot.

The other thing that astonishes me about golf is that half of these separate and distinct methods are the precise opposite of the other three, and all of them work equally well. On – that is – their limited day.

I should have thought, after so long an apprenticeship, that one particular method would finally have risen to the top, and that with it, in the middle eighties, I should have been allowed quietly to play out my time.

But no. As I stand on the first tee in the first round of, say, the Amateur Championship, at 8.30 a.m. with a nippy oblique breeze off the sea, I can strike the new ball in front of me in no fewer than six different ways, and that after a week of careful practice.

With this first shot there are three things I want to do. I want to get it off the ground. I want to be able to find it after I've hit it. And, rather specially, I want to avoid the one which shoots off the toe through the roof of the starter's tent.

I might try the Hogan crouch. I got the Hogan crouch from looking at pictures of Ben Hogan, and with it drove the second green at Coombe Hill in March 1951.

In the Crouch the knees are bent throughout the duration of the performance. The back is hollowed, and the buttocks (Hogan's word not mine) are thrust out in a sitting position. It certainly gives a feeling of exceptional power and mobility. But with the Crouch I must continue to crouch. If the knees should suddenly straighten, owing to centrifugal force, the clubhead passes over the ball, resulting in the clean miss (Wentworth, April, '51; Stoke Poges, April, '51; Walton Heath, April, '51; Sunningdale, April, '51, etc.).

The Upright Classical might be a wiser investment. I got the Upright Classical from looking at pictures of Henry Cotton, and with it nearly reached the ditch from the first tee on the first hole at Deal in a year I don't remember, because every Halford Hewitt, in retrospect, looks to me exactly alike.

The difficulty with the Upright Classical is that my left leg, at impact, seems to have the rigidity and length of a telegraph pole, and a follow-through of more than a foot guarantees a permanent injury. This is the one which, incorrectly played, passes low over the heads of people not paying attention at cover point.

The Blacksmith's Convulsive has, of course, stood me in good stead before now, notably when I arose from the poker table at 9.10 one morning – previous best 6.30 p.m. to 8.15 a.m., Ballybunion, '38 – and slashed one right down the middle, five minutes later, in a West of Ireland championship at Rosses Point.

The essence of the Blacksmith's Convulsive is to seize the club so tightly that the forearms become numb, and then let drive, disregarding pivot, weight-shift and any attempt to cock the wrists. The wrists, if cocked, snap off. The value of the Convulsive is that the stroke is always completed, one way or an-

John Betjeman at his beloved St Enodoc

other, before the audience have had time to observe its finer points.

The Convulsive's companion, and, of course, direct opposite, is the Sensitive. A French word, pronounced 'sonsitive'. The thing about the Sensitive is that it relaxes me right down to the ground. The club is held so lightly in the fingers, and so marked is the absence of tension, that upon my word I'm in danger of dropping off to sleep.

I discovered it one summer evening at Portmarnock, in 1936. We were fooling about on the practice ground, when I had occasion to tell one of my companions that he was trying to hit too hard. 'Just *drop* the clubhead on the ball,' I said, 'like this.' I dropped the head of a No. 5 on to the ball and it took off like a bullet, to crash full pitch through the secretary's window – as we paced it out later – 207 yards away.

I could certainly use it now, except that with the Sensitive the backswing gives me the impression of going on for ever. I have a tendency to lose my nerve, and to wonder if the ball will still be there when, like General MacArthur, I return. Under these circumstances I'm inclined to lash out suddenly from the level of the waist, and off she goes in that special kind of hook so quick that the ball becomes egg-shaped in its efforts to take the bend.

Round about now, on the first tee in the opening round of the Amateur Championship, I often begin to wonder which hand goes on top of the club, in the grip which I am accustomed to use. But this is only a passing phase. I have more serious things to consider. Whether, for instance, at this eleventh hour, to use the Utterly Inside Out, or the Retired Colonel's Up and Down.

I once played the Utterly Inside Out by accident, into the heart of the green at Calamity Corner, Portrush. There was a gale blowing from the sea. To keep the clubhead as close to the ground as possible, and thereby out of the worst of the weather, I drew it back stealthily in a half circle round my legs. I had no expectation that anything very much was going to happen, but without warning, and for the first time in my life, I felt that if we were to be fortunate some time in the future to return to the target area I was going to have a solid left side to hit against. I could actually see my left shoulder, as large as life beneath my chin. An astounding spectacle, in view of the fact that I'd never been privileged to get more than a glimpse of the elbow before.

Round we came. And off she went – actually boring in from the left, to pitch downwind, check, and finish 3 feet from the hole.

At the next, I tried it again, with the driver. We gave up looking for it almost immediately. Another couple was pressing behind. But the caddie, in that rather charming Belfast accent, said that never before in his life had he seen a shot which had travelled 270 yards without actually crossing the front of the tee.

With only a few seconds left before my name is called I decide it will have to be the Retired Colonel's Up and Down.

This is the simplest style at my command.

I stand in front of the ball and hold the club just firmly enough to stop it falling out of my hand – a semi-Sensitive – and then I pick it up and move it back and when I think I've got it back far enough I move it forward again, and if the ball, however briefly, manages to get itself tangled in the lot I do swear I'm well pleased.

But the Retired Colonel's Up and Down got me drummed out of the preliminary trials for the Walker Cup. From the first tee at Temple I nicked one so finely with the Retired Colonel, off the toe, that it would have carried away the starter's tent *and* the starter, if the starter and his tent had been there. As it was, it nearly felled three members of the selection committee.

Discussing the technicalities of the thing afterwards, Mr Raymond Oppenheimer told me that it had seemed to him and his fellow selectors that my best prospect of making contact with the ball, as from the top of the swing, was to strike at it vertically, downwards, keeping the head well back and out of harm's way.

But now it is my turn. The die has been cast. The name has been called. After two attempts I tee up a new ball.

I initiate the backswing with a slight forward press – and suddenly every one of my six systems become fused!

From the Hogan Crouch, with a grunt, into the Upright Classical! Sensitive at the top of the swing! The club is lying on my collarbone! Quick – the Blacksmith's Convulsive – take hold!

We're coming down. Ease her in. More. A little more. The Utterly Inside Out. Too much! I'm going to strike my hip! Quick! The Retired Colonel! The Up and Down! Level her off! I've *got* it! *CONTACT! SHE'S AWAY!*

A low snakey thing, scorching the rough all along the lefthand side of the fairway. And all of 150 yards.

Well, by God, that's one I haven't seen before.

(From *The Golfers' Year*, edited by Tom Scott and Webster Evans, Nicholas Kaye, 1951)

Tournament Golf
BOBBY JONES

Tournament golf! It's different from just golf, especially when it leads at last into the cage of championship. I read a line somewhere, or a title, 'the Cage of Championship'. It *is* something like that. Something like a cage. First you're expected to get into it, and then you're expected to stay there. But of course nobody can stay there. Out you go – and then you're trying your hardest to get back in again. Rather silly, isn't it, when golf – just golf – is so much fun?

Still, championship has its compensations. There was that sight of New York harbour, in 1926, when I was bringing the British Open Championship cup home; New York harbour, and the *Macom* coming out, with the home folks aboard and the band playing 'Valencia'.

I've been awfully lucky. Maybe I'll win another championship, some day. I love championship competition, after all – win or lose. Sometimes I get to thinking, with a curious little sinking away down deep, how I will feel when my tournament days are over, and I read in the papers that the boys are gathering for the National Open, or the Amateur ... Maybe at one of the courses I love so well, and where I fought in the old days ... It's going to be queer.

But there's always one thing to look forward to – the round with Dad and Chick and Brad; the Sunday morning round at old East Lake, with nothing to worry about, when championships are done.

(From *Down the Fairway*, Allen & Unwin, 1927)

Bobby Jones – arguably the greatest of them all

Seaside Golf
JOHN BETJEMAN

How straight it flew, how long it flew,
  It clear'd the rutty track
And soaring, disappeared from view
  Beyond the bunker's back –
A glorious, sailing, bounding drive
That made me glad I was alive

And down the fairway, far along
  It glowed a lonely white;
I played an iron sure and strong
  And clipp'd it out of sight,
And spite of grassy banks between
I knew I'd find it on the green.

And so I did. It lay content
  Two paces from the pin;
A steady putt and then it went
  Oh, most securely in.
The very turf rejoiced to see
That quite unprecedented three.

The Mind of a Golfer

PETER ALLISS

Golf is a peculiar game. I almost said a funny game, but then it is not meant to be that. But it does pose problems for the performer different from those of almost any other sport I can think of. For one thing, it is played with a stationary ball. This simple fact in itself creates tensions, constrictions and inhibitions so peculiar that they make golf almost unique. A stationary ball means in essence a stationary performer. In games played with a moving ball, the movement of the performer is mandatory and instinctive, and this very physical movement creates its own relaxations. In such sports movement is incidental, incidental to the pattern of play or the final product of the game. In golf, movement is calculated, wilful, total. In golf, the achievement is concentrated into one fleeting, conscious action and is then over and done with beyond redemption. In other, moving-ball, sports the movement is continuous and intrinsic and for the performer acts as a stimulant and tranquillizer combined. The golfer has to act in cold blood. From a motionless posture he must generate a swift, sudden, powerful but rhythmic action which is complete in itself in perhaps three or four seconds. Golf is a solitary game. A golfer walks alone. In team play, in football, cricket, rugby and the others, the very existence of other team members gives the player a release, a safety valve for his tensions, an excuse, a scapegoat readily to hand. The final responsibility is only partly his, whereas in golf, finally, it all gets down to the player, the club and the ball, and no other people. If you consider that the golf swing, the calculated shot at the ball, will take a generous four seconds, and if you further calculate that you will do it 72 times in a round, there is a total time *in action* of some four and a half minutes in a round which can take more than three hours to play. And in the intervals between the actions, the game is stopped absolutely. The ball has flown, rolled, come to rest. The golf course remains passive. Action is suspended. Thus, for the competitor as he walks forward for the next action, there is an intolerable amount of time for thinking, or, rather, being subject to the mental process, regarding the shot he has just made, the one he is about to make, the bad shot he had made three holes back, the problems of the most difficult hole which will be coming up five holes ahead, the shifts of the wind, the people in the crowd, the face of a pretty girl in the crowd, a silly pop tune charging around in his mind, some reflections on a poor breakfast he had in the hotel and will dinner be any better, what his best route home through the traffic might be, how the children are at home, and so on. A round of golf lasts many hours. A tournament goes on for days. It is played at a low physical pressure, but always at a dangerously high mental pressure. Other sports make demands on the instincts and reflexes. Golf makes its demands on the mind. Thus a golfer is terribly exposed, exposed in almost every way. The final responsibility is his, and there is no way to camouflage this, no hope of jettisoning it.

(From *Alliss through the Looking Glass*, Cassell, 1966)

Think Positively

GARY PLAYER

If you think of yourself as an unlucky golfer, if you're sure you'll get a bad bounce, if you think you will land in the water, then you *will* be unlucky and get the bad bounce and land in the water. But if you keep telling yourself that you are a good putter, that you can beat anybody, that you are not scared of the golf course, then you really have a head start on the whole thing. What you think, you will be. Think defensively, and you will play defensively. Think positively and you will play positively. At Indianapolis one year, I thought the course was in poor condition, with the fairway grass over long. I said this to a journalist, that there was no way I could win on a course like that, that I would be hitting fliers out of the long grass because no one could control the ball, and so on. Sure enough, it appeared in print, and I was a little less than popular. But the night before the tournament started, I got to thinking about what I had said, and I decided I had been busy making excuses for myself before we had even started. I was well along the way to talking myself out of any hope of winning. So I started to think along the lines that the golf course was perfectly all right, that of course I could hit good shots off these fairways, and why shouldn't I win the tournament. I won.

I believe that within this business of shaping a good positive thought process, one can visualize the golf shot, complete and whole. By that I mean one can have a vision of the stance, the continuous physical swinging motion and strike at the ball from beginning to end, and the actual flight pattern of the ball, the whole thing related to the environment. I believe one can visualize what is to be done, how it is to be done, the consequence of doing it, and this I now practise in my mind on every shot, as I am coming up to the ball. I am trying to make the point that this is something quite definitely different from thinking of the technical points of the swing, such as lining up, and keeping the head still, and taking the club straight back, and so on, but is rather a complete mental photographic pattern of one golf shot, from set-up until the ball stops rolling, and the whole thing related to the environment at the same time.

(From *Grand Slam Golf*, Pelham Books, 1966)

Gary Player – perhaps the most positive player

Patience

BOBBY JONES

I had a different attitude. Some way, I wasn't in that frantic hurry about getting those strokes back. It was as if something deep in my consciousness kept counselling patience. Patience! Somewhere lately I heard or read that the greatest asset of Harry Vardon was his perfect realization of the cold fact that no matter what happened, there was only one thing for him to do – keep on hitting the ball. I hadn't heard or read that at Flossmoor; and I cannot say that such a plan was in my mind. Indeed, I had no plan. Instinctively or otherwise, I managed to keep on hitting the ball, and not trying to wrench back those strokes immediately. And presently – presently they came back to me, in a sort of normal and ordinary manner, and some more with them.

So maybe that is the answer – the stolid and negative and altogether unromantic attribute of patience. It is nothing new or original to say that golf is played one stroke at a time. But it took me many years to realize it. And it is easy to forget now. And it won't do to forget in tournament golf . . .

Maybe that is the answer – patience. Whatever I possess of it now must have been cultivated, as I assuredly did not have it at first, and the number of years required to hammer it into me is a sorry commentary on my native intelligence . . .

After all, it's Old Man Par and you, match or medal. And Old Man Par is a patient soul, who never shoots a birdie and never incurs a buzzard. He's a patient soul, Old Man Par. And if you would travel the long route with him, you must be patient, too.

I really think that is good advice.

I hope I may be able to follow it, occasionally.

(From *Down the Fairway*, Allen & Unwin, 1927)

Time for a Change of Life
PAT WARD-THOMAS

A golfing acquaintance recently declared that he had reached the change of life. He was, of course, referring to his golf and not a bizarre circumstance of nature. When I sought explanation he said that the time had come when he was inclined to remember the good shots in a round rather than the bad, thereby achieving some consolation for his efforts, however paltry the overall outcome might be.

This was surprising. The last time we had played in the same match his attitude had been quite different. He had played far below his best until about the turn, when he produced a remarkable recovery stroke. The ball was on a steep, downhill, sandy lie. Between it and the flag, no more than twenty yards away, was a deep bunker, above which was a sheer little shelf to the edge of the green. It would be hard to conceive a more testing stroke: it had to be thrown up very steeply so that it would land softly. The slightest under- or over-hit would be fatal.

Gary Player, as skilled in shots from sand as anyone I have seen, could not have played the shot better. It fell gently and rolled to within inches of the hole. Whereupon his partner remarked that it made up for some of the previous errors. But the hero would have none of it, declaring that nothing could really compensate for them. From a practical viewpoint he was right; but why, as he came to realize later, not savour the triumphs, few though they may be, and forget the tragedies?

Many golfers never progress beyond this stage and sensibly recognize that in all probability they never will. In a way they are to be envied because they return to the clubhouse not dissatisfied with their round. Perhaps their driving was steadier than usual, they may have mastered a hole that normally defeated them, one or two long putts may have fallen, maybe a bunker shot finished dead or a rare victory was won against an old rival.

A few such happy moments are sufficient to make their day even though they may have taken an awful number of strokes. They will have crowned the joy of treading smooth turf, the feel of the summer breeze, the music of birdsong, the sense of escape from mundane reality and the pleasure of being with friends. And when the round is done, how eagerly they look for someone to whom they can impart the glad tidings.

Occasionally it happens that the listener is a much more accomplished golfer and is equally anxious to unburden himself, but for very different reasons. He is seeking a sympathetic ear into which he can bemoan

Pat Ward-Thomas – a beautiful writer who had a true love–hate relationship with the game

the strokes that spoiled his day. 'It's incredible,' he will say, 'but I had a 6 at the eighth, the easiest hole on the course, fluffed a chip and took 3 putts. Admittedly, my 5 iron to the eleventh was pushed into that bunker, but it didn't have to finish in a heelmark. You know how well I've putted lately – well, I missed three from inside 4 feet. The greens are a bit rough, but 78 was terrible the way I was hitting the ball. The permutations of misfortune, real or imagined, are infinite.

The victim of this recital, having no idea of how many strokes he himself had taken, could retort that he would happily settle for so few problems and would give anything to go round in 78. If ever he did pass such a landmark he would be in ecstasy, but if thereafter he did so fairly often he, too, would probably find himself dwelling overmuch on his mistakes, thinking that the 78 should have been 75, and so on, down the scale. Once a golfer has reached the stage where horizons are clearly defined and ambition sharpened, he is less likely to be satisfied with his handiwork.

Wise is the golfer who remembers that every round, however low the score, includes one or two shots that are not perfectly struck. For the great player they may only be slight errors of timing or judgement, but a matter for regret none the less. Accustomed as the tournament golfer is to striking the great majority of his strokes truly, he will naturally recall the few that were not, but will accept them as part of the unforeseeable day-to-day variations of form. The club golfer who is often restricted to one weekly round or less finds such a philosophy hard to acquire.

(From *Country Life*)

The All-Absorbing Challenge

BOBBY JONES

I began playing golf a few months after I became six years old. I began life as a sickly child, and at the age of forty-six was stricken by a crippling ailment. Even so, to this day, golf has been the major interest of my life.

No one could possibly owe a greater debt to the game than I do. With all the odds on the health side against me from the beginning, I know that I can thank golf for having given me forty years of active life filled with exciting experiences and warm human contacts. I know that my physical affliction was not derived in any sense from playing the game, and I doubt that without this playing I should ever have lived to see a full maturity. I am convinced, too, that golf has taught me much about life and provided for me a philosophy, a treasure of memories, and an appreciation of human attachments which have immeasurably enhanced both the reality of the past and the prospect of the future. The game for me will always be, as it has been in the past, a consuming interest.

Throughout the period when my physical faculties were unimpaired, I was always an ardent player of the game. I was somewhat of a student or analyst, I suppose, but mainly I liked to play. And whatever thoughts I had about the game were directed towards enjoyment of competition. This did not have to be formal competition, because I could throw myself as enthusiastically into a fourball match for a dollar Nassau as into a tournament for a national championship. I admit the strain was not so great, nor the prize of such importance, as to inspire the intense concentration of tournament play. Nevertheless the zest was still there. The proposition is thus very clear to me that golf is a game meant to be played, and played as a contest worthy of the best effort of any man alive.

Golf has a very great and sometimes mystifying appeal to busy men. Some of its most ardent devotees are men of affairs whose lives are filled with responsibilities for making important decisions. To those who know little of golf, it is difficult to explain how a game so apparently frivolous could interest such men as these.

To those who know something of the game, there is no mystery at all. Golfers know, and have known for a long time, that when playing golf it is almost impossible to think of anything else. The most complete rest for the mind, and the most effective renewal of mental keenness and vigour, comes not from thinking of nothing, but from putting one's mind completely upon fresh and stimulating activities. It is, therefore, the all-absorbing challenge of golf which makes it such an effective agent of mental therapy.

In this view, then, it seems to me that we are defeating or detracting from the effectiveness of the game as a recreation when we urge people to relax, take it easy, or be casual and carefree on the golf course. I think we should urge them to do just the opposite – to put themselves wholeheartedly into their play. What they want and need most from the game can be had only when the intense concentration upon the play helps to sweep away the problems, worries, and even troubles of everyday life.

(From *Golf Is My Game*, Doubleday, 1959)

And next some writing about a few great players – or just those who have had great enjoyment from the game.

One Hero

PAUL GALLICO

The sportswriter has few if any heroes. We create many because it is our business to do so, but we do not believe in them. We know them too well. We are concerned as often, sometimes, with keeping them and their weaknesses and peccadillos out of the paper as we are with putting them in. We see them with their hair down in the locker rooms, dressing rooms, or their homes. Frequently we come quite unawares upon little meannesses. When they fall from grace we are usually the first to know it, and when their patience is tried, it is generally to us that they are rude and ill-tempered. We sing of their muscles, their courage, their gameness and their skill because it seems to amuse readers and sells papers, but we rarely consider them as people and, strictly speaking, leave their characters alone because that is dangerous ground.

Also, we grow up with them and see them change from pleasant and sometimes unspoiled youngsters into grievous public pets, boors, snobs and false figures. I am, by nature, a hero worshipper, as, I guess, most of us are, but in all the years of contact with the famous ones of sport I have found only one that would stand up in every way as a gentleman as well as a celebrity, a fine, decent, human being as well as a newsprint personage, and who never once, since I have known him, has let me down in my estimate of him. That one is Robert Tyre Jones Jr, the golf player from Atlanta, Georgia. And Jones in his day was considered the champion of champions – in other words, better and more perfect at playing his game than any of the other champions were at theirs. He was the best golf player the world has ever known, and still is, because no one has yet appeared capable of challenging his record [of course, Nicklaus since has].

Probably no celebrity in sport ever attracted quite so much attention or was so dominating a figure and yet remained completely unspoiled. Jones even had his own personal Boswell, Mr O. B. Keeler of the *Atlanta Journal*, one of the better sportswriters. For a great many years Keeler reported on Jones almost exclusively. Jones was hero worshipped by Atlantans and the golf public generally nearly ad nauseam, and yet he never lost his head or permitted it to swell. In Scotland and England, where he played in tournaments, the natives practically made a god out of him. He remained unaffected. He was exposed to the attacks of the most ill-bred and ruthless pests in the world, the curiosity-seeking golf nuts and autograph hunters, and his privacy was assailed from morning until night. He never in all his career could engage in a friendly golf match (except on his home course) without being followed and swamped with attention and, more often, annoyance. Yet I never heard of his being deliberately rude. The only thing I think he ever permitted himself to do when chivvied and harassed beyond human endurance, particularly during an important tournament, was quietly to turn and walk away.

He has a record of some ten years' contact with press and public and the golf world, in which, to my knowledge, he never once said the wrong thing in any public utterance or interview, never insulted anyone or hurt the feelings of any sect, organization, or people. I have never known him deliberately to lie to the press, the common fault of every newspaper celebrity. He had a gorgeous instinct for doing the right thing – such as asking to be permitted to leave the trophy representing the British Open Championship in the keeping of the Royal and Ancient Golf Club at St Andrews, Scotland, where he won it. He made the Scots love him as one of their own.

He was a good loser, but even a better winner. And he had the almost unbelievable intelligence and grace to quit after his greatest accomplishment, his grand slam of 1930, when he won the Amateur and Open championships of Great Britain and the United States, the four major tournaments of the golf world.

He was born Robert Tyre Jones Jr, but millions of people knew him merely as Bobby – Bobby Jones. And he hated the name Bobby. If he knew you well, he would sometimes dryly request that you call him Bob, and not Bobby. From the crowd he accepted the Bobby as it was meant, a diminutive of affection. This is a trivial and unimportant item until you try to picture yourself going through life eternally being hailed by a name that you thoroughly detest.

Before I knew Jones well, early in my sportswriting career, I was sent down to Atlanta by a national magazine, assigned to play a round of golf with him and report what it was like to play with the great one. Bob agreed to a game. (I was still a cub then and quite unknown as either a writer or columnist, but it made no difference to Jones. Later, on a similar assignment, Helen Wills refused to play with me.) He invited two of his friends and we went out to East Lake, his home course. Nervous, self-conscious and badly frightened, I blew up on the first tee and stayed blown for the entire eighteen holes except that I went higher each hole. I doubt whether I ever suffered so acutely in all my life. But I learned something about Jones in that round. Towards the end, after taking 9 to get close to the green, I botched my niblick approach, cutting the legs out from under the ball instead of hitting it properly, but with astonishing results, because the ball rose into the air, dropped 2 feet from the pin, and stayed there. Jones sneaked a great sigh of relief and said, 'Fine shot, partner. Well played.' And then we looked at each other. His face was all properly regulated respect and mingled admiration and serious pleasure at having been permitted to witness such a miraculous demonstration of a difficult game, but there was something funny going on at the corners of his mouth. I guess I must have had a strange expression too, because suddenly we both fell down on the green and howled with laughter, and after that everything was all right.

I suspect that the Jones humor has been what has really got him through all these trying years – and if you don't think it is trying to be a celebrity in our country, wait until you manage to chin yourself four hundred times or outsit everyone else on a flagpole – when at times the assaults on his nerves, good nature and good manners would otherwise have been unbearable. It would not be fair to say that Jones never took himself seriously. When he entered a tournament he entered to win. He was quite willing to admit that he did not like to lose. But his sense of the eternal ridiculous lay very close to the surface and I think he often saw himself as a slightly comic figure that did things that amused him vastly. People who are able successfully to laugh at themselves are able to take a great amount more of punishment and abuse than the humourless crew. It takes much more to snap the temper of a man who can read something funny into any and every situation. Well, what more can I say for my hero? He was a gentleman and there was laughter in his heart and on his lips, and he loved his friends.

(From *Farewell to Sport*, Knopf, 1937)

The Great Golfer
FRED CORCORAN

Hogan never made any effort to win a popularity contest. He was a chilly, withdrawn person who didn't want anyone patting him on the back. There was a lot of Ted Williams in Hogan, and a lot of Hogan in Williams. They were a couple of guys who preferred to walk alone. Cheers meant nothing to Ben. He looked upon hero worshippers with little regard, and even regarded his tournament galleries with disdain.

For all this, he was one of the most honest and sincere persons I have ever known. He detested phonies. His friends were few, his intimates rare. He always preferred the company of his wife, Valerie, to anyone else.

Hogan could win under any and all conditions. He had a fierce competitive drive that was almost frightening in its intensity. And he mastered the difficult art of concentration, blanking out everything but the immediate problem – the hole he was playing, the shot he was making.

Nothing ever changed Hogan. He was the same in defeat as in victory. He filed them both away in some mental locker box after carefully analysing them, then went right along with the business of surviving.

I had enormous respect for him and, because of it, could overlook the cold aloofness which at times exasperated me as a publicity-minded promoter. I never fully broke through that wall of reserve and never felt completely at ease with him. I was never sure, when he bared his white teeth in the suntanned face, whether he was smiling or unhappy. Mirth was a luxury he denied himself except on the rarest occasions, as though he were afraid it might corrode his zeal. Compete and work, compete and work ... on the practice tee and on the practice green ... then putt in the hotel room until bedtime while the others were relaxing. He even practised in the rain so he could hold his game together under these conditions. Actually, Ben didn't leave himself much time for laughter.

He could learn more about a golf course in one round than others could in ten. I saw the best demonstration of this during the 1956 Canada Cup matches when Hogan and Snead represented the United States. I recall we were flying to England and Ben came down the aisle and slipped into a vacant seat next to Snead.

Fred Corcoran – a gentle man and the first real sporting entrepreneur

'Sam,' he said, 'you've played this Wentworth course. Tell me something about it.'

Sam gestured vaguely. 'Well,' he said, 'what can I tell you? It's tough, that's all. It's a tough tricky course.'

Hogan was silent for a few moments. Then he said, 'Sam, I could make you the best player in the world.'

Sam cocked his head alertly.

'How's that?'

'Well,' said Ben, 'I'll give you one tip and you'll win every tournament.'

'Even the Open?' Sam grinned.

Hogan didn't crack a smile.

'Even the Open.'

Snead straightened up in his seat.

'What is it?'

But Ben waived him off.

'Not now,' he said, 'I'll tell you sometime during the tournament in England.'

Arriving in England, we went directly to Wentworth for a practice round and, on the way back to the hotel, Hogan said, 'Sam, you don't play this course right.' Snead had played the course many times and Hogan had just completed his first round over it.

'To begin with,' he went on, 'you ought to leave your driver in the bag. It only gets you into trouble here. Now you take the first hole. You've got to be down the right side to come into the green. On the second hole you've got to be short ... all the way. Come into that green short of the flag. They're going to stick the pin up front and it's a whole lot easier putting uphill than to come in high and have to putt down to the hole ...'

And Hogan went on, hole by hole, until he came to the 17th.

'Sam,' he said, shaking his head, 'you don't play that 17th hole right at all.'

Snead had lost his singles match to Harry Weetman in the 1953 Ryder Cup matches at Wentworth, losing four of the last six holes.

'Use your four wood from the tee, or an iron,' said Ben. 'Stay on top of that hill because you'll never get a good lie if you go over the brow to the far slope.'

Hogan set an all-time record for Wentworth, 31-36-67, on his second time around the course and both he and Snead shot final round 68's to win the Canada [now World] Cup for the United States. That evening I saw Sam and said, 'Sam, did Ben ever tell you anything?'

'No,' said Sam, 'not that I can recall.'

'Didn't he give you that tip he promised you during the tournament?'

Sam brightened.

'Yeah,' he drawled. 'Come to think of it, on the last round he told me to point my left toe down the fairway.'

'Did it help?' I asked.

'Naw,' said Sam, 'I don't think so.'

He had just shot a 68 on a tough course by pointing his toe down the fairway and unblocking his stance.

Hogan is a strange one. If he were a judge, I believe he would give you the benefit of the doubt on your first offence, but he'd never let you off the hook twice. He would condemn you to death without batting an eyelash. But we had a few laughs together. I remember flying with Ben and Jimmy Demaret from Houston to Dallas in a terrible storm. The plane was tossed about like a basketball. Ben never changed expression and stepped off the plane as if he'd just come down in the elevator from the fifth floor in Macy's. Demaret staggered off the plane and croaked, 'Lindberg got a ticker-tape parade for less than this.'

This brought a bleak smile from Hogan.

'Excuse me a minute,' I said, 'I'm just going in and dig my rosary beads out from under my fingernails ...'

The wintry smile broke into a full-throated laugh. Hogan's usually icy shell shattered. Later he said the mental image of me actually digging my rosary beads out from under my fingernails was too much.

I can't recall him ever finding humour in anything that happened on the golf course. Golf was his business – a tough business, full of disappointments.

(From *Unplayable Lies*, Duell, Sloan & Pearce, 1965)

The Good Old Days

GENE SARAZEN AND HERBERT WARREN WIND

The life of a professional athlete is precarious at best. Win and they carry you to the clubhouse on their shoulders; lose and you pay the caddies in the dark. I was playing erratic golf in 1924–25, and I realized that my income had to be placed on a more stable basis than hit-or-miss slices of the tournament pot. I snapped up the chance to become the professional at the Fresh Meadow Club in Flushing, Long Island. As my assistant, I hired my great friend and booster from the old days at Beardsley Park, Al Ciuci. Al was an inspired salesman. My predecessor at Fresh Meadow, Anderson, had grossed about eight thousand dollars annually from pro shop sales. By astute promotion, Al and I were able to quadruple this figure. In the winter months when Fresh Meadow was closed, I worked with Leo Diegel on promotional jobs in and around Miami Beach to supplement the prize money I picked up in the Florida tournaments.

During our first hibernation in Florida, Mary and I lived in a cottage in Hollywood Beach with Diegel as our perpetual house guest. In all my years in golf, I have never seen anyone whose devotion to the game could match Leo's. It was his religion. Between courses at the table, Leo used to get up and practise swings. Every night he went to bed dreaming theory and every morning he awakened with some hot idea that was going to revolutionize the game. The best known of Leo's innovations was his putting style. He bent over the ball like a man seized with cramps and putted with his elbows extended and stiff. Leo was a fine orthodox putter but he adopted this new contortion because, as he explained, 'There are fewer nerve centres in the elbows than in the wrists so there'll be less chance of my stabbing a putt under pressure.' Leo never departed from this style. You could always tell where he had been when you gazed out on a course and saw the members Diegeling away all over the place. Leo's other passion was bridge. He was a brilliant player, and with Wild Bill Mehlhorn he made up a team that entered and did well in the country's leading tournaments.

Leo was for ever worrying about his golf. Imaginative and high-strung, during tournaments he tortured himself with wild musings about rounds yet to be played. At the 1925 Open in Worcester, for instance, he would lie in bed chain-smoking, fretting about the large tree that stood on the edge of the fairway on the twelfth hole. 'That tree shouldn't be there,' he would say, half to me, half to himself. 'I want to play a left-to-right tee shot on that hole, but if I do I'll come awfully close to that tree. I ought to sneak out some night and chop that tree down, or else I'll hit it before this tournament is over.' Leo did hit that tree on his fourth round, the first of a series of errors that lost him his chance for the championship.

Diegel and I played as partners in the Florida tournaments. Before the 1925 Miami-Biltmore International Fourball got under way, we learned that the bookmakers' odds on us were 9 to 1. We didn't see the team in the field who could beat us, and placed one hundred dollars apiece on Sarazen and Diegel to win. We made our way to the final where, with four holes to go, we led our opponents, Farrell and Cruickshank, 2 up. While Leo and I were thinking about how we would spend our nine hundred dollars, Bobby and Johnny took two of the next three holes and had squared the match with the long home hole coming up. Both Bobby and Johnny missed their drives and their seconds. With Leo on the front edge in 2, and myself in a shallow trap to the right of the green in the same number, the match seemed in the bag. Cruickshank's third was nothing to worry about, but Farrell playing a full mashie out of the rough, pumped a towering approach beautifully onto the green, less than a foot from the pin. Leo and I exchanged a wordless fight talk and tried to regather our concentration. My shot from the trap left me a 10-footer. We decided that I should try my putt before Leo attempted his 30-footer. I missed, and you could see the pressure plopping itself on Leo's shoulders and invading those celebrated nerve centres of his elbows. Leo must have smoked at least two cigarettes before he was ready to putt. When he eventually did, he struck the ball too timidly, leaving himself a 3-footer to halve Farrell's birdie 4. Leo had gone through another cigarette before he was finished studying his 3-footer. He tapped that putt a fraction off line. It caught the rim of the cup, swerved off, stayed out. For three or four days after this, Mary and I didn't see Leo at the cottage. We were about to ask the police to conduct a hunt for the missing pro when Leo showed up, tired, unshaven, apologetic, and wild about a new theory he had worked out for sinking 3-footers.

A diligent organizer, Leo whipped up the series of annual matches between the pros wintering on the east coast of Florida and those on the west coast. The roads across the peninsula at this time were unpaved and bruising. Leo and I decided, after some deliberation, that our solution was to purchase a cottage in the town of Sebring to serve as a stopover on all our junkets. I think we spent one night there and somehow never used our halfway house again. Hagen, during this period, used to travel to his matches in his private Pullman car. His train would be met by a chauffeur driving a Locomobile and a footman-caddie watching over his clubs and his luggage.

Leo Diegel and I were partners in a few other extracurricular activities which seemed as normal as breakfast when you were living in the fabulous atmosphere of the Florida boom. Everybody else seemed to be cleaning up on Florida real estate and I agreed to go in fifty-fifty when Leo got hold of an inside tip that some wonderful seaside land at Dania Beach was going at only $3000 an acre. We purchased five acres. A few weeks later, we thought we ought to give our property the once-over. The real estate promoter drove us to Dania Beach where we changed into a rowboat. I liked the look of that strip of seashore. 'Leo, you're to be congratulated,' I said, slapping him on the shoulder. 'Now this is what I'd call a topnotch stretch of seashore.' I turned to the real estate man and asked him to point out exactly where our property stood. He pulled at the oars a few strokes more and then pointed into the water. 'We're right over it now, boys,' he said cheerfully. Leo and I had a chance a few months afterwards to sell our five well-watered acres for $20,000, but Tommy Armour advised us against it. 'You fellows don't know when you're sitting pretty,' Tommy lectured us. 'After that land is reclaimed, you'll be able to get $80,000 to $100,000 for it.' I don't know how Armour fared in his investments, but Leo and I never got a nickel back on ours.

We had better luck, Diegel and I, in our second

underwater deal. In 1926 we were signed to represent Golf Park, a grandiose project that was slowly taking shape in the wilderness behind Miami. We were each to get $5000 a year for three years, plus a private cottage adjoining the million-dollar clubhouse that was going to have a tower higher than the Miami-Biltmore's. We asked the promoter, a Mr Davis, when he thought the golf course would be completed. 'Next winter, boys,' he answered, 'and let me tell you, there won't be a sportier course in the whole state. The soil – richer than Morgan.' After the hurricane of 1926, Leo and I drove out to see if Golf Park was still standing. The fortress of a clubhouse had not been seriously damaged, but the course was inundated. The caretaker rowed us mournfully up the first fairway and down the placid waters of the eighteenth. At Dania Beach we had lost our shirts, but Mr Davis was as good as his contract and paid Leo and me $5000 apiece for three winters when we were home professionals with no home course. The Golf Park plant finally opened in the winter of 1949, a quarter of a century behind schedule.

That was a nice slice of the century to be young in. The times were good, the parties were frequent, the girls were pretty, the drinks were long, the days were sunny, the nights were cool, and the stock market was as strong as an ox.

(From *Thirty Years of Championship Golf*, Prentice-Hall, 1950)

Psychology
FRED CORCORAN

A typical Hagen story is an account of his match with Joe Turnesa at Dallas in 1927. Hagen was the master of applied psychology and always said he liked the head-to-head character of match play. He said he always knew exactly where things stood.

On this occasion, Walter arrived at the clubhouse thirty minutes late and was sharply scolded by the tournament officials. Hagen knew he was wrong. He apologized humbly and hurried off to dress.

On the first three holes he grandly conceded putts of varying lengths and Turnesa quickly went 3 up. Then Hagen said, 'There, that makes up for the thirty minutes I was late. Now we'll play . . .'

Well, the match rocked along until they reached the seventeenth hole – the thirty-fifth of the match – and Joe had a fairly easy putt. But Hagen made no gesture of conceding it. In fact, he was elaborately helpful to Joe in lining it up. Joe missed it and the match was all even.

They came to the last hole and Hagen put his second shot off to the right in some tall grass, partially screened off from the green by some trees. Turnesa was in good position in the middle of the fairway. Walter studied the line of flight, paced back and forth several times, tentatively drew three or four clubs from his bag. Then he turned and waved Turnesa back into the gallery.

'Joe,' he called, 'I may have to play this safe.' Later he chuckled, 'I could have driven three Mack trucks up to the green through those trees.'

Then he settled down and played his shot, sticking the ball within 12 feet of the flag. Turnesa, kept waiting and watching this strange performance, finally stepped up to his easy shot and dunked it in the trap

1926 – Abe Mitchell, on the left, looking very conventional, but Walter Hagen already setting sartorial trends

flanking the green – and Walter had won his fifth PGA Championship.

Curiously, Hagen's grandstand performance thoroughly delighted Turnesa, as it did the gallery. One of the remarkable things about Walter Hagen was the fact that, even in their defeat, his opponents all had tremendous affection for him. In fact, Turnesa tells this story with complete admiration for Hagen.

(From *Unplayable Lies*, Duell, Sloan & Pearce, 1965)

James Bruen

PAT WARD-THOMAS

Of all the golfers I have watched down the years there was one whose game had a quality of excitement that was incomparable. Hogan and Cotton could stir the imagination and command attention by virtue of their presence alone; Thomson and Snead could create an awareness of beauty, and all the other great ones in their different ways made a powerful demand on the senses, but the golf of none of these men had a greater dramatic appeal for me than that of James Bruen, citizen of Cork.

Although few of the present growing generation saw him play, and many indeed may scarcely have heard of him, those that did could never forget. The image of his swing, surely the strangest that modern first-class golf has known, remains clear in my mind to this day. There can never have been a style quite like it. He drew the club back outside the line of flight and turned his wrists inward, to such an extent that at the top of the swing the clubhead would be pointed in the direction of the tee box. It was then whipped, no other word describes the action, inside and down into the hitting area with a terrible force. There was therefore in his swing a fantastic loop, defying all the canons of orthodoxy which claim that the back and downswing should, as near as possible, follow the same arc. There must have been a foot or more between Bruen's arcs of swing.

The first sight of him was positively startling – and anyone, unaware of his identity, must have been inclined to scoff, but not for long. In this method of his Bruen had an instrument of tremendous power. The action of his hands was identical to that of wielding a whip, and one has but to try this to realize how much greater is the acceleration into the hitting area, whether it be with a whip, a club or throwing a ball.

I certainly would not recommend anyone to loop deliberately in the quest for power, few if any of the greatest golfers have found it necessary, but with Bruen it was; and wisely at the time no one attempted to change his style. Cotton has said that he has made Bruen try a normal method and that he hit the ball well – but without the great length that his own swing produced. To what extent, if any, his swing was responsible for the injury to his right wrist that hastened his departure from tournament play can never be known. Bruen denies that golf had anything to do with it. Soon after winning the Amateur Championship in 1946 he was lifting a tile in his garden when he felt a sudden pain. Thereafter it was always liable to be troublesome, and none of the expert advice and treatment he sought could cure it. Whatever the cause, there was no doubt that the wrist had to withstand a considerable shock every time he hit a full shot, such was the force of impact.

Bruen, an only child, started golf when about eleven years old and pursued his own natural way of hitting the ball. He was fat in those days and weighed something like 14 stones. At sixteen he murdered all opposition in the boys' championship. It was obvious that an extraordinary talent had arisen. Two years later he was in the winning Walker Cup team at St Andrews and, aside from halving his foursome with Harry Bentley, there was no doubt that his presence and the formidable golf he played in the practice had a strong psychological influence on the outcome of the match. The following summer he led the qualifiers in the Open, also at St Andrews, finished thirteenth in the championship – and was narrowly beaten in the last eight of the Amateur. He was only just nineteen.

There was no limit to what he might have achieved had the war not come, and had he so desired. His power was prodigious – he hit the ball enormous distances with a vast, soaring flight that gave him a great advantage on heavy courses, and his powers of recovery and strength from deep rough and sand were almost incredible. The nature of his swing brought the club into the hitting area at a remarkably steep angle and he could cut the ball huge distances out of places where normal men simply heaved and prayed. This ability to recover was essential, for his swing could not be expected to repeat with absolute consistency. Suddenly a drive would boom away towards extra cover into country where others neither ventured nor reached, but invariably the ball would emerge. The deadly willow scrub of Birkdale must have shrunk at his approach when he beat Robert Sweeny in the final of the first Amateur after the war.

All this was terribly exciting to watch; there was an unexpectedness and a variation to his golf that has not been surpassed on such a high level. Yet it would have been unfair to describe him as erratic, in the usual meaning of the term, and certainly in no sense was he crude. There was an almost hypnotic quality about his play; its very strangeness was compelling, its power and unusual beauty fascinating. Bruen had a wonderful rhythm that concealed the explosive violence of the club's impact on the ball, and this was most noticeable in the lovely, soft, slow action of his pitching, and in a beautiful, delicate touch when chipping and putting. Several of the strongest golfers, like Carr and Weetman, have been similarly blessed and Bruen at his finest was a great putter.

Thus, as a very young man, he had everything. No course, whatever its length or difficulty, was safe from destruction, and how terribly disconcerting he must have been to play against. It was sad that his career should have been so brief, for he might well have won an Open Championship. As it was he appeared but little after 1946. Three years later he played in the Walker Cup and in 1950 won the *Daily Telegraph* Foursomes with W. D. Smithers. I often think that this was the most attractive tournament of its time, with leading professionals and amateurs paired out of the hat and no strokes involved. Bruen and Smithers made a perfect combination that year at Formby, for Smithers revelled in the challenge that some of his partner's driving would set him. I shall never forget how Bruen, three times out of perhaps five attempts, carried the range of dunes that crosses the tenth fairway, with no great wind to help. This was huge hitting. The following summer he played again in the Walker Cup match at Birkdale but his wrist betrayed him in the foursomes and competitive golf saw him no more, save just once for an hour or so at Portrush nine years later.

Bruen was there as an Irish selector, he had been playing well and had entered the Amateur. His wrist had begun to hurt in practice but, after some hesitation, he decided to play. His golf was still impressive, even though its old power had gone, and he was soon in a winning position; but the wrist was swollen and he withdrew from the match, rather than scratch after winning. This glimpse, brief though it had to be, was infinitely worth while for it stirred memories of the most fascinating golfer I have ever seen, or probably ever will see. There will never be another quite like him.

(From *Masters of Golf*, Heinemann, 1961)

Championship Golf
BOBBY JONES

Championship ... championship. I thought it over in a kid's way. Not beating a great player now and then. Not winning a medal round here and there. Not drubbing the boys back home in a state or a sectional tournament ... Championship – championship. Seventy-two holes of medal play in the National Open, or beating five men, in succession, in the National Amateur. So that's it. No matter how prettily you play your shots. No matter how well you swing or how sweetly the ball behaves – after all, it's only championship that counts, the way most of us have come to look at it.

Please don't understand me as being unappreciative of my good fortune in the matter of championship. But that is part of what I mean. There was so much of fortune, so much of luck, in my winning that I now feel more than ever that the popular value of championship is a factitious thing; and that golf is too great and too fine a game, and too much an epitome of life itself, for such a ranking to do it justice ... I can speak frankly about this now that I have won my spurs. I can say with all my heart that it means a great deal to me, for my name to be on three of the four major golfing trophies of the world. And I can say with all my heart that I think it's a rotten shame for us to overlook so readily the fine fellows and the truly great golfers who for one reason or another have never got within that charmed circle of National Championship ... I think they do not overlook them so readily in Britain as we do; I think we are more enamoured of championship over here. And they have the better view, it seems to me. It appears a poor thing that the late Jack Graham should be ranked an inferior golfer to some of us champions, simply because he lacked the plain brute endurance to play through a long gruelling tournament. A strong back and a weak mind and a lot of this stuff they call the will to win – another name for stupid persistence, frequently – have made many a golfing champion who hadn't the shots or the heart or the character of Jack Graham, and a lot more I could name, who never got into the newspaper headlines ... The road to championship was a hard one, for me, and it took seven years in the climbing. And when I got there, at Inwood, my first feeling was that nothing mattered – I had broken through. And next, when I missed some of the elation I had expected, I just said to myself, 'You lucky dog!' I think no golfer ever properly appreciates the amount of luck needed to win a championship until he has been on the inside and won one.

(From *Down the Fairway*, Allen & Unwin, 1927)

At the opening of the nine-hole course at Wentworth, September 1959.

Lord Brabazon, on the right, next to Sydney Hine of brandy fame, partnering Max Faulkner, Open Champion, 1951, and Tom Haliburton, professional at Wentworth

'Brab'

HENRY LONGHURST

The death of Lord Brabazon of Tara will leave an absolutely unfillable gap in the lives of all who had the good fortune to know him. He was completely unique. His eighty years of life, ten better than the established par of three score and ten, covered more radical changes in human existence than any other two centuries put together and it seemed as though he was in at the birth of them all. He was the most 'interesting' man – in the sense of stimulating one's own interest – I ever met and I doubt whether anyone could remember having spent a dull moment in his company.

The walls of his office told his early story. Here, for instance, was Aviator's Certificate No. 1 of the Fédération Aéronautique Internationale, dated 8 March 1910 – thirty years after which the holder started the craze for 'personal' car numbers by securing FLY 1.

Next to it a young man with gumboots, Norfolk

jacket and slightly prominent teeth is seen grasping the levers of a Heath Robinson flying machine – none other than the 'biplane pusher with bamboo and ash framework', which was the first all-English aeroplane to fly. With it Brab won £1000 from the *Daily Mail* for a circular flight of 1 mile, average height 40 feet.

Another picture, surely a unique galaxy of aeronautical pioneers, shows under the heading 'First English Aerodrome, Mussel Manor, Shellbeach, Sheppey, 4 May 1909', a knickerbockered group including all three of the Short brothers, Wilbur and Orville Wright, young Moore-Brabazon, and the handsome, ill-fated Charlie Rolls, of Rolls-Royce, whom Brab was later to see killed in an air display.

'The only gentleman's way of leaving the ground,' he used to say 'is ballooning,' and in another picture he is standing in the basket with Charlie Rolls, waiting to ascend from Battersea Gasworks (45,000 cu ft £4 10s, 'including labour and bags of sand: holders-down extra').

Other pictures reveal him, in chauffeur's cap, waiting to crank the first Rolls-Royce, with the Duke of Connaught sitting bolt upright as passenger, and at the huge, high steering wheel of the Minerva with which he won the Circuit des Ardennes in 1907.

Beside one of the most remarkable pictures ever taken of the Cresta toboggan run are, curiously enough, two of a main-line railway station. Only very close inspection reveals them to be models, reminders of younger days when Brab had the best model railway in England. He would have! He ran it with his brother-in-law, Clarence Krabbe, and when they had an accident they stopped and held an 'inquiry'.

One day I chanced upon Brab at Turnberry, at breakfast, poring over what appeared to be a football pools coupon. It would have been in keeping with him if it had been, as he would have undoubtedly just worked out a completely novel system of permutations and combinations. As it happened he was engaged in a chess match by post with Lady Powerscourt in Dublin and was filling in his next move. This was in mid-summer. I asked him how he was getting on. 'I lost a bishop in February,' he said, 'and have been in difficulties ever since.' I did not see him again till about September. I again asked him how he was getting on. He looked round with an almost conspiratorial air, as though to make sure that no one was listening, and said, 'I was mated last week.' We agreed that he might now add to his many other distinctions that of being the only peer ever to have been mated by post.

Among the many other firsts in Brab's life was that, as a boy at Harrow, he was walking down Grove Hill when a few yards away from him a motorist put on the brakes too hard, ripped the spokes from his wheels, and became the first man to be killed in a motor accident. While others stood back, waiting for the infernal machine to blow up, Brab stepped forward and turned off the ignition burners. He was the only person who knew what they were. Afterwards he gave a lecture to the school scientific society on 'The Motor Car'. 'A treasure now lost to the world,' he called it.

Brab was the complete pioneer. He was one of the earliest riders on the Cresta, and certainly, in his seventies, the oldest. In the first war he became without question the Father of Modern Air Photography. He once turned up at Cowes with a kind of rotor arm attached to the mast of his yacht instead of a sail. It was he who, somewhat ridiculed at the time, pulled the first trolley up the first fairway at St Andrews.

Later he was to be led out by the past captains at eight o'clock on a September morning to drive himself in down the same fairway, as captain of the Royal and Ancient. He had previously been observed making surreptitious practice swings in his shirtsleeves behind the bandstand, but, when he executed one or two on the first tee, I remember remarking to my companion that, if the real thing were to turn out like these, no great good could come of it.

In fact, he hit it all along the ground towards mid-wicket and the ball had long been stationary before the first of the caddies could reach it. Afterwards he described his opening stroke as a 'noble gesture of self-denial which has given pleasure to thousands'.

With his booming, unmistakable voice he would hold an audience anywhere, whether in the Commons, the Lords, after dinner, or, particularly, in the United States. Proposing the toast of the Open champion at a dinner, he opened with: 'It is only appropriate that a Member of Parliament whose constituency borders upon Liverpool and Merseyside should be asked to get up on his hind legs and propose the toast of Cotton.'

It was he who in the Commons likened the Opposition to 'a lot of inverted Micawbers waiting for something to turn down'. Nor did his own side escape, for it was them, I seem to remember, whom he meant when he referred to the 'snores of the Front Bench reverberating throughout the land'. It was certainly the then Archbishop of Canterbury whom he accused, when His Grace had made a speech on finance, of 'talking through his mitre'.

When Prince's, Sandwich, was used as a target range in the war, Brab declared that it was 'like throwing darts at a Rembrandt'. When Royal St George's was waterlogged and too little, he thought, was being done about it, he put a suggestion in the book 'That the water in the bunker at the thirteenth be changed.'

People who worked with him were always astonished at the variety of subjects on which he could truly be described as expert. Yet in many ways he was an example of that rare, invaluable and almost extinct species, the Universal Amateur.

Of the more serious side of Brab's long life – his work as Minister of Transport during the Blitz and later of Aircraft Production, as President of the Royal Institution, and on the board of many eminent companies – I must leave it to others to write.

For those who pursue the humble game of golf, however, it is nice to think that a man of so many parts and of such immense distinction should have written in his autobiography: 'When I look back on my life and try to decide out of what I have got most actual pleasure, I have no doubt at all that I have got more out of golf than anything else.'

(From the *Sunday Times*, 1971)

The Caddie Who Won the Open

GENE SARAZEN AND HERBERT WARREN WIND

After a few days in London, I went down to Prince's to practise. The first person I met, right at the gate, was Daniels. He was overjoyed to see me. While we were exchanging news about each other, I could see that the last four years had taken a severe toll of him. He had become a very old man. His speech was slower. That shaggy moustache of his was much greyer, his limp was much more obvious. And his eyes, they didn't look good.

'Where's your bag, sir?' Daniels asked, hopping as spryly as he could towards the back seat of my auto.

'Dan,' I said – I couldn't put it off any longer though I almost didn't have the heart to say it, 'Dan, this bag is too heavy for you. I know you've been in bad health, and I wouldn't want you to try and go seventy-two holes with it.'

Dan straightened up. 'Right-o, sir, if you feel that way about it.' There was great dignity in the way he spoke, but you couldn't miss the threads of emotion in his voice.

'I'm sorry, Dan,' I said, and walked away. I had dreaded the thought of having to turn old Dan down, but I had never imagined that the scene would leave me reproaching myself as the biggest heel in the world. I attempted to justify what I had done by reminding myself that business was business and I couldn't afford to let personal feelings interfere with my determination to win the British Open. It didn't help much.

I was a hot favourite to win. The American golf writers thought that I had a much better chance than Armour, the defending champion, and the veteran Mac Smith, the other name entry from the States. George Trevor of the *New York Sun*, for example, expressed the belief that 'Prince's course, a 7000-yard colossus, will suit Sarazen to a tee, if you will pardon the pun. It flatters his strong points – powerful driving and long-iron second shots.' The English experts were likewise strong for me until, during the week of practice, they saw my game decline and fall apart.

The young caddie from Stoke Poges did not suit me at all. I was training for this championship like a prizefighter, swinging the heavy club, doing roadwork in the morning, practising in weather that drove the other contenders indoors. My nerves were taut and I was in no mood to be condescended to by my caddie. He would never talk a shot over with me, just pull a club out of the bag as if he were above making a mistake. When I'd find myself 10 yards short of the green after playing the club he had selected, he'd counter my criticism that he had under-clubbed me by declaring dogmatically, 'I don't think you hit that shot well.' I began getting panicky as the tournament drew closer and my slump grew deeper. I stayed on the practice fairway until my hands hurt.

Something was also hurting inside. I saw Daniels in the galleries during the tune-up week. He had refused to caddie for any other golfer. He'd switch his eyes away from mine whenever our glances met and shuffle off to watch Mac Smith or some other challenger. I continued, for my part, to play with increasing looseness and petulance. The qualifying round was only two days off when Lord Innis-Kerr came to my hotel room in the evening on a surprise visit. 'Sarazen, I have a message for you,' Innis-Kerr said, with a certain nervous formality. 'I was talking with Skip Daniels today. He's heartbroken, you know. It's clear to him, as it's clear to all your friends, that you're not getting along with your caddie. Daniels thinks he can straighten you out before the bell rings.'

I told his Lordship that I'd been thinking along the same lines myself. Daniels could very well be the solution.

'If it's all right with you, Sarazen,' Lord Innis-

Kerr said as he walked to the door, 'I'll call Sam the caddiemaster and instruct him to have Daniels meet you here at the hotel tomorrow morning. What time do you want him?'

'Have him here at seven o'clock ... And thanks, very much.'

Dan was on the steps of the hotel waiting for me the next morning. We shook hands and smiled at each other. 'I am so glad we're going to be together,' old Dan said. 'I've been watching you ever since you arrived and I know you've been having a difficult time with that boy.' We walked to the course, a mile away. Sam, the caddiemaster, greeted me heartily and told me how pleased everybody was that I had taken Daniels back. 'We were really worried about him, Mr Sarazen,' Sam said. 'He's been mooning around for days. This morning he looks ten years younger.'

Dan and I went to work. It was miraculous how my game responded to his handling. On our first round I began to hit the ball again, just like that. I broke par as Dan nursed me through our afternoon round. We spent the hour before dinner practising. 'My, but you've improved a lot since 1928!' Dan told me as he replaced my clubs in the bag. 'You're much straighter, sir. You're always on line now. And I noticed this afternoon that you're much more confident than you used to be recovering from bunkers. You have that shot conquered now.' After dinner I met Dan by the first tee and we went out for some putting practice.

The next day, the final day of preparation, we followed the same pattern of practice. I listened closely to Dan as he showed me how I should play certain holes. 'You see this hole, sir,' he said when we came to the eighth, 'it can be the most tragic hole on the course.' I could understand that. It was only 453 yards long, short as par 5s go, but the fairway sloped downhill out by the 200-yard mark, and 80 yards before the green, rising 25 to 35 feet high, straddling the fairway and hiding the green, loomed a massive chain of bunkers. 'But you won't have any trouble on this hole,' Dan resumed. 'You won't have to worry about the downhill lie on your second shot. You have shallow-face woods. You'll get the ball up quick with them. I should warn you, however, that those bunkers have been the graveyard of many great players. If we're playing against the wind and you can't carry them, you must play safe. You cannot recover onto the green from those bunkers.' Yes, I thought as Dan spoke, the eighth could be another Suez.

That evening when the gathering darkness forced us off the greens and we strolled back to my hotel, Dan and I held a final powwow. 'We can win this championship, you and I,' I said to Dan, 'if we do just one thing.'

'Oh, there's no doubt we can win it, sir.'

'I know, but there's one thing in particular we must concentrate on. Do you remember that 7 at the Suez Canal?' I asked.

'Do I!' Dan put his hand over his eyes. 'Why, it's haunted me.'

'In this tournament we've got to make sure that if we go over par on a hole, we go no more than 1 over par. If we can avoid taking another disastrous 7, Dan, I don't see how we can lose. You won't find me going against your advice this time. You'll be calling them and I'll be playing them.'

Mac Smith and Tommy Armour were sitting on the front porch when we arrived at the hotel. 'Hey, Skip,' Armour shouted. 'How's Eugene playing?'

'Mr Sarazen is right on the stick,' Dan answered, 'right on the stick.'

The qualifying field played one round on Royal St George's and one on Prince's. There isn't much to say about my play on the first day at Prince's. I had a 73, 1 under par. However, I shall never forget the morning of the second qualifying round. A terrific gale was blowing off the North Sea. As I was shaving, I looked out of the window at the Royal St George's links where I'd be playing that day. The wind was whipping the sand out of the bunkers and bending the flags. Then I saw this figure in black crouched over against the wind, pushing his way from green to green. It was Daniels. He was out diagramming the positions of the pins so that I would know exactly how to play my approaches. I qualified among the leaders. You have to play well when you're partnered with a champion.

The night before the Open, the odds on my winning, which had soared to 25-1 during my slump, dropped to 6-1, and Bernard Darwin, the critic I respected most, had dispatched the following lines to *The Times*: 'I watched Sarazen play eight or nine holes and he was mightily impressive. To see him in the wind, and there was a good fresh wind blowing, is to realize how strong he is. He just tears that ball through the wind as if it did not exist.'

On the day the championship rounds began, the wind had died down to an agreeable breeze, and Daniels and I attacked from the very first hole. We were out in 35, 1 under par, with only one 5 on that nine. We played home in 35 against a par of 38, birdieing the seventeenth and the eighteenth. My 70 put me a shot in front of Percy Alliss, Mac Smith and Charlie Whitcombe. On the second day, I tied the course record with a 69. I don't know how much Dan's old eyes could perceive at a distance, but he called the shots flawlessly by instinct. I went 1 stroke over on the ninth when I missed a curling 5-footer, but that was the only hole on which we took a buzzard. We made the turn in 35, then came sprinting home par, par, birdie, par, par, birdie, birdie, birdie, par. My halfway total, 139, gave me a 3-shot margin over the nearest man, Alliss, 4 over Whitcombe, and 5 over Compston, who had come back with a 70 after opening with a 74. Armour had played a 70 for 145, but Tommy's tee shots were giving him a lot of trouble – he had been forced to switch to his brassie – and I didn't figure on too much trouble from him. Mac Smith had started his second round with a 7 and finished it in 76. That was too much ground for even a golfer of Mac's skill and tenacity to make up.

The last day now, and the last two rounds. I teed off in the morning at nine o'clock. Three orthodox pars. A grand drive on the fourth, and then my first moment of anguish: I hit my approach on the socket. Daniels did not give me a second to brood. 'I don't think we'll need that club again, sir,' he said matter-of-factly. I was forced to settle for a 5, 1 over par, but with Daniels holding me down, I made my pars easily on the fifth and the sixth and birdied the seventh.

Now for the eighth, 453 yards of trouble. So far I had handled it well, parring it on both my first and second rounds. Daniels had given me the go-ahead on both my blind second shots over the ridge of bunkers, and each time I had carried the hazard with my brassie. On this third round, I cracked my drive down the middle of the billowy fairway. Daniels handed me my spoon, after he had looked the shot over and tested the wind, and pointed out the direction to the pin hidden behind the bunkers. I hit just the shot we wanted – high over the ridge and onto the green, about 30 feet from the cup. I stroked the putt up to the hole, it caught a corner and dropped. My momentum from that eagle 3 carried me to a birdie 3 on the ninth. Out in 33. Okay. Now to stay in there. After a nice start home, I wobbled on the 411-yard thirteenth, pulling my long iron to the left of the green and taking a 5. I slipped over par again on the 335-yard fifteenth, three putting from 14 feet when I went too boldly for my birdie putt and missed the short one coming back. I atoned for these lapses by birdieing the sixteenth and the eighteenth to complete that long second nine in 37, 1 under par, and the round in 70, 4 under. With eighteen more to go, the only man who had a chance to catch me was Arthur Havers. Havers, with 74-71-68, stood 5 strokes behind. Mac Smith, fighting back with a 71, was in third place, but 8 shots away. Alliss had taken a 78 and was out of the hunt.

If the pressure and the pace of the tournament was telling on Dan, he didn't show it. I found him at the tee after lunch, raring to get back on the course and wrap up the championship. We got off to an auspicious start on that final round – par, birdie, par, par. On the fifth I went 1 over, shook it off with a par on the sixth, but when I missed my 4 on the seventh I began to worry about the possible errors I might make. This is the sure sign that a golfer is tiring. The eighth loomed ahead and I was wondering if that penalizing hole would catch up with me this time. I drove well, my ball finishing a few feet short of the spot from which I had played my spoon in the morning. Daniels took his time in weighing the situation, and then drew the spoon from the bag. I rode into the ball compactly and breathed a sigh of relief as I saw it get up quickly and clear the bunkers with yards to spare. 'That's how to play golf, sir,' Daniels said, winking an eye approvingly. 'That's the finest shot you've played on this hole.' He was correct, of course. We found out, after climbing up and over the ridge, that my ball lay only 8 feet from the cup. I holed the putt for my second eagle in a row on the hole, and turned in 35, after a standard par on the ninth.

Only nine more now and I had it. One over on the tenth. Nothing to fret about. Par. Par. Par. A birdie on the fourteenth. Almost home now. One over on the fifteenth, 3 putts. One over on the sixteenth, a fluffed chip. Daniels slowed me down on the seventeenth tee. 'We're going to win this championship, sir. I have no worries on that score. But let's make our pars on these last two holes. You always play them well.' A par on the seventeenth. On the eighteenth, a good drive into the wind, a brassie right onto the green, down in 2 for a birdie. 35-39-74, even par. There was no challenge to my total of 283. Mac Smith, the runner-up, was 5 shots higher, and Havers, who had needed a 76 on his last round, was a stroke behind Mac.

Feeling like a million pounds and a million dollars respectively, Daniels and I sat down on a bank near the first tee and congratulated each other on a job well done. Our score of 283 – 70, 69, 70, 74 – was 13 under par on a truly championship course, and it clipped 2 strokes off the old record in the British Open, Bob Jones's 285 at St Andrews in 1927. (Incidentally, 283 has never been bettered in the British Open, though Cotton equalled that mark at Sandwich in 1934, Perry at Muirfield in 1935, and Locke at Sandwich in 1949.) Much as I was thrilled by setting a new record for a tournament that had been my nemesis for a decade, I was even more elated over the method by which I had finally reached my goal. I had led all the way. I had encountered no really rocky passages because I had had the excellent sense to listen to Daniels at every puzzling juncture. Through his brilliant selection of clubs and his understanding of my volatile temperament, I had been able to keep my resolution to go no more than 1 over par on any hole. The eighth, which I had feared might be a second Suez, had turned out to be my best friend. I had two 3s and two 5s on a hole on which I would not have been unwilling, before the tournament, to settle for four 6s.

(From *Thirty Years of Championship Golf*, Prentice-Hall, 1950)

A Question of Identity

PETER ALLISS

Golf pros are sometimes accused of not having much sense of humour. A completely untrue story of four pros – myself, Dai Rees, Christy O'Connor and Eric Brown – has us playing an exhibition match in Aberdeen at the time of a blowout at one of the oil rigs. We were sitting in the Station Hotel in Aberdeen having a drink. I looked up and saw a group of characters in stetsons and cowboy boots at the bar, and said to the assembled company, 'That's Red Adair.'

'Och, no,' said Eric Brown, 'that's no' Red Adair, for Christ's sake.'

I said, 'I think it *is* Red Adair.'

'No, I'll go and ask him,' said Eric. So he went over. 'Is that right you are Red Adair?'

'Yeah, yeah, boy, I sure am.'

'Well,' said Eric, 'I want to shake your hand. You are doing a great job, you're saving our oil before those sassanachs manage to take it all. You are going to have a drink with me.'

Adair thanked him very much and had a large bourbon. Eric returned to the table.

'You're quite right. That's Red Adair.'

'No, no, no,' said Dai Rees, 'I'm sure it's not Red Adair.'

'Go and ask him.'

So Dai went up.

'Now then boyo – nice to see you up yere. You can tell I'm not from these parts, you see, look you, but Eric Brown and I are golf pros – a bit long now in the tooth but he tells me that you are this great man who comes and puts out oil fires.'

'Yeah, indeed boy, I sure am. I reckon I've done a pretty good job here.'

'Well, it's not often we buy drinks you know, but I would like to buy you one as I think we in Wales might be a bit short of oil, we have plenty of coal but not much oil. You had better have something with me.'

So Adair had another little taste of the bourbon.

Dai came back and I said, 'Was I right?'

'Yes, you were right.'

Christy O'Connor quietly said, 'No, no, lads. I am quite sure it's not Red Adair at all.'

I said, 'Eric's satisfied it is. I know, and so does Dai, so why don't you go and ask?'

So Christy goes over.

'Excuse me, sorr, I'm sorry to be interrupting you but they tell me you are this great man Red Adair.'

Red by this time was getting quite flushed with the bourbon and quite pleased with all the adulation.

'Yeah, you're quite right boy. I sure am Red Adair. What do you want to know?'

Christy leaned over the table and said, in that light soft brogue, 'Tell me, what twas it really like dancing with Ginger Rogers?'

(From *Bedside Golf*, Collins/Willow, 1980)

Underneath the Arches

IVOR BROWN

My favourite among the elder golfers has always been J. H. Taylor, partly because he is a great and good man, golf apart, partly because he was at Royal Mid-Surrey where I not only played but was privileged to play with him. He was not within miles of being a Golf Snob, that numerous breed who regard a long handicap as a fly fisher regards a worm fisher. He was most tolerant of the rabbitry and I have never forgotten overhearing, on leaving the tee, his comment on my style. 'Mr Brown somehow forces them away.'

There was no forcing in the sweet rhythm of his own methods; he was never very long, never at all crooked, and never demonstrative or showy. He was always your companion as well as your partner on a round. I once, owing to a friend's embarrassingly ambitious arrangement, had Henry Cotton for a partner in a match with Abe Mitchell and another amateur.

Fortunately it was a fourball, otherwise I should have refused and fled in terror. Fancy leaving Henry to rescue your foozled drive!

It did not matter what I did, but, by an outrageous fluke with a long putt, I won the first hole from the lot of them. That certainly was something dropped from heaven. It was as glorious as being made an LD of St Andrews. Luckily, I never heard Cotton's comment on my style. Probably he made none. Some things lie too deep for tears, too low for words. He just went his way and I plodded on with my rabbitry, picking up discreetly when I had taken 3 to his 1.

But I must get back to John Henry Taylor, with the broad shoulders, with the eyes already spectacled but so keen and friendly, with his love of any game and any companionship, not just 'tiger' company, and with the solid settlement of his booted and trousered self – no finery for him – on teeing ground or fairway. He has gone back to ripen – not to age – in his West Country: rightly, for he has always remained in my eyes a countryman, not a suburban, despite his long years in Richmond and his nice little London house there, with the garden opening onto the slice-catching trees beside the second green.

In a welcome letter recently he reminded me how he preferred to play his golf 'in boots of an agricultural character'. His belief that we should be rooted to the soil was justified by the magnificence of his own stand-fast and get-right-down-to-it game.

So I think that he would sympathize with a book I have just been reading called *Golf After Forty*. (Why only forty? Golf after eighty is very handsomely and victoriously accomplished by some chirpy veterans of my acquaintance.) This opus has been written by Mr H. A. Hattstrom and is an exposition of what he calls the Flatfoot Method. He is a Taylorian in all but his choice of appropriate footwear. Since his photographs were taken during an American summer, he demonstrates his doctrine in the white flannels of his climate and in the particoloured shoes of our time instead of in the tackety clodhoppers advocated by our surviving Triumvir.

I cannot understand why the flatfooted, heels-in-the-mud technique should not suit the under-twenties as well as the over-forties, but doubtless the young do not look so silly if they prance into the game emulating Danny Kaye as he sings 'Tiptoe Through the Tulips'.

Mr Hattstrom is an aesthete as well as a professor. 'The spectacle of the older and more rotund golfers attempting to execute a full and complete pivot is a fearful thing to behold.' Let those who are putting a paunch as well as a punch in it glue themselves to the clay and get the mud well stuck beneath the arches; then the odious spectacle (and the calamitous drive) of stout men pirouetting on the tee will be averted. Obese sportsmen cannot overswing and so become objects of horror to the eye, as well as murderers of their game, if they are well grounded and unquestionably down at heel.

'You know my methods, Watson,' said Holmes. And Mr Hattstrom can echo the same whenever he sees a pair of feet as flat as paving stones. Of his own golf in a torrential rainstorm he writes exultantly. 'Here the Flatfoot Manner saved the day as I sloshed home winner of a state service club competition.'

Sloshed home! I like the frankness. There is a tremendous satisfaction in all games for the man who does it all wrong and gets, occasionally, the right results. It is pleasant, if unkind, to watch a highly professional fisherman, complete with ghillie and all the costliest equipment, expertly casting for a salmon all day and all in vain; then a clumsy companion turns up and gauchely heaves a fly at the water. And, lo, the prize, so long denied to the maestro, falls to the raw hand, the careless lout.

So with golf. All we moderate players have surely, on one day or another, 'sloshed home'. Our short-handicap rivals drove vastly – into the jungle; they made a mighty recovery – and just caught the rim of the bunker on the edge of the green. The perfectly dressed, the men who carried a full load of ironmongery, the lissom swingers were all in trouble. One dug one's toes in, got the arches well down, and 'somehow forced it away', in J. H. Taylor's phrase, or 'sloshed home' in Mr Hattstrom's.

It is all very maddening for the people who walk delicately, stand and swing so neatly, who do the correct, the decorative thing. How they must loathe the beetle-crushing 'slosher home'! But, after all, they have their rewards, they do win nine times out of ten. They must put up with the humiliations of that tenth day, when the louts come lurching through, when the Flatfoot bangers not only keep to the fairway but hole the decisive putts.

Hail then to the heroes of the Fallen Arch, which, on the eighteenth green, is, just once in a while, the Arc de Triomphe.

(From *The Golfers' Year*, edited by Tom Scott and Webster Evans, Nicholas Kaye, 1951)

Michael and Angela Bonallack – a unique partnership both on and off the course

The Decisive Shot

PETER ALLISS

The eighteenth, 430 yards long, ran along the clifftop. But it was the green itself which posed the greatest threat. It was fronted by a wide ravine. There were deep bunkers to the right and also at the back, while any shot to the left fell into the ocean. To compound the problem still further, the flag had been placed 12 feet from the front of this awesome green.

Cornell showed his class and his courage with a drive straight down the centre of that narrow fairway which left him perfectly positioned for his second shot onto the green.

Duke, that great messiah of adventurous golf, played a 1 iron which finished 30 yards short of Cornell. The shot was accurate enough as 1 irons should be off the tee, but the light applause reflected the crowd's sympathy. The old hero's nerve had seemingly deserted him in his hour of need. Alabaster, remembering a distant day in Arkansas, had already sensed what was to come; and at the thought, the hairs rose on the nape of his neck.

Duke was experiencing that old heady sensation of walking on the waters. He was about to gamble as no one had ever gambled before. He was about to play the two million dollar shot. But more than that, much more than that, he wanted to break Cornell. He wanted to put this pretender to his throne to the ultimate test.

He strolled down the fairway, came to his ball and still in no hurry asked for a 2 iron. Then he smiled at Alabaster. 'Go on ahead, old pal,' he said, 'and stand by the flag.'

Even Alabaster hadn't expected that, but he smiled and nodded, understanding completely. The smile built up slowly. 'Sure, Duke. You gonna bounce it off my chest or my feet?'

Alabaster began to walk slowly towards the ravine, the bag slung over his shoulder, knowing precisely what Duke wanted him to do, keeping his pace leisurely, letting the tension build up.

At first the crowd didn't understand; and then as

they watched this huge black man walk across the bridge, a sense of wild excitement swept through the massed ranks. Alabaster looked down to the rocks far below and despite himself he shuddered. And then as he moved onto the green and stood with his hand on the flag, everyone realized the full measure of the gamble Duke was about to take. To play a long iron over a ravine into the teeth of the wind, hit the edge of the green and stop it within 6 feet was the stuff of which the impossible dreams were made. To play it with world supremacy and two million dollars at stake took it into the realms of wild and wonderful fantasy.

But even in this buccaneering mood, Duke had made his calculations, based his faith upon the very strength of that wind and the softness of the green. Now that the moment had finally come, he didn't hesitate. He rifled the shot straight at the flag. There was a brief buzz from the crowd, quickly stifled as a fresh gust of wind held the ball in flight; and for a moment it hung motionless high above the ravine, then it was arching downwards. Everyone in the stands had risen to their feet, but there was still barely a sound. Then suddenly the roar came as the ball hit the edge of the green, biting with the backspin, and began to roll towards the hole. Alabaster lifted the flag; but even Duke couldn't quite walk on the water. The ball stopped just 6 inches short of the cup.

If the shot hadn't already broken Cornell, the cheers did as they rumbled like thunder across the canyon. He had no options left. If he was going to get down in 2, he had to attempt the same madcap shot.

Twice he stepped up to the ball, twice he stepped back. He deliberated for a while, pacing restlessly, then debated whether to play a 3 iron or a 4, decided on a 4. But for once the cold heart betrayed him. The swing was just a shade too tentative. The ball soared towards the flag, then dipped in the sunlight and fell straight into the ravine.

(From *The Duke*, New English Library, 1983)

This book has already contained a great deal of instruction. Perhaps I've overburdened you, but here are just a few final thoughts, one or two with tongue in cheek.

Congenital Slice

HENRY LONGHURST

We have served out our self-imposed fourteen-day sentence and, subject to good report by the governor and the chaplain, will be issued with our civilian suit and released in the morning. It has been, as always, an interesting and beneficial experience. Like any other delicate piece of machinery, the human body has from time to time to go in for repairs and what the soldiers always called 'maintenance', and this for the past fortnight is what we have been doing at the so-called 'health farm'.

The rations have been meagre in the extreme – an orange for breakfast, tomato juice for lunch, tea for tea, and a cup of soup for dinner, which is 'on', roughly speaking, at 6.59 and off at 7. No alcohol, of course, but to a near teetotaller like myself this is of little account – though I confess to a suspicion that, having so often walked past it with pious and averted eye during the morning exercise, I shall not readily pass by the nearby White Hart Inn during opening hours again.

One of the objects of this curious business, though by no means the only one, is the melting of our too,

Dear Henry, as I remember him

too solid flesh and those who go through life admitting cheerfully that they are 'a stone (14 pounds) or two on the heavy side' may come to reflect that a stone represents, within an ounce or two, a full set of fourteen golf clubs and a medium-sized bag. Touching on this at Rye the other day with a stout and rubicund friend, I shook him, I like to think, by observing that he was caddieing permanently for half the British Walker Cup team.

At any rate, mounting the scales is an essential item of the daily routine and great are the sacrifices, not least in dignity, that we make to ensure a favourable reading. We even sit, in corpulent rows, in little 'sitz baths' of hot water with our feet in a bowl of cold, each watching his own little clock for the dread moment when it 'pings' to tell him to go and sit in the cold one with his feet in a bowl of hot. Still, it has its rewards, and I shall not lightly forget the jubilation of the noble naked lord who, on the sixth day, declaimed that he had 'lost all the irons and two of the woods'.

Smoking is frowned upon, and addicts are herded together to puff furtively in a communal cell. I mention it only in order to pass on a simple, perhaps rather childish but remarkably effective way of cutting one's smoking by half at a cost of twopence. When the cigarette is halfway through – which is all you want at a time anyway – you lay the lighted end on a penny. You then lay another penny gently on top. Within seconds the cigarette goes out – don't ask me why – and may be relit later, tasting exactly as good as before. With this I have been able to keep easily within the daily quota of ten, except for one day when James Mason's thriller, *The Man Between*, combined with a Hollywood film so moronic as to defy description, cost me the whole of the unexpired portion of the day's ration and I had to open another packet.

Though golf was to be forgotten, the past fortnight may have had for me a profound golfing significance. On alternate days we go to have our necks ricked and such like – 'never broken one yet' – by the osteopath. The other day, lying on the slab, I presented so interesting a phenomenon that he called his colleague from the adjacent cubicle to come and look. They peered learnedly together at I knew not what. No doubt about it, apparently. Yes, yes, of course. You could see it without even measuring. Right leg shorter than the left.

No wonder I have had a slice all my life! Now I know, dammit, I was born with it!

(From the *Sunday Times*, 1957)

The Hitting Area

BOBBY JONES

Now the hitting area in the downstroke does not begin at the top of the swing, and the first motion of the club should not be inspired by the wrists; that is, the clubhead should not start first, which would use up some valuable wrist action before hitting is possible. For me, as near as I can work it out, the correct way to start the downstroke of any full shot is a slight sway to the left. The arms get under way with the wrists still cocked, or wound up. It is a difficult sort of speculation, but it seems to me that the hitting area starts at that part of the stroke when the right hand begins to assert itself, the right arm begins to straighten out and the wrists begin to unwind. In my stroke, this seems to be when the club is about parallel with the ground and the hands opposite the right leg. I suppose the speed of the club, from a gradual beginning, has been sharply accelerated to this juncture, and then the unwinding wrists and the straightening right arm provide the punch in the stroke.

It seems fearfully complicated, this trying to take a swing to pieces and see what makes it tick. I'd hate to try to learn to play golf synthetically. These attempts at analysis are quite puzzling enough. But it has been deeply interesting to me, in my feeble efforts at analysis, to encounter so many times, and in so many ways, the factor of bodyturn in all shots.

One bit of earnest admonition. Stewart Maiden maintains that he cannot think of any of these details, or of any other details, during the execution of a shot – that is, if the shot is to come off. He adds that he does not believe anybody else can think of these or other details and perform a successful shot. I find this to be the case with my own play. I have to do all my thinking as I prepare to play. Once the swing is under way, the only thing I can think of is hitting the ball. To attempt to think of anything else is the most certain method of courting absolute ruin.

(From *Down the Fairway*, Allen & Unwin, 1927)

Be Free
BOBBY JONES

In my own case, I am persuaded that the instinctive need for a free bodyturn is responsible for the closeness of my feet together in all shots. The critics say my feet are closer together than anyone else's. But I never am conscious of any lack of balance, and if I attempt a wider stance, I simply cannot get a free enough bodyturn.

If there is any special merit in my style of play, it is the free bodyturn. Of this I am convinced.

(From *Down the Fairway*, Allen & Unwin, 1927)

Putting
BOBBY JONES

Now I haven't said much about grip or stance because I've changed mine a good many times and may change them again and, anyway, I do not think the secret of putting, if there is a secret, is in the mechanics, granted that the swing can be made smoothly and to a fair degree automatically. I do say that for me there must be some flexibility, and hence movement, of the knees and body, and of the arms, in putts of some length. I keep my hands opposed; that is, with the palms opposite and the wrists thus working exactly against each other, which is not done in the bigger shots, where my left hand is more on top of the shaft and my right also a bit farther over.

But as I see it, the thing that hurt my putting most when it was bad – and it was very bad at times – was thinking too much about how I was making the stroke and not enough about getting the ball in the hole. I have always been a fair approach putter, and I am not so bad at holing out now, though not in the class of a number I could name. But I have concluded that, having acquired a fairly smooth and accurate stroke, the thing for me to do is to forget it as far as possible and concentrate on getting the ball in the cup.

Which seems to have been the original object, in golf.

(From *Down the Fairway*, Allen & Unwin, 1927)

Advice from on High
FRED CORCORAN

Coming home, we made the Grand Tour, stopping off in Rome for what Sam called an audition with the late Pope John. I suggested facetiously that Sam might bring his putter along and have it blessed. I argued that a papal blessing might help steer in some of those six-foot sidehill putts.

Sam was impressed. I remember we were met in the vestry of St Peter's by a monsignor whose eyebrows flitted up into his tonsure when Snead checked in with his clubs. But he turned out to be a 100-shooter himself and he immediately went to confession to Sam about his putting problems. Sam sighed, picked up his clubs and headed back to the car.

'If you're this close to the Pope and you can't putt,' he drawled over his shoulder, 'he ain't gonna be able to do anything for me!'

(From *Unplayable Lies*, Duell, Sloan & Pearce, 1965)

Heavenly Golf
PETER ALLISS

A keen golfer went to Heaven and was very surprised to find that they had the most beautiful golf course there. It was built on rather American lines with water hazards, tree-lined fairways, big bunkers, white sand ... it really was a joy. The new arrival was being shown round by St Peter, who, as we know, was a very keen golfer. They came to the eighth, which was a short hole of about 195 yards, and stopped to watch a couple up on the tee.

The first player stood up and hit a No. 4 wood. He hit it well and it landed nicely on the putting surface. The second chap seemed to umm and ahh for a bit, then he took out an iron which looked very lofted. He gave the ball the most enormous whack but the ball didn't even reach halfway over a lake running across in front of the green. He took out another ball and gave it a tremendous crash. In the water again. He did this five times and on every occasion the ball landed in the water, 30 or 40 yards short of the green.

The new arrival in Heaven couldn't resist any longer, and he turned to St Peter and said, 'Who on earth does he think he is? Jesus Christ?'

St Peter replied, 'Actually, that is Jesus Christ. The trouble is, he thinks he's Arnold Palmer.'

A very enthusiastic golfer had a friend who was a noted clairvoyant, and he was always badgering his friend to contact someone from the beyond to see whether there was a golf course in Heaven. If there was, he wanted to know what sort of sand was in the bunkers, which were the out-of-bounds holes, how difficult the course was, what was par, whether there was a grill room, a good pro's shop, and so on.

The clairvoyant eventually said that when he had his next seance he would make some inquiries. So he did that, and about three weeks later the keen golfer saw the clairvoyant and asked whether he had any news.

'Yes,' said the clairvoyant, 'I have some good news and some bad news. The good news is that there is the most superb golf course in Heaven. It's beautiful. It has Bermuda grass on the fairways and Penn Cross on the greens, the most beautiful crushed marble in the bunkers. There is a superb clubhouse with a grill room, a marvellous men's locker room, a splendid pro's shop, golf carts, etcetera. It is really tip top.'

'That's great,' said the golfer. 'But what's the bad news?'

'I booked you a starting time for next Tuesday at two o'clock.'

I noticed once on our 'Pro-Celebrity' series that Lee Trevino seemed to have the idea that it was possible to interfere with a golf ball while it was in flight. Lee's sense of the supernatural manifested itself to me after he had hit a tee shot and was standing there giving the ball rather a lot of verbal encouragement.

'Be up! Be up! Be up!' he kept calling.

But his caddie, Willie Aitchison, evidently disagreed because he was shouting, 'Come down! Come down! Come down!'

Lee could not stand competing for the attention of the gods, so he turned to Willie and ordered, 'Leave it alone, Willie! Leave it alone!'

(From *Bedside Golf*, Collins/Willow, 1980)

He Doesn't Know What It's Like to be Me

HENRY LONGHURST

I sometimes wonder whether the likes of me – I will not say us – can really be helped by the likes of Jack Nicklaus. He cannot have any conception, fortunately enough, of what it feels like to be me. Tuck a pillow in the front of his trousers, enfeeble his left eye, drain three-quarters of the strength from his hands and fingers, make him pant when walking up slopes and cause the blood to rush to his head if the ball falls off the tee and he has to bend down to pick it up again, and he might begin to get the idea.

On the other hand, it is nice for the likes of us to imagine what it must be like to feel like Nicklaus, who glories in his strength and cheerfully invites the young to do the same. My own generation was always taught to try to cultivate a good swing and let distance come later. Nicklaus thinks exactly the opposite.

'The first thing I learned was to swing hard, and never mind where the ball went. That is the way Arnold Palmer was taught, too, and I think it is the right way. A youngster first trying golf will enjoy the game more if allowed to whale away at the ball, and he will be developing the muscles he needs to become a strong hitter. Once he has achieved distance, he can learn control while still hitting a long ball.'

The most important factor in long hitting, he thinks – and it would be interesting to know how many long hitters feel the same – is strength in one's legs, and this is developed by hitting hard when one is young. 'If a golfer does this while young, he will get the leg strength needed to hit very long shots. I know that my distance is due more to the strength in my legs than to any power I might be getting from my arms, hands or fingers.'

Meanwhile, spring draws us from our winter lairs and a few tentative swings may soon be made with the special weighted club, if we can find it. 'Swing 250 to 270 yards to a fairway 35 yards wide; long irons over 200 yards to within 36 feet . . .' I can see them all! As rendered by Nicklaus.

(From the *Sunday Times*, 1968)

And now for some thoughts on how to behave whilst on the golf course.

Dressing the Part

FRED CORCORAN

The good golfer is always impeccably neat. He dresses well. He doesn't have towels flying from his bag like flags of capitulation. He takes pride in his grooming and his appearance. Hagen, for example, always wore a silk shirt and necktie. And he always managed to maintain that crisply fresh look. I can remember him playing in a North and South Open Championship at Pinehurst when a storm broke. Others came in from the eighteenth green muddy and bedraggled, but not Hagen. His clothes were rain-spattered, but he strolled off the last green under an umbrella as handsomely groomed as when he had stepped off the first tee.

(From *Unplayable Lies*, Duell, Sloan & Pearce, 1965)

Henry Cotton – for the third time Open Champion. Muirfield, 1948

Taking Root

JOHN REECE

Eight thousand people saw the start of slow play in this country. They were present at Walton Heath in 1938 for the greatest challenge match ever played.

This was the historic confrontation between Cotton and Reg Whitcombe, the reigning Open champion, and Bobby Locke and Sid Brews for £500, winners take all. The first round of the four took three hours and forty minutes, the third lasted ten minutes longer, and the aggregate of the third and fourth was seven and a half hours. If the spectators were enraptured by the play they were disillusioned by the pace. Locke was the culprit.

The horrifying fact of the matter is that the speed of each round by the four would beat by many minutes a top single at today's going rate.

There had been instances of individual slow play up to that time. Cyril Walker, a Mancunian who went to America from Hoylake before the first war and won the U S Open in 1924, was criticized for slowness, but the most notorious in this respect was Phil Perkins, a Warwickshire amateur who won the English championship and later went to America and turned professional. I did not see either player, but I wonder how relatively quick they were compared with the modern Chartist movement.

Creeping paralysis began to grip the younger school of British players immediately after the Second World War, and when Cotton left Southport after the 1946 tournament he was constrained to say he would 'like to whip some of them for the time they are taking to play'.

The state of greens in general left a lot to be desired after seven years of cursory treatment but it was the same for everyone, which is always the case in this wonderful game.

I wrote then that there is no pay in putt, putt, putt. And I remain convinced that slowness is largely to blame for much of the three-putting that goes on. My contention is that if everything else is done at a normal rate then slowness on the greens is not concentration but a pose. It is a misguided attempt by the player to convince himself that he is leaving nothing to chance, and he ends up by concentrating so hard on concentrating that he forgets what he is supposed to be doing.

Locke may have been culpable at Walton Heath, but as he grew older and filled out to the more familiar shape of the postwar years he was not so much slow as tediously deliberate. To his unhurried short pacing he attached an unfailing routine. Whatever the putting problem, once he had made up his mind he took two practice putts which bore every relationship to the stroke he had in mind, stepped forward and struck the ball – usually into the hole.

He was like Old Father Thames.

He never seems to hurry,
But he gets there just the same.

Apart from the climate, slow play remains the greatest threat to the game in this country.

In club life Saturdays used to be the occasion for two rounds, a pot of tea with a poached egg, and nine more holes squeezed in for good measure. However, there is a great deal of difference between six hours of enjoyment and nine or ten of torture. As one wag has put it: 'What used to be a doddle has become a dawdle.'

Eventually the Americans put their house in order and not before time – when they imposed a system of two hundred dollar fines on the spot. The effect was immediate. Tournament players began to complete a round in four hours and discovered that life was still worth living. Incredibly, it seemed a better way of life.

Deane Beman, commissioner of the American professional tour organization, said, 'I am particularly gratified to hear comments from our players about how much they are enjoying the tour because of their shorter days on the course.'

The thought struck me as reasonable that if the American could reduce five hours to four, we should be able to cut four and half to three and a half without endangering anyone's chances of earning a living, on the one hand, and enjoying himself, on the other.

The European Tournament Players' Division tackled the problem as if they meant business. A professional deemed guilty of slow play would be fined £50 without preliminary warning. If he should persist he would be fined £100. If the poor chap should then be reduced to a state of paralysis, benumbed by fear of what his bank manager might say or whether he would be able to eat that night, he would be fined £200 for immobility unless his playing partners should pick him up and break into a gallop.

The main problem is definition. The most important one after that is finding the discipline to deal with it. Who is to be judge? And who is to be executioner? The slowest play I ever endured as an onlooker was in a tournament in which Peter Oosterhuis, Nick Job and South African Tertius Claassens, none of whom I would label as slow on his own, were involved in a threeball starting at two o'clock in the afternoon. At four o'clock, with everything out of sight ahead of their match, they reached the seventh green. It proved to be a study in almost still life and yet it would have been difficult to point a finger of guilt at one of them. Collectively they were farcically slow. Each was as bad as the others; each affected by the others. If the system of fines had been in force the tour administrator of the day, George O'Grady, would have cried all the way to the bank. I cried all the way home.

How often do we see the young professional waffle about with a sheaf of notes, looking for his yardages only to find he has brought Stoke Poges with him instead of Muirfield?

I took root one day beside a young professional's ball as it lay in the centre of the fairway 150 yards from the flagstick. I knew it was 150 yards, and so did he. His notes told him so, and he had played the hole the previous day from almost exactly the same place. And 150 yards yesterday is the same as 150 yards today. The only significant difference was a wind in his face.

He stood up to the ball without a club in his hands and went through a lateral sway with his arms a foot apart. Having satisfied himself that some sort of stroke was a possibility, he bent and picked up all the loose bits of vegetation he could muster, throwing the handful into the air, only to realize that as there was a wind blowing into his face he should have pitched the stuff higher. He rubbed his hands on a towel provided by his caddie, who had lowered the bag burden because he had a shrewd idea of what was yet to come. It was rest time for him.

Yardage was one thing; a chart was another. It called for exploration, and our young character walked forward to within 40 yards of the green. As he retraced his steps, the following match walked onto the tee, there to reflect on the beauties of nature and ponder the result of the 2.30. Meanwhile, back beside the ball, there was fresh activity. Our man did another clubless swing before moving over to the bag of clubs, now held upright by the reinvigorated caddie. When the player placed a hand among the clubheads I thought a decision had been reached, but I was wrong because the two of them struck up a conversation.

It was still a long time before he addressed the ball. There had to be one or two practice swings to see if he could remember what to do. When the ball eventually plunged into a bunker, short and to the right, I walked forward because I thought the next stroke would take even longer and I wanted to time it, surreptitiously, of course. Strangely, he took no time at all, having become disenchanted with this way of trying to make a living. He blasted the ball right over the green, chipped back and then went for a walk with his putter. Eventually, when his first putt from 8 yards sidled up to the hole and stopped 6 inches away, he looked as if sentence had been passed. I believe we shared similar feelings at that moment. For different reasons.

Every time I watch a tournament I see at least one player arrive on a green and stand over his ball, fumbling in a trousers pocket for a marker. He used it on the previous hole, but even so, in order to find it, he has to remove everything from the pocket, filling his palm and poking about like a little boy looking for his marbles. Having marked the ball, he throws it off stage to some out-fielder who gives it a shampoo. In the meantime he goes for a walk in the opposite direction. He looks so bored and when, minutes later, he returns to putt dead from 15 yards it clearly brings him to the edge of nervous breakdown. These greens should be ploughed in; all these wormcasts, how can a guy putt? A lack of human sympathy and the noise of the butterflies are all too much for the poor chap.

I venture the opinion that fining is no good at all. Impose penalty strokes and cure the ill immediately. It is a way I would have in a wider field of law enforcement, but we are dealing with golf. Consider the competitor in a professional championship who found himself standing on the tenth green three hours and ten minutes after starting the round. There was no indication that the situation would improve and so he did what appeared to me to be perfectly reasonable. He walked in, leaving his understanding partners telling their beads on the eleventh tee. The unfair aspect of this act came when he was ultimately charged with 'misdemeanour' and the slow ones went scot free.

A leading West Country figure, Denis Scanlan, has an idea as good and realistic as any I have come across. In general, if players fail to reach the sixth green in one hour, each will be penalized 2 strokes. It would happen again at the twelfth, and even unto the eighteenth.

At some stage in his life between 1864 and 1925, Willie Park Jr, who knew as much about golf as any man, wrote: 'Golf is a businesslike game, and should be gone about in a brisk, businesslike way.'

(From *Golf of Course*, Redcliffe, 1983)

Bad Temper

HENRY LONGHURST

Being a traditionalist at heart and having been brought up in an age when the bad language of golfers was always good for a laugh in the humorous magazine *Punch*, I was secretly, and of course most improperly, delighted to read that the language of some of the golfers of the Rushmere Club at Ipswich had so much offended the susceptibilities of a number of passers-by as to cause them to make official complaint. Well done, gentlemen. Splendid stuff! This, as I once heard Mr Churchill describe it, is a 'mealy-mouthed, purry-purry, puss-puss age', and a few strong words do much to restore our self-esteem.

In my early days it was only the club golfer who permitted himself to give vent to his feelings; the professional never. In the intervening period we have had such characters as Tommy Bolt, a past US Open champion, who was constantly being fined for failing to hold his feelings in check. But the conduct of the great millionaire professionals today, which sets the pattern for the rest, is almost solemn in its righteousness.

This 'correctness' has now passed itself on to the golfing rank and file, but it still does not alter the fact that, to me at any rate, the most exquisitely satisfying act in the world of golf is that of throwing a club. The full backswing, the delayed wrist action, the flowing follow-through, followed by that unique whirring sound, reminiscent only of a passing flock of starlings, are without parallel in sport. Many is the time I have done it, and seen it done by better men than I – but now, alas, we should probably be drummed out of the club.

The classic club-throwing story is, of course, that of the fellow who, on returning from an unsatisfactory mission in Scotland, threw his clubs one by one from the carriage window into the Firth of Forth while crossing the Forth Bridge. I never believed this to be true until I met a fellow who with the utmost seriousness assured me that he was the man. (Immediately on returning home, he confessed to me, he went out and bought another set.) There was also the hero who, on chipping three times into the Swilken Burn at the first hole at St Andrews, when playing it as the nineteenth, beckoned silently to his caddie, lifted the clubs from his shoulder and threw them into the burn. Then he threw his caddie in. Then he jumped in himself.

Many, many years ago, I was playing in a Bedfordshire Northants Alliance meeting in company with a partnership consisting of the then vicar of Northampton and a gentleman whose complexion indicated either good living or shortness of temper, or both. They were doing rather well and at the seventeenth were in with a definite chance. At this point the vicar's partner had only to loft a short pitch over the bunker onto the green, when, alas, up came his head, out came a lump of turf, and the ball dropped feebly into the bunker. The man lifted his niblick to heaven. '*******!,' he cried, and '*******!' and '*******!' Then, pulling himself up with a jerk, he began to make embarrassed apologies. The vicar's reply remains in my mind as though it were yesterday. 'Brother,' he said, slowly and gently, 'the provocation was ample.'

The best swearing 'incident' in golf must surely be the conclusion of P. G. Wodehouse's story, 'Chester Forgets Himself'. (If any reader is so golfingly illiterate as not to possess, and be able to quote from, *The Heart of a Goof* from which book this story comes, and the original *The Clicking of Cuthbert*, let him at once go out and get them.) Chester, it may be remembered, stifling his normal flow of strong language for the sake of the girl he hopes to marry, has to get down in a chip and a putt to break the course record. At the eighteenth he has at last managed to get through that immortal fourball known as 'The Wrecking Crew' and is about to play his chip, when one of them, I think it was the First Gravedigger, the one who 'never spared himself in his efforts to do the ball a violent injury', took his usual swipe at the ball and for the first time in his life did everything right at once. His shot hit Chester on the seat of his plus-fours at the crucial moment, thus causing him to fluff his pitch, whereupon he let forth a blistering succession of asterisks and exclamation marks. The girl, wondering how all this time she could have 'so misjudged this silver-tongued man', folds him in her arms and, a moment later, of course, he nonchalantly holes his final chip for the record.

The man who got really cross at golf – strange as it must seem to those who only knew him by the gentleness of his writing – was Bernard Darwin, who enjoyed, if that is the word, a kind of love-hate relationship with the game for the best part of seventy years. A friend of mine was once playing in a foursome with him at Rye when, at a rather crucial moment on the sixteenth, Bernard missed his second. He wandered off into the rough and started banging his club repeatedly on the ground. He thought he was out of earshot but my friend heard him muttering savagely to himself. 'Why do I play this ******* game? I do hate it so.'

It was Bernard who told me what remains one of my favourite golfing stories, of a well-known Scottish amateur before the first war. Though a big man, he had made the discovery, as people do from time to time, that you can putt remarkably well, one-handed, with a little putter about the size of a carpenter's hammer. As always happens, it lasted splendidly for a while but proved fallible in the end. The climax came when he missed a tiddler with it on the ninth green at Muirfield. Raising himself to his full height, he flung it against the grey stone wall bordering the green. 'You little *******!' he cried. 'Never presume upon my good nature again!'

(From the *Sunday Times*, 1965)

Anger

BOBBY JONES

My Byers and I played terribly. He was a veteran and I was a youngster, but we expressed our feelings in the same way – when we missed a shot, we threw the club away. This habit later got me no end of critical comment, some of which hurt my feelings deeply, as I continued reading references to my temper long after I had got it under control to where there was no outward evidence of it except my ears getting red, which they do to this day – for I still get as mad as ever, missing a simple shot . . .

I was a year or two more getting my turbulent disposition in hand. It wasn't an easy matter. It's sort of hard to explain, unless you play golf yourself. You see, I never lost my temper with an opponent. I was angry only with myself. It always seemed, and it seems today, such an utterly useless and idiotic thing to stand up to a perfectly simple shot, one that I *know* I can make a hundred times running without a miss – and then mess up the blamed thing the one time I want to make it. And it's gone for ever, an irrevocable crime, that stroke ... And when you feel so extremely a fool, and a bad golfer to boot, what the deuce can you do, except throw the club away? Well, well, Chick Evans, writing years later, said I had conquered my temper not wisely but too well; that a flare now and then would help me. I liked that of Chick. But I could have told him I get just as mad today.

Returning to my first match at Merion in 1916, after this bit of *apologia* – which may not be in the best of taste – I repeat that My Byers and I played very wretchedly and I think the main reason I beat him was because he ran out of clubs first. Somebody playing behind us said later that we looked like a juggling act.

(From *Down the Fairway*, Allen & Unwin, 1927)

Manners Maketh the Golfer

IAN WOOLDRIDGE

It was quarter past eight before Tom Watson was through with the media rituals and free to walk the 300 sunlit yards back to the Marine Hotel at Troon.

There were just Tom and his wife and a couple of friends. No one plagued them or dogged their footsteps or yelled 'Attaboy' or jabbed autograph books at Tom's face.

There were probably a hundred people drinking on the long terrace in front of the Marine as Tom came up the steps and they gave him the kind of gentle applause accorded brief speeches at private dinner parties. Tom smiled.

The Marine head porter, in dark green frock coat, exercised the privilege invested in all great head porters through their close attendance on the mighty. He offered Mr Watson his hand. 'Well done, sir,' he said. 'Thank you!' said Tom, richer by a fourth British Open title and ultimately £1 million than when he had first shaken the man's hand a week earlier.

It is all very well saying Watson was handed it all on a sacrificial plate. The truth is that Mr Modesty Incarnate is just about the hardest man you will meet in a long year's march through sport. He stayed ice cool while the tyros got their brains scrambled in the pressure cooker.

The point of this little homily, however, is that, short of actually threatening to deprive Mr Watson of a tenner, let alone a title, you'd never know.

The manners are impeccable, the chivalry enduring, the courtesy to women and servants and pestering reporters infinite.

And so, mostly, is it throughout golf. After weeks with those snarling footballers at the World Cup, days with those squeaking trade-union second-raters at Wimbledon and off-duty hours in the pouting, complaining presence of the only son of Mr and Mrs McEnroe, I gratefully confirm that the British Open Golf Championship remains much more than a major sports event.

It is an annual refresher course in admirable behaviour. It is a reassurance that traditional sporting

Tom Weiskopf – the most elegant of players

virtues can survive outrageous commercialism. It is the denial of the widely held modern theory of professionalism that you have to be an ill-mannered pig to win.

The crowds reciprocate. The atmosphere for four days is one of warm mutual regard.

No incident reflected it more than out on the seventh hole in the second round when Jack Nicklaus made such a ghastly mess of a wedge shot that even I could have been its perpetrator. It pitched lamentably short and fell away into the semi-rough.

Some 2000 people were watching from the hillsides and no one made a single sound. It was like being witness to a biblical miracle going wrong. Nicklaus, expressionless, walked on. When he was 50 yards from the green, now well distanced from the evidence of fallibility, the crowd rose and applauded him for fully thirty seconds.

It was homage to the greatest golfer who ever lived and Jack stood there for a moment and looked at them, deeply moved by their affection and understanding.

Bobby Clampett, a young genius too green to comprehend that Troon and tension are the ultimate taskmasters, and Nick Price, broken by the awesome burden of merely having to play the last four holes in par to vault from unknown journeyman to millionaire, must have felt it too.

The ovations they received as they moved into the great canyon of spectators down the eighteenth fairway will live with them for many years. The applause acknowledged their panache and unpatronizingly invited them to come back and try again.

There were other aspects of the Open that reminded you that sport is not entirely annexed by the unspeakable.

Tom Weiskopf brought his family from America to the birthplace of golf and Mrs Weiskopf clearly understood what that meant. Their small son, probably eight, was dressed for dinner like a City banker. Their daughter was straight out of Jane Austen. Tom presided over the family table, sitting as erect as a Victorian father.

Across the dining room Jack Nicklaus hosted dinner for twelve. By the window Arnold Palmer, relaxed now in the knowledge that the galleries will still follow him if he returns to Scotland when he's eighty, was holding court.

He didn't so much play golf at the Open as allow a younger generation to get a glimpse of him, touching his cap from time to time to acknowledge their veneration.

Across the table Ed Sneed was unutterably depressed. He'd missed the cut, an expensive lapse when you've come from America. He was superbly dressed. His wife could have been photographed for *Vogue*. And they didn't bitch.

Ben Crenshaw didn't even suffer the disappointment of finishing second this time. He didn't finish anywhere that counted. You would never have known. Ben smiles even at breakfast and always stands to speak to ladies.

But it was Tom Watson's championship again and even if he didn't repeat for American television what he said on BBC – namely that the British Open is the greatest championship in world golf – all is forgiven. He was the gracious winner of an exercise in manners.

No one sprayed champagne over innocent bystanders, no one punched the air, no one blasted the officials or effed and blinded in public. The 111th Open Championship merely passed into history, and golf and sport itself was strengthened by it.

(From the *Daily Mail*, 20 July 1982)

During the forty years I've been seriously 'into' golf, the reporting of the game has changed a very great deal. More and more, over the years, the players have been asked to comment on their performances in tournaments and championships, virtually unknown until more recent times. I remember an incident in 1951 as Max Faulkner emerged triumphant in the Open Championship at Royal Portrush.

It was announced that the champion was about to give a press conference. Said Bernard Darwin, the man from *The Times* and the greatest golf writer of his day, 'No one is interested in what Faulkner thinks about the way he played. They want to know how *I* think he played.'

Those were the days when reporters roamed the course and reported on what they saw. Now, of course, successful players come to them – largely through press-tent interviews. Throughout an event, there is also TV, a flow of information and a huge scoreboard which gives the press the hole-by-hole results as the pars, birdies and bogeys go down on each competitor's card.

Peter Dobereiner traces the development of quotes from professional golfers and reveals the hidden meanings of what they say.

Talking a Good Game

PETER DOBEREINER

Once upon a time before you and I were born it was the custom of newspapers to carry reports of sporting events. Our correspondent would go along to, say, a cricket match and describe what he saw. 'Grace dispatched the crimson orb to the confines for the full complement.' And much, much more in similar captivating style.

These days readers are not interested in what a player did. Unless a sportsman can talk a good game he is nothing. I am old enough to remember when a craze for quote journalism first fired the imagination of sports editors and, as a practitioner in the field, it was uphill work, I can tell you.

At a tournament in Yorkshire Neil Coles and Bernard Hunt were playing together. Of course, being professionals, they were never favoured with the use of their Christian names, thereby becoming the source of frequent nightmares for the late Henry Longhurst, the pioneer TV commentator.

Coles and Hunt were professionals of the old school, brought up in the tradition that sportsmen should be seen and not heard. They simply could not take to this newfangled idea of answering questions; and in those early interviews they responded mostly with embarrassed grunts. On this occasion they had both scored well and were duly wheeled into the press tent to be grilled for the day's quota of quotes. Hunt first. 'Drive, 6, 2 putts. Drive, wedge, 2 putts.' At this point Coles, who was just beginning to grasp the fundamentals of the new journalism, gave a faint cough and raised one eyebrow about a millimetre. Hunt stopped his recital and looked at Coles in bewilderment.

'Aren't you going to tell them about the fourteenth?' whispered Coles.

Neil Coles wasn't always sombre. What do *you* think Brian Barnes said to him?

'The fourteenth?' said Hunt. 'Regulation par.'

'No', hissed Coles, 'you know ...' (Say what you like about us sportswriters, but we can sniff a story.)

'What happened at the fourteenth?' we bayed. It was like drawing teeth; but we persisted and bit by bit it came out. As he was addressing the ball for his approach shot, Hunt's club was struck from his hands by lightning.

Eventually we had our story, justifying the new system – for it was almost as good as if we had seen the incident for ourselves. But try as we might we

Bernard Hunt, a good friend

couldn't get much of a quote out of Hunt. 'What did you do when the lightning hit you?'

'I picked up the club and hit the ball. Front left, about 20 feet.' It was a start.

How times have changed. Ten years later the players had mastered the art of the quote. When Lee Trevino was hit by lightning at the Western Open he did thirty minutes of stand-up patter without drawing breath and he had a column of quotes in every newspaper. That is why he is a superstar.

These days young professionals are taught the art of the quote at the American qualifying school and they have to sign a declaration agreeing to cooperate with the media at all times, meaning that they must be ready with a quotable quote at the drop of a tape recorder.

The most important time for quotes is before a tournament when the newspapers are obsessively devoting columns and columns to reports of what is going to happen. This is one of my favourite journalistic exercises and I live for the day when I master the art of prognostication to such a degree that it will not be necessary to report the actual event at all. I shall simply write: 'The Open Championship was played yesterday and turned out exactly as I forecast five days ago. Back numbers are available from the circulation department.'

Arnold Palmer is the absolute master of the quote and I cherish particularly his reply to a quote-hungry writer before the U S Open Championship. 'Do you think the guys can shoot low on this course, Arnie?'

'Waaall, any time you drive the ball in the fairway, hit all the greens and make a bunch of putts, then you have a chance to make a score.'

That is straightforward enough, but there are pitfalls in the golfing quote and it may be helpful if I offer a little advice on the art of interpretation.

Thus the sentence 'This is a magnificent test of golf' can be translated as 'I hold the course record.' Likewise, when Dave Hill is quoted as saying 'This course is nothing but a cow pasture' he is really saying 'I missed the cut.' Beware too of Gary Player's favourite quote: 'This is the finest golf course I have ever seen, of its kind.' That is verbal shorthand for 'The Commissioner has warned me that the next time I criticize a host club in public he will have my guts for garters.'

When professionals are talking about their own play their remarks can only be properly understood if you happen to know their scores. I have therefore invented a new form of punctuation which I hope will be universally adopted by newspapers for golfing quotes. Here is how it works.

Jerry Pate led the first round and said: 63 I really enjoyed playing this superb course which has been beautifully prepared for the championship 63. Or: Larry Nelson commented: 75 They could do with lowering the cutters of the fairway mowers: I had a lot of flyers 75. Or: Lanny Wadkins snarled: 82 I'd like to get hold of the clown who set those pin positions and give him a lobotomy – with my wedge 82.

By now we experienced hands, both players and writers, have refined the quotes business to a fine art. I glance at the scoreboard and notice that David Graham, for instance, has been posted with a score of 76. A few years ago this would have required a complicated ritual involving a tape recorder and laborious transcription, followed by the editing out of any fruity adjectives and then the writing of the rough draft. Now, under the mutual trust system, the process can be streamlined.

Self: How?
Graham: Tripled five.

I can now go straight to the typewriter and begin: David Graham's challenge faltered with a third round 76. An otherwise solid performance was marred by a torrid 7 at the innocuous 370-yard fifth hole where the players enjoyed the help of a light following breeze. Graham reeled from the course ashen-faced and groaned: 'I played that hole like an arthritic granny.'

You may purse your lips and mutter about a decline in journalistic ethics but it is necessary to invent quotes more and more these days because professional golfers are gradually losing the power of speech. Already adverbs have been eliminated entirely from their vocabulary. 'I hit the ball super but putted just horrible.'

Some of these semantic murderers have gone farther and limit themselves to the use of one adjective only, employing it on every possible occasion and sometimes in the middle of a word, thus: 'I played a low com-xxxxxx-pression ball.'

These developments in the world of golf reporting have transformed our lives. We cannot waste time enjoying the sunshine and fresh air on the golf course because hard necessity requires us to produce quotes. For reasons which I have explained, we mostly have to invent such quotes, putting a gigantic strain on the imagination. The only way this can be achieved successfully, day after day, is by the use of artificial stimulants. Greatly against my natural inclination, and indeed to my abhorrence, I myself have occasionally to resort to the use of hallucinatory drugs, of which alcohol is the only form available in golf clubs. So if you should happen to see a golf writer in the bar while a tournament is in progress, please suppress that unfortunately common instinct to remark sneeringly, 'I thought you reporter chappies were paid to watch the golf.'

We are sensitive to such ignorant jibes. Just remember that as we force ourselves to swallow that hateful amber fluid through clenched teeth we are actually performing a difficult and distasteful task *for your benefit* and in order to support our families.

(From the *Observer*, 1981)

When I came into golf commentating, Henry Longhurst was established as the leading practitioner. Here he recounts some of his experiences.

Up in the Tower

HENRY LONGHURST

Life is a mixed bag – chances offered and taken, more often chances missed or not even noticed. Successes are sometimes to be scored by honest toil and solid worth, more often by happening to be standing somewhere, thinking of nothing, at exactly the right time. In the latter category may be placed my entry into broadcasting, which for about thirty-five years has been one of the most pleasurable activities of my life.

Television is, by comparison with radio, a push-over. In television – I am talking, of course, of golf – in times of local difficulty, which means quite often, you can always intersperse what Sydney Smith, referring to the loquacious Macaulay's conversation at dinner, called 'brilliant flashes of silence', and, indeed, as I hope to show in due course, this may gain you much merit. In other words, you can always sit back and let them look at the picture. In radio, if your mind goes blank for three seconds, they think the set has gone wrong. Is is essential, therefore, in an emergency to possess the ability to 'waffle on', and with this from the first I never had any great difficulty – on the radio or anywhere else, come to that!

I believe I can claim to have done the first live outside radio broadcast on golf when the BBC set up a glass box on stilts at some vantage point far out on the Little Aston course outside Birmingham, overlooking two greens and three tees. In a way we were not unsuccessful. We saw plenty of play, chopping and changing from one hole to another, and had an added piece of good fortune when a past British Open champion, Arthur Havers, completely fluffed a short approach shot in front of our window. Perhaps he was unnerved by the thought of being on live for the first time in history.

Then the BBC brought in a portable apparatus with which it was to be possible actually to follow the golf, and here the initiator, at the English Amateur Championship at Birkdale the year before the war, was the doyen of our profession, Bernard Darwin. He set off onto the course accompanied by two engineers, one carrying a portmanteau-shaped apparatus strapped to his back with a long aerial sticking up vertically behind his head, and the other lugging around the batteries. I naturally listened with professional interest, having been invited to carry out a similar venture at the Amateur Championship at the Royal Liverpool Golf Club at Hoylake later on.

It was soon pretty clear that the venerable Darwin

was finding it heavy going and it was no surprise when he declared, on returning to the clubhouse, that golf, so far as he was concerned, did not lend itself to this type of broadcasting.

At Hoylake on the morning of the Amateur Championship quarter finals, we tried to follow the play but soon came up against the elementary stumbling block that in order to describe the play you had to see it, and in order to see it you had to be within range of the players, and they could therefore hear what your were saying, which was not only extremely embarrassing but led to persistent cries of 'Sshhhh' from the silent spectators. For the afternoon semifinals, we set ourselves up on a knoll beside the fifth fairway, well out of the way but with a reasonable view of the distant play. It seems incredible today but the signal for us to start was to be the lowering of a white handkerchief by an engineer perched on the roof of the Royal Liverpool clubhouse.

The exact hour of the broadcast in those days had to be printed in advance, so there was no flexibility in time. The first semifinal came to us and passed, then came the second. At this point the engineer raised the white handkerchief and we were under starter's orders. He lowered it briskly and we were 'off' – whereupon the second match vanished from sight, leaving our little trio silent upon a knoll in Hoylake, unable to move since our range was only a mile. I state with confidence that I gave an absolutely splendid and dramatic eyewitness account of the play, understandably interspersed with a good deal of the 'Wish you were here ... lovely view across the bay' sort of stuff, and I could not help feeling that not everyone could have waffled continuously or to such effect for ten whole minutes about nonexistent play. I thus returned to the clubhouse feeling that a congratulatory hand or two might well be extended. Instead, we met the engineer. He was most apologetic. 'We had to fade you out after a minute or two,' he said, 'on account of a technical hitch.'

Much as I respect the club, Hoylake has never been my happy hunting ground for either radio or television. In 1936, when golf on the radio was comparatively new, the engineer and I were stuck in a tiny, glass-fronted box situated among the guyropes at the back of the refreshment tent, with barely room for ourselves and a suspended microphone. First, one day's play in the Open was cancelled on account of a snowstorm – in July – and I had to do three ten-minute pieces on a programme going out across the British Empire, filling in for a whole day's play that had never taken place. Then a couple of friends espied me from afar and with schoolboy delight advanced upon our humble box.

I was in full spate when they came and made rude two-fingered gestures outside the box, pressing their noses against the glass and generally carrying on as though provoking a monkey in a cage. Finally, when once again we were in full flow, a waitress came out behind the refreshment tent carrying an enormous pile of plates. The strange spectacle in our little box so distracted her attention that she tripped over a guyrope and sank with a crash that reverberated throughout the Empire. I explained what it was and gather that it gave innocent pleasure as far away as New Zealand.

The first serious attempts in Britain to televise live golf were directed by Antony Craxton, who used to do the Queen's Christmas broadcasts. Many were from Wentworth, which, in summer, with the trees in full glory and a shirtsleeved crowd moving from hole to hole enjoying themselves in the sunshine, can present a magnificent picture. I remember Craxton saying how golf even then attracted quite a large rating by comparison with what had been expected, and how many housewives on housing estates said that they knew nothing about it but liked to watch because 'it seemed such a lovely place'. Nowadays, of course, this holds good to a much greater extent and some of the scenes in colour – on British television so much superior to the American colour, for once, due to different line standards – can be really heavenly.

For myself I always thought the 'beauty shots' and the little irrelevancies – though we seem to have time for few of them these days – added to the appeal of golfing programmes: the 360-degree panorama of, say, Turnberry, with the Clyde and the Isle of Arran and the long encircling arm of the Mull of Kintyre and Ailsa Craig; or Muirfield, with the distant tracery of the two great Forth bridges and the Kingdom of Fife on the other side of the Firth; or St Andrews and the bay and the snow-capped Cairngorms; or, again, the small boy at the eighth at Wentworth who, immediately after the last match had passed by, emerged from the undergrowth and started fishing in the pond; or the lark's nest focused upon by an alert cameraman at Muirfield during the Open. The producer had to sacrifice this camera for quite a while before the mother lark returned to the nest to feed the young, and there were many who afterwards said that this was the best bit in the programme, never mind Jack Nicklaus. The same cameraman's roving eye and telephoto lens discerned a couple on the sandhills just outside the course and it was nip and tuck whether their subsequent union would appear, live and in colour, for the first time on this or any other screen. If only the producer had been under notice from the BBC at the time, he might have risked his arm and given the world a most entertaining exposure – and I sometimes wonder what I should have made of the commentary.

(From *My Life and Soft Times*, Cassell, 1971)

Though I sometimes find it very hard to understand why, undoubtedly, many duffers enjoy their golf, here's one who claims he doesn't.

Golf: Who Needs It?

TOM KEARNEY

First Hole

Usually people who have never played golf before resolve never to play it again after they've suffered the agony and humiliation associated with this hole. I will not attempt to describe it, other than to say that once you've mastered it, then Ben Nevis, Snowdon and even perhaps Everest are yours for the taking.

My first encounter with it was shameful and mortifying, lessened only by the fact that I was on my own and, as far as I could discern, there were no witnesses to the succession of disasters that befell me. I suppose my teeshot set the scene really. I did everything right in my opinion, club facing right way and gripped firmly in both hands, stance perfect, muscles flexed, breathing rhythmic, eyes fixed alternately on glistening brand-new Spalding and dead crow on stick (marker) in far distance and then a graceful upswing followed by a downward movement of considerable velocity which, in the few seconds that this was happening, led me to believe that I hadn't lost the old magic of yesteryear.

In point of fact and in the interests of veracity, for which my family is revered, I have to report that the result of this explosion of energy was a golf ball sitting up nicely on the fairway almost exactly 3 yards away and a tee which needed a pair of pliers in order to extract it from Mother Earth.

My next attempt to get the ball airborne propelled it another 3 yards or so while a considerable sod of earth fell to the ground like a dead buzzard.

So far, 2 shots. Distance approximately 6 to 7 yards.

I won't bore you with the next three efforts because all I need to say is that they were almost identical with the first two and the air was black and blue – black with flying divots and blue with language, the like of which I'd never heard before and can only assume it came from some previous existence.

It was at this stage that I began to wonder what I was doing wrong and then it came to me in a flash. What I was doing wrong was, very simply, being on the golf course in the first place.

Be that as it may, I decided to carry on; I was determined to get to the green at any cost. So I picked up my ball, hurled it about 25 yards or so and repeated this until I was on the green, where I four-putted, and I must admit it was a nice feeling, picking the ball from the hole.

Second Hole

This is an easy one – par 3. You stand on a sort of plateau and there below you, not very far away, is the green and, as with the first green, someone has thoughtfully placed a flag in the hole so you could tell where it is.

An unusual feature of this particular green today, however, was that it was almost completely covered by sheep who appeared to be involved in some annual general meeting or other and I began to wonder when it might occur to them that if they didn't move, and pretty damn quickly, they stood a good chance of being blasted off the green and into a neighbouring county minus a few vital organs.

D'you know, they totally ignored me and I began to imagine a conversation they might be having which was probably something like this: 'I say, girls, there's simply no need to panic, we're quite safe as long as we remain on the green. I mean, just look at the way that eegit's standing, there's no way he could get anywhere near the green.' I thought to myself, right you bastards, you've asked for it, and I let fly. It was a good ball, rather high trajectory and, because of the sun, I lost sight of it momentarily but was in time to see two of the animals on the green leap into the air with a few startled oaths and, before you could say Sandy Lyle, the rest of the flock was on the outskirts of Abergavenny.

Third Hole

This is rather a long one with a slight dogleg to the right except that, when I played it, it developed a dogleg to the left. Earlier in the game I had discovered a tendency to dispatch my Spalding to the left, so, in order to counteract this, I decided to stand facing in a starboard direction thus giving my ball a better chance of landing on the fairway. Not so. The ball rocketed off to the right and, in the process, joined that vast legion of lost Spaldings, Dunlop 65s, Top Flights, Warwicks, etc.

Later that day in the clubhouse, when I was talking to a wizened but kindly member, I described certain facets of my game and he introduced me to words like shanking, hooking, slicing and fresh-air shots. I found it all very interesting and I thought to myself at least I've now got the terminology right and will feel more qualified to bore the Y-Fronts off people when I corner them in the bar after the game.

Fourth Hole

This is laughingly referred to as a par 3 and I can only assume that the idiot who classified it thus knows absolutely nothing about the game or else has possibly worked on the theory that, if you can see the flag from the tee, the hole automatically becomes a par 3.

I am prepared to concede that it could be regarded as a par 3 by people like, say, Ballesteros, Nicklaus and Faldo, but only just and certainly not on one of their off days.

All I can say about this dreadful hole is that, had it been a par 10, I would have birdied it.

Fifth Hole

This is a long one, at least you think it's a long one because, at this stage, you have no way of knowing what's in store for you later on at the fourteenth and fifteenth.

If you don't mind, I'd rather not dwell on what happened to me on this hole and, in fact, I haven't even told my wife.

Incidentally, an interesting aspect here is that a fire-alarm system has been installed on the fairway between the fifth and the sixth. This is in the form of a large fire-alarm bell which has a handle which requires to be turned in order to sound the alarm. Presumably this has something to do with the Fire Precautions Act (1971) and, if this is the case, I am rather curious to know why there isn't the statutory notice displayed telling one where to assemble in the event of a fire breaking out between the fifth and sixth. Funnily enough, when I was discussing this later with the chief fire officer for Powys and a bit of Gwent, he made it very clear that, under no circumstances would he issue, or cause to be issued, a fire certificate until such time as all holes were completely interconnected with fire-alarm points and bells, par 3s excepted. He was also in sympathy with the club steward, who complained about having to run to the fifth to sound the alarm in the event of a fire breaking out in the clubhouse.

Sixth Hole

This is another short one, par 3, and looks made to measure for a reasonably deft execution with a 7 iron.

I must say I made good contact and managed, quite effortlessly, to hit a jeep which was parked on the side of the road left of the green. I didn't know it at the time, but apparently there was a young couple in the back of the jeep engaged in rather advanced biological experiments and I imagine that the impact of my ball may have momentarily disturbed their momentum.

It was as I approached the green here that I was accosted by none other than Peter Alliss himself and I noticed the BBC van close by. Peter clipped a microphone onto my raglan overcoat and we had quite an amusing chat about my golf. This apparently will be going out later this month on BBC2 in his series, 'Laugh with Alliss'.

Seventh Hole

This is a funny hole because my first tee shot disappeared into the Cairn Tea Rooms, narrowly missing a waitress who didn't know that the place had been closed since 1963. Anyway we had a pleasant chat, a cup of tea and a drag and I'm taking her to a disco at the Pavilion on Saturday if the floor hasn't collapsed in the meantime.

My second tee shot went into a pond nearby and, although I could see it quite clearly (the word Spalding slightly distorted by the current), I couldn't get at it so I came back later in the day with my wellies and fished it out. I eventually got to the green and, with minimal trouble, four-putted.

Eighth Hole

This hole is designed in such a way that, although you *think* you're playing the eighth, you are in reality using the seventh fairway and you only become reconciled with the eighth when you finally reach the green, which you are able to identify because of a sign which points to the ninth. An interesting innovation on the eighth near the tee is a ball-washing machine, but I can't help feeling that most men golfers would probably prefer to wait and enjoy a nice hot shower after the game.

Ninth Hole

Decidedly tricky. From the tee, the green is unsighted and you are immediately confronted by a ravine which is littered with abandoned caddie cars and the whitened bones of golfers who didn't make it. Just a cursory glance at these remains suggests that most of them belonged at one time or another to members of the fair sex and nobody will be surprised to know this. Halfway along the ninth there is a pleasant little café where one can dally over a nice cup of tea or something stronger if desired.

Well, it's not exactly a café in the true sense of the word. It is, in fact, Pam and Nora's bungalow and they will tell you that, over the years, they have had more than their fair share of errant golf balls on the premises. Nora relates that one sunny afternoon recently, while she was lying in bed with a mild dose of flu, a Dunlop 65 7 bounced through the doorway and landed on her chest, where there were already installed a cup of Typhoo and a plate of assorted biscuits, courtesy Huntley & Palmer.

Shortly after this, a rather agitated golfer, the owner of the Dunlop 65 7, burst on the scene and had the nerve to ask Nora if he could play his ball from where it rested because, as he explained, he was involved in a competition and didn't wish to forfeit a stroke if he could help it. Well, Nora, in perfect English, told him what he could do with his Dunlop 65 7 and, of course, he had to scratch from the competition.

Forgive me if I digress here, but I'm sure you would like to know about a diary which recently came into my possession and which dates back to 1927. The story goes that it belonged to a Mrs Clara Jones and it seems that at the time she was inordinately proud of her husband's prowess at golf, so much so that she followed him devoutly around the course every time he played, carrying his clubs, filling in her diary on each hole and generally ministering to him as any normal wife would be only too delighted to do. Midway through 1927, however, the diary comes to an abrupt and sad end with three cryptic entries as follows:

'Parred first.'
'Birdied second.'
'Dropped dead third.'

Tenth Hole

A slice here puts you in no-man's-land between this hole and the ninth, an area of dense jungle-like growth in summer where you would not be at all surprised to come across a black fellow wearing nothing but a loincloth, carrying an assegai and addressing you as 'Bwana'. If, on the other hand, by some hitherto unrecognized talent for hitting the ball straight, you manage to get the line right, then it is almost certain that your ball has landed in a ditch which is unsighted from the tee and which runs the full length of the fairway at this point.

Do not overshoot the green here because, if you do, the chances are that you will meet another ebony gentleman, carrying an assegai and yelling 'Bwana'. The place is crawling with them.

Eleventh Hole

This is a Par 3 and looks relatively simple. I reached the green with a 3 iron, that is to say I had a 3 iron in my hand when I arrived at the green. My ball was some 50 or so yards back in some hairy stuff.

I foozled my first shot and swore, foozled my second shot and swore, overshot the green with my third, thought seriously about an overdose to end it all, decided against it and, being in such a confused mental state by now, putted out eventually using a 9 iron.

Twelfth Hole

Long and straight par 4 and no place for the Happy Hooker. In fact, quite soon you will be a very unhappy hooker because if you play this hole often enough you will in time find yourself on nodding terms with quite a few cows and sheep who infest the field which runs alongside the left of the fairway.

As a matter of interest, I know of a fellow who missed a 2-footer on the twelfth green and complained that his concentration had been broken by the din being made by two butterflies in this same field. He reckoned it cost him the match.

Thirteenth Hole

There is a 15- to 20-foot-high bank about 100 yards ahead of you here, which in order to surmount, you tend to try to take the skin off the ball with the sheer ferocity of your swing and this inevitably results in your ball plugging deeply into the bank. This is certainly not one of those caring banks you hear so much about. No, this bank is unrelenting and if a penknife has not become part of your equipment by now, then you have no business being on Llandrindod golf course and should turn your attention to, say, scrabble or even wife swopping.

Fourteenth and Fifteenth Holes

Absolutely diabolical. Both par 5s and total distance, as crow flies, about 1100 yards. One of the few good things to be said about these two route marches is the existence of a small trading post about midway between the two. This is run by a Pakistani gentleman called Mr Patel who, he tells me, has supplies flown in by helicopter every fortnight or so. One or two points here for your guidance. It's advisable to have with you, apart from your golfing gear, the following: a flask, sandwiches, AA book, compass, overnight bag, identity disc, and it wouldn't be a bad idea either to inform your next of kin.

I believe that it has been known for fellows (usually with matrimonial problems) to set off on the fourteenth and never be seen again.

One final point before we leave this disaster area. At the fourteenth green you are sufficiently close to the Bridgend pub in Howey to be able to pop in for a restorative bevvy while your opponent is still looking for his ball. As a matter of passing interest, I must tell you that on Wednesday last a friend of mine was plodding wearily through the fifteenth when he heard the sound of gunshot in the distance and it was only later in the clubhouse he discovered that some poor unfortunate member had unwittingly tried to cut across a fourball. The funeral is tomorrow, apparently.

Sixteenth Hole

After what you've been through this is, in relative terms, a doddle. Here again there is a bell situated halfway along and you spend most of your time on this hole wondering if this is connected to the bell on the fifth, or is it perhaps there to summon an ambulance to rush those that didn't make it on the fourteenth/fifteenth to the intensive care unit at Hereford.

Seventeenth Hole

This is a dogleg to the right, the green is on a hill and is unsighted, and the funny thing is that you don't give a damn any more. By now your arms are leaden, your legs are someone else's and your mind, or what's left of it, has temporarily left its moorings.

All you want to do is to lay your head on a soft capacious bosom somewhere, between silken sheets, and, to the gentle strains of a caressive lullaby, sleep for at least forty-eight hours nonstop. This, of course, you can't do. This is not to be. You grab the nearest club, not caring any more, and, as you bend down to place your ball on the tee, a slight puff of wind knocks you sprawling and you are only glad that your opponent, who died suddenly on the fifteenth where he had a nice lie on the fairway, isn't there to add to your misery and humiliation by laughing hysterically.

By some miraculous piece of good fortune your ball goes over the rise and, having crawled up the hill on all fours, you are weakly overjoyed to see your ball only about 25 yards from the green and you remember one of Sam Snead's golden rules which was: 'Never have your back to the green when playing an approach shot.' Well, I didn't but I might as well have. I went down in nine, or was it ten? Who cares.

Eighteenth Hole HURRAH!

It is obvious at this stage that you are beginning to hallucinate because from the tee you can see the clubhouse and, if you listen intently, you fancy you can hear the clinking of glasses and the sheer rhapsody of a large Scotch being poured; the conviviality of it all is only marred by a huge, gaping chasm which separates you from it and, until such time as the proposed cable car is introduced here, there is very little chance of you reaching the clubhouse on the same day as you set out.

It will not surprise you to know that I lost three balls here and searched well into the twilight for them before repairing to the clubhouse and sobbing uncontrollably in the gents' toilet.

Finally, a tongue-in-cheek attack on golf from Michael Parkinson, a man who was at one time president of the Anti-Golf League but later took up the game and appeared on my 'Around with Alliss' show.

Golf Blight

MICHAEL PARKINSON

The scientists and the doom watchers have got it wrong. The greatest problem facing the world today is not overpopulation, or nuclear proliferation or pollution it is golf blight. This disease, which has reached epidemic proportions over the past decade, means that our natural habitat is rapidly becoming turned into one huge golf course.

One could, if one so desired, play golf from coast to coast across the United States. A man getting off a train in Newcastle could tear up the return ticket and golf all the way home to Torquay.

Recent research shows that in Britain an increasing number of people play golf more times each week than they have sex – and, in the main, get more enjoyment out of a hole in one. Moreover, it is calculated that more man-hours are lost through executives practising their golf swings in office hours than accrue during an outbreak of typhoid.

But, most significantly, there are now more golf clubs in the world than Gideon bibles, more golf balls than missionaries and, if every golfer in the world, male and female, were laid end to end, I for one would leave them there.

I am president of the Anti-Golf Society, a position I have held for many years in the face of stiff opposition from friend and foe alike and in spite of the aforementioned spread of golf blight.

My society would not ban golf, it would simply provide rehabilitation centres where people could be taught that there are more important handicaps than golfing ones, that practising swings in public places is antisocial and that the reason why golfers' wives soon lose their girlish enthusiasm for love and marriage is that they know better than most exactly what a golf bag is.

Unlike other human beings golfers do not live at home, they live at the golf club. They are happier in these establishments because they guarantee their peace of mind by barring outsiders and only giving shelter to people of similar pigmentation of skin, background and religious and political views.

Thus there are clubs exclusively for Jews, and clubs where a Jew could only gain admittance if he arrived on the doorstep with Moshe Dayan at his side supported by a regiment of Israeli paratroopers.

Michael Parkinson, *circa* 1971, before he discovered the trials and tribulations of the game of golf

This unhealthy state of affairs can only damage the move towards better international understanding and will undoubtedly lead to dire consequences. Indeed, it is my belief that the Third World War will start at a golf club – probably the deliciously titled Honourable Company of Edinburgh Golfers – when Sammy Davis Jr arrives at Muirfield unannounced and uninvited with Arthur Scargill as his partner.

It is difficult to find any justification whatsoever for golf. The people who play it might disagree with the criticism that it is simply an elaborate device for ruining a good walk. But they would be hard pressed to convince me of its claims as a sport, particularly one to be watched.

One of life's great mysteries is just what do golfers think they are playing at, but even more mysterious is what those spectators who traipse around golf courses are looking for? They, at least, can claim the exercise as an excuse, but what about those noddies who sit at the eighteenth hole all day long? All they see – and I know because I observed them on television – is an alleged athlete fretting over sinking a 2-foot putt.

There is more excitement and spectacle in a competition to decide the world's largest parsnip.

It is during events like those of last week that some of us despair for the future of the human race. The golfers are taking over, vast regiments of people whose only justification can be that they provide employment for people who make sad and gaudy trousers.

At such times I feel isolated but not alone. There are a few of us left to fight the rearguard action. Not all of us have been brainwashed.

Watching the Open on television – actually I was fretfully waiting for them to go back to a real game, cricket – my wife came into the room as some golfer was practising his swing. 'He missed the ball,' she exclaimed. I felt a new, stirring love for her. She looked more closely at the box. 'Also he's lost a glove,' she said. At that precise moment I knew I had married the right person.

If there is hope it is in my wife's unsullied innocence, plus the expert backing of people like the environmental correspondent of the *Observer*, who recently suggested that in the national interest, all golf courses should be ploughed up and made into allotments.

There can be no arguing with this outstanding piece of common sense. Vegetables are more important than golfers and, aesthetically speaking, I'd rather watch a cabbage grow than a man worrying his guts over a 2-foot putt.

(From the *Sunday Times*, 13 July 1975)

14 Glossary of Terms

Address To take up a stance and ground the club before striking.

Albatross Taking 3 strokes under par for the hole.

Apron The area round the green that is not mown quite as closely as the green itself.

Birdie Taking 1 stroke under par for the hole.

Bisque Stroke conceded in form of a handicap. It may be taken at any point in a match.

Bogey Now taken to mean, especially in America, 1 stroke over par. It is still used to mean a par, particularly by older golfers.

Borrow Allowance needed on a putt that is not going to run straight towards the hole, usually because of the gradient of the green.

Bunker A deliberate hazard, either an area of bare ground, or more usually a depression that is filled with sand.

Caddie One who carries or handles a player's clubs and otherwise assists him.

Carry The distance between the point of the hitting of ball and its first bounce on landing.

Casual water Temporary accumulation of water.

Chip A low running approach to the flag made from close to the green.

Cut-up High shot played with side spin.

Divot Small strip of turf taken out of the ground in playing iron shots.

Dogleg Shape of a hole turning from left to right or right to left.

Dormie Term used in matchplay when a player is as many holes up as there are holes left to play.

Draw A shot, made intentionally, which, for a right-hander, bends slightly to the left.

Eagle Taking 2 strokes under par for the hole.

Fade A shot which, when hit by a right-hander, is intentionally bent slightly to the right.

Fairway The specially prepared area of turf between tee and green.

Forward press A slight movement forward of the hands before beginning the swing.

Fourball A match in which four players compete, each playing his own ball.

Foursome A match in which four players compete in pairs, each playing alternate shots with the same ball. Sometimes used to describe four players playing together.

Green The part of a golf hole specially prepared for putting.

Greensome A variation of foursomes in which each player is allowed to hit from the tee, the best shot then being selected.

Handicap System of awarding bonus strokes which enable golfers of differing levels of ability to meet on equal terms.

Hole The playing area from tee to green.

Honour A player entitled to play first from the tee through having won the previous hole is said to have the honour.

Hook A shot which when hit by a right-hander curves to the left; more pronounced than a draw and unintentional.

Iron Club, the head or striking part of which is made of metal.

Matchplay The method of deciding a match by the number of holes won as distinct from the number of strokes taken in a round.

Medal play (also **strokeplay**) A match or competition decided by the total number of strokes taken in a round and not by number of holes won.

Par The number of strokes required by a first-class player at each hole.

Pitch A lofted approach shot to the green.

Pitch and run A shot pitched short and allowed to run up to the flag.

Birdie! Seve becomes the 1984 champion as he holes his birdie putt on the seventy-second green in the British Open at St Andrews

Pull A straight-flying shot which, when hit by a right-hander, goes to the left of the line intended.

Push A straight-flying shot which, when hit by a right-hander, goes to the right of the line intended.

Rough The area within the course not specially prepared for play and cut only occasionally.

Run of the green When ball in motion is stopped or deflected by an outside agency.

Sand wedge A broad-soled club mainly used for playing from sand.

Scratch A handicap of nought. The player neither gives nor receives strokes in a match.

Semi-rough Rough bordering the fairway cut to a height of approximately 2–4 inches.

Slice A shot which, when hit by a right-hander, curves to the right; more pronounced than a fade and unintentional.

Stance To take up position before hitting a shot.

Strokeplay See **Medal play.**

Wedge A broad-soled iron having maximum loft for hitting short, high shots, usually to the green.

Woods Clubs, usually of four different kinds, whose heads are made with wood. Used for the longer shots.